THE  TIMES

GUIDE TO

JAPAN

About the authors

David Watts was bureau chief in Tokyo for *The Times* from 1984 to 1988. He became Diplomatic Correspondent of *The Times* in 1991. In 1992 he was appointed Deputy Foreign Editor.

Joanna Pitman read Japanese at Cambridge University. She was appointed Tokyo correspondent of *The Times* in 1990.

Geoffrey Bownas established the The Department of Japanese at Oxford University in 1954. In 1965 he was appointed the first Professor of Japanese Studies at Sheffield University. Professor Emeritus of Sheffield University since 1980, he has worked as a consultant to numerous organizations, British and Japanese. He is currently Director of the Centre for the Study of Modern Japan at Gyosei International College in Britain.

Author's acknowledgements

Barry Keehn, Professor of Japanese Studies in the Oriental Studies Faculty of Cambridge University, gave invaluable assistance and friendship in writing this book, as did Julian Howard, resident partner in Macfarlane's law office in Tokyo. Others too numerous to mention have also contributed to this guide through their ideas and inspiration. I owe a particular debt to my wife, Shizuko.

THE  TIMES

GUIDE TO

JAPAN

UNDERSTANDING THE
WORLD'S NEWEST SUPERPOWER

by DAVID WATTS

TIMES BOOKS
A Division of HarperCollins*Publishers*

First published by Times Books
A division of HarperCollins *Publishers*
77–85 Fulham Palace Road
London W6 8JB

© Times Books, London 1993

British Library Cataloguing-in-Publication Data
A catalogue record of this book is available
from the British Library

ISBN 0-7230-0495-1

Typeset by Tradespools Ltd.,
Frome, Somerset

Printed by WSOY, Finland

CONTENTS

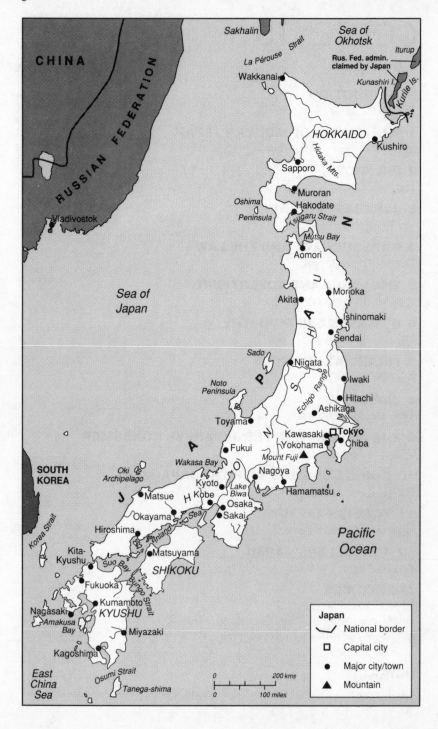

CHINA

RUSSIAN FEDERATION

Sakhalin

La Pérouse Strait

Sea of
Okhotsk

Iturup

Rus. Fed. admin.
claimed by Japan

Wakkanai

Kunashiri I.

Kurile Is.

HOKKAIDO

Kushiro

Sapporo

Hidaka Mts.

Vladivostok

Muroran
Hakodate

Oshima
Peninsula

Tsugaru Strait

N

Mutsu Bay

Aomori

Sea of
Japan

Morioka

Akita

H

Ishinomaki

Sendai

Sado

Niigata

Iwaki

Noto
Peninsula

P

Hitachi

Echigo Range

Ashikaga

Toyama

N

Kawasaki

Tokyo

Fukui

Yokohama

Chiba

SOUTH
KOREA

A

Wakasa Bay

O

Mount Fuji

Nagoya

Oki
Archipelago

Kyoto

Hamamatsu

J

Matsue

H

Kobe

Lake
Biwa

Osaka

Okayama

Sakai

Hiroshima

Inland Sea

Korea Strait

Kita-
Kyushu

Suo Bay

Matsuyama

SHIKOKU

Pacific
Ocean

Bungo Strait

Fukuoka

Kumamoto

KYUSHU

Nagasaki

Amakusa
Bay

Miyazaki

Kagoshima

East
China
Sea

Osumi Strait

Tanega-shima

Japan

National border

Capital city

Major city/town

Mountain

0   200 kms

0   100 miles

INTRODUCTION
The challenge of the future

By the turn of the century Japan aims to be a member of the Security Council of the United Nations. Few doubt that Japan will achieve that ambition given the same dedication and determination its people have shown over nearly 50 years in rising from the ashes of World War II to the front rank of the world's economic powers.

This achievement will mean much more than just a tick against another of the many goals that the Japanese people have set themselves. It will be, despite much earlier US presidential rhetoric, the true beginning of a new world order, with Japan perhaps taking her seat alongside Germany and Russia. It will mean the arrival of a new power with its own world view – one that, at times, may seem markedly different from those of its Western mentors; a power that has clung to the notion that disputes should always be settled by peaceful means. Such an approach has often earned opprobrium from other nations convinced that all Japan wants is peace and a quiet life without responsibility so as to pursue its mercantile aims. The image of a world taxpayer afraid to do little more than sign the cheques, with minimal say in how the money is spent, and of a nation whose political system, to the outsider, appears rotten to the core has grown wearisome to the Japanese. It has grown wearisome, too, to the Americans and others who for years have been urging Japan on to greater things, to sharing a greater burden of responsibility.

But despite support from the United States for a Japanese Security Council seat and the obvious need for Japan to play a more responsible role, the learning curve will be a steep one. Certainly, Japan has a remarkable record for absorption and assimilation of foreign ideas, especially in a field where its role is likely to remain controversial for some time – peacekeeping. Moreover, Japan's neighbours are concerned that it may show the same single-mindedness about the pursuit of its interests through the United Nations that it once reserved for conquest and, given its economic reach, might eventually wield an economic influence that could, in more subtle ways, match or even surpass that of the United States. In any event Japan will be able to offer a powerful rallying-point for the nations of Asia and elsewhere which up to now feel that their views have been under-represented at the United Nations. It will be the standard-bearer for the countries of the Pacific Rim as they become wealthy in this, the fastest-growing region of the world economically, at a time when the United States is showing all the signs of wanting to concentrate on its own problems. Lessening interest in the Asian

Development Bank by the United States and American blockage of the Organization for Economic Cooperation and Development's plans to develop expertise on China would both seem to point in that direction.

A trend to expansion of Japanese investments in Asia will reinforce the perception that Tokyo increasingly sees the importance of focusing more on its part of the world, taking advantage of China's helter-skelter ride through what must surely be the dying years of communism in that country. But Japan knows equally well that, alone, it cannot manage some of the potential economic, social and political fallout from the most populous country in the world. This illustrates Japan's need for one, and preferably both, sides of the supporting of the US–EC–Japan triangle in a complementary role.

Japan's relationship with Europe, and indeed the United States, is likely to be defined, at least in part, by what happens elsewhere. Ironically, Russia has already helped to introduce distance and tension into the relationship between Japan and the United States on two levels. First, the ending of the Cold War markedly reduced Japan's political and military dependence on the United States and so increased its options. Second, there was the dispute over Japan's contribution to economic assistance for Russia, which put a brake on the proceedings and eventually compelled President Clinton to change tack. This was a telling lesson for world diplomacy, just as the financing of the Gulf War against Saddam Hussein's Iraq had earlier shown the growing economic limits to the use of US power and the increasing dependence on Japan for more than mere technology.

Although, on the face of it, the EC–Japan relationship is the weakest part of the triangle, events in Russia could quickly change that. If, for instance, Boris Yeltsin were to fall and be replaced by a hardline regime, that could propel Europe and Japan into a closer relationship in response to the potential new threat. Equally, if the US drift from Asia continues and Asia goes on developing at its present speed, there will probably be no alternative for Europe but to become more involved in that region.

Although it is early to speculate on the ultimate effect of the defeat of Japan's Liberal Democratic Party, which had ruled uninterrupted since 1955, it is clear that it too fell victim to the effects of the end of the Cold War. But it seems likely that this heralds the development of a more pluralist democratic system. Ironically, during the Cold War the LDP had played a similar role *vis-á-vis* the Americans to that played by the eastern European Socialist and Communist parties, who acted as the channel of communication with Moscow. Just as that role has disappeared in eastern Europe, giving rise to other voices, so it did in Japan, which had hitherto maintained a united front under the LDP but now feels less need to do so. With Russia no longer perceived as such a threat, and the umbrella of US protection no longer needed, the Japanese are fast reassessing their relationship with the Americans. The result of this gradual sea change will most likely be a much less predictable Japan and one less easy for allies and friends to deal with. It may also mean a more nationalistic country as its deference to

Washington declines and it espouses more independently-minded foreign and economic policies.

On the domestic front, Japan can be expected to move more of its productive capacity in the motor, electronics and other industries offshore to take advantage of lower costs in other parts of Asia. Jobs requiring lower skill levels would probably go to China, Vietnam and Indonesia, while the higher-skill investments will be made in South-East Asia. For the medium term it is clear that there will be fewer Japanese investments in Europe and the United States because of the lower profit levels that those countries now yield. But whatever the emphasis of policy, Japan is likely to remain a key engine of the world economy, however much its responsibilities grow and become a demand on the domestic economy.

1 THE MAKING OF MODERN JAPAN
Mystical origins to economic superpower

Japan's historical origins are as scarcely credible as its rapid rise to the status of a late 20th-century technological and economic superpower. Its early history is still shrouded in myth; myth akin to the Arthurian legends of England but carrying more weight in a country where it has only relatively recently been conceded that the ruler is not divine. According to Japan's mythical ancient chronicles, when heaven and earth began, a god named Izanagi and the goddess Izanami together gave birth to the islands of Japan. On Izanami's death, Izanagi miraculously gave birth to the Sun, Moon and Storm.

In reality the origins of the people who now inhabit the islands is a good deal more prosaic, and a somewhat sensitive matter. Today, despite the ardent belief of many Japanese that they are a 'pure' race, the polyglot origin of the modern people is obvious from the fleshy, rounded faces of those of Chinese descent to the more sharply-hewn features of those with Korean ancestry.

It is from the Korean peninsula that modern Japan's history springs. The peace and quiet of the rural, agricultural lifestyle of the native Ainu who inhabited the islands from time immemorial was invaded by people moving into Japan from China and Korea. They brought with them their culture, a written language and other skills of China along with the religion of India – Buddhism. Ever since, Japan has lived in the cultural shadow of China.

According to the traditional version of Japanese history – the *Nihon Shoki* – the first 17 emperors of Japan had an average age of 100 years. But it is not until the beginning of the Christian era that any dates can confidently be ascribed to rulers and not until the end of the 5th century that an historical basis can be established for measuring events in Japan against those in the rest of the world.

During the first four centuries AD the descendants of the first emperor, Jimmu, gradually assumed greater authority throughout western Japan. They even found resources to stage an expedition to Korea led by the Empress Jingo, who founded a Japanese colony on the tip of the peninsula. The colony provided a channel through which the Chinese language was absorbed, along with such vital skills as metalworking and the culture of silkworms. By the middle of the 6th century there were some 100,000 Koreans and Chinese from Manchuria living in Japan, many of whom were better

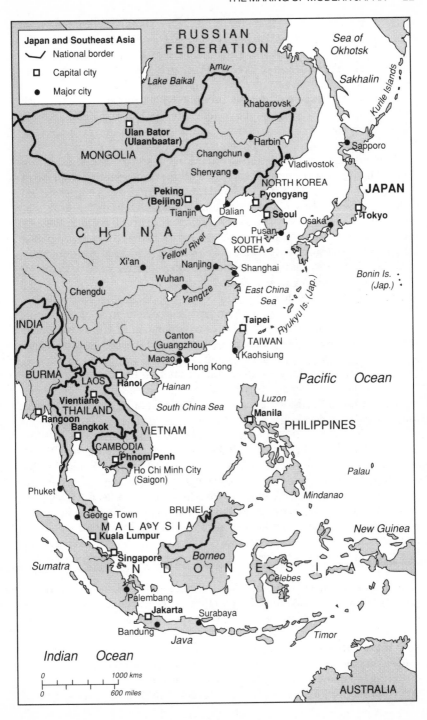

educated than the native Japanese. The skills they brought with them were so valuable and important that barely 200 years later about one-third of the noble families in Japan claimed either Chinese or Korean continental descent (quite unlike the status of Koreans in Japan today, who though they are Japanese in all other respects are not recognized as such in law).

The same continental arrivals brought with them Buddhism which then, as now, is practised happily alongside the native religion, Shinto, without noticeable detriment to either. Buddhism's adoption by the powerful Soga clan, and by the imperial house of Shotoku Taishi, ensured its survival and ultimate success. He absorbed the moral and philosophical nature of the religion, which contrasts sharply with the more emotional appeal of Shinto. The latter implies certain standards in its rites but incorporates no written code or body of ethics such as those associated with the great 'religions of the book'. The absorption of a foreign religion and the adoption of a written language that was ill-suited to reproducing the native spoken tongue were milestones in Japan's development. A history of assimilation of foreign influences has given rise to today's extraordinary ability to absorb and 'Japanize' anything from outside.

At the turn of the 7th century, the crown prince Shotoku Taishi spread Buddhist thought and art throughout Japanese society, in AD 604 promulgating the 'Constitution of 17 Articles' or ethical maxims. 'The management of state affairs', he said, 'cannot be achieved unless it is based on knowledge, and the sources of knowledge are Confucianism, Buddhism and Shinto.' Earlier there had been a good deal of opposition to Buddhism. This coincided with increasing rivalry between some of the great clans competing for influence around the imperial throne. The imperial family's favour shifted towards the Soga clan.

After the prince's death the Soga clan's power increased to such an extent that they seemed poised for a take-over of the imperial throne. However, the Soga were themselves overthrown by Fujiwara Kamatari, the representative of a family whose name still has a noble ring to this day. He endeavoured, with mixed results, to give Japan an administrative system based on that of Tang dynasty of China, by setting up a highly centralized government. This was intended to make things more difficult for would-be usurpers of the throne. The system succeeded for several hundred years but eventually the power of the regional clans reasserted itself and much of his work was undone. The adoption of Tang culture did, however, leave lasting mementos – the ancient capital of Nara built as a replica of the Chinese Tang capital of Ch'ang-an and a wonderful collection of 8th-century furniture, ornaments and personal effects used by the imperial family.

The Heian period

Starting in 794, the Heian period saw what was probably the most luxuriant flowering of Japanese culture. From the establishment of the imperial court at Kyoto, the capital, the culture was confined to a small elite who paid meticulous attention to the formal and the elegant in both life and art. Here, at the beginning of the 11th century, arguably the world's first novel was written. *Genji Monogatari* (The Tale of Genji) was a romance penned by a court lady, Murasaki Shikibu.

Throughout the Heian period the real rulers of Japan were the Fujiwara. Their rule was marked by a relatively humane approach and they can be given credit, largely, for the Japanese enthusiasm for study and improvement which trickled down from the rarefied atmosphere of the capital during their 300 years of influence. But an equally important development was the relative decline of the power of the monarchy, as the Fujiwara ruled first as regents and later as civil dictators. At the height of their influence it was not unusual for the emperor of the day to abdicate his power to the Fujiwara by the time he reached his thirties.

This relative lack of power and the feeling that the emperor was above the clouds was in marked contrast to the situation in China. There, the emperor wielded real power and was deemed the ruler so long as he held the mandate of heaven. Consequently, China was ruled by numerous dynasties as each lost this mysterious authority and had to concede to rival claimants whereas the Japanese claim to have had a single ruling line since the institution of emperor began. Paradoxically, in Japan the emperor's lack of power has protected the throne from controversy and contributed to its long-term viability.

There have been various attempts by the political right in Japan to restore the powers of the emperor but in modern times they have not succeeded. Since World War II the extreme right wing of the ruling Liberal Democratic Party has continuously pressed for such a restoration. Moreover these pressures are likely to increase as Japan remains relatively weak politically but economically very strong.

But in a democratic Japan they are unlikely to achieve their aim for two reasons. First, the character of the present emperor militates against any such move. Second, the public perception of the role of the monarchy in World War II remains ambivalent. The fact that the emperor of the day apparently did little to prevent his country from being engulfed in war is always likely to be held against both him and the institution, as the Japanese seek other, more democratic, avenues for self-expression.

The age of the shoguns

In the background of Fujiwara influence the power of great military families was growing. The two outstanding ones, the Minamoto, who wielded authority in the east of Japan, and the Taira, who controlled the province bordering the Japan Sea, were increasingly called upon to keep order. In the 12th century, conflicts within the Fujiwara clan over political appointments led to the two military families being employed by different factions to promote their aims. Sadly for the Fujiwaras, when the quarrelling was over they found that power had fallen into the hands of the two military houses who were supposed to be supporting them.

The Taira were in the ascendant for some 25 years before they, too, were overcome by the power of the Minamoto family. The climax came in 1185, in a sea battle fought in the Straits of Shimonoseki, which is now part of the great romantic age of chivalry in Japan re-enacted countless times in television drama.

To escape what were seen as the corrupting influences of the court in Kyoto, the leader of the Minamoto now moved the administrative capital of the country to Kamakura, south-west of Tokyo. There he established a system of government known as the *Bakufu*, literally 'camp office' – a sure sign that the levers of power were now controlled by the military. In 1192 the leader of the Minamoto, Yoritomo, received from the hands of the emperor, then a boy of 13, the title of *Sei-i tai-shogun*, or Great Barbarian-Suppressing General. The Bakufu was primarily a means of regulating the shogun's men, but it soon became apparent that it was a system superior to the nominal government of the day. The emperor reigned, but the shogun ruled. The Bakufu was to continue for 150 years and left a lasting impression on Japanese methods of government and on the culture.

But the dominance of the Yoritomo was over by the time that Japan faced its most severe foreign challenge of that period – the great armadas sent by the Mongol emperor Kublai Khan. There were two attempts to subdue Japan into joining the great Mongol empire which then controlled vast areas of the Asian land mass. After attacking islands in the Strait of Tsushima between Japan and Korea, in 1275 the Mongols made a determined landing on the southern island of Kyushu. However, a storm blew up, forcing the invaders to withdraw. Six years later, 150,000 Mongol troops landed in Kyushu and established a bridgehead, which they held for a considerable period before 'divine intervention' again saved the Japanese islands. The Mongol fleet was virtually wiped out by a typhoon, which the Japanese called *kamikaze*, or Divine Wind.

The often chaotic era of the shogunates, during which the fortunes of the imperial house fluctuated wildly, continued through to the 15th and 16th centuries. At one point the impoverished emperor was reduced to selling examples of his calligraphy on the streets of Kyoto. Not surprisingly, things were often much worse for the ordinary citizen at the bottom of the hierarchy. Below the feudal lords in this rigidly stratified society were the samurai, the warrior class who alone were permitted to bear arms. The warlords and their samurai composed some 7 per cent of the population while rice-growing farmers made up 80 per cent. Below these came the ordinary people and, later, the merchants.

The coming of Christianity

As the 16th century drew to a close, the Japanese were already established as seafaring traders and pirates, the scourge of almost the entire length of the Chinese coast. Contact with the Chinese increased, particularly by Japanese from the Kansai area, through the city of Osaka and its port of Sakai. Today Sakai is almost swallowed up in the massive urban megalopolis which is Osaka, but in those days it was an open port, trading vigorously with the mainland from what was Japan's industrial and economic heartland. Japan was by then a booming economic power, but with its political structure still some way from maturity. Independent rulers and even monks joined the new boom in trading, while local warlords still struggled with each other for supremacy.

Amid this turmoil, however unobtrusively at first, came the first contact with Christianity and the West. The first Westerners set foot on Japan's soil in either 1542 or 1543. They were Portuguese sailors whose junk was blown ashore on a small island off the coast of Kyushu. Some six years later, in 1549, the most distinguished Christian visitor, the Spanish Jesuit Francis Xavier, arrived. The impact of Christianity was then, as now, relatively small, but those early Portuguese traders brought with them something far more potent – the musket. The arrival of the weapon gave an immediate advantage to the *daimyo* (warlord) Oda Nobunaga, who was then in the ascendant in central Japan. By 1578, he was the leading power in the land. However, he did not last long and was killed at the age of 49. Had he lived longer he might have unified the entire country. Oda Nobunaga was also important for another reason. Disliking the Buddhist priesthood, he gave a welcome to the Jesuits who, in their turn, wrote favourably of him in their reports back to Lisbon and Rome. He gave land for a Christian seminary and wrote of the missionaries, 'These are the men whom I like; upright, sincere and who tell me solid things.'

The first to achieve a unified nation was the great warlord Toyotomi Hideyoshi, who built on Oda Nobunaga's legacy and successfully quelled rivals throughout the country and opposition among the Buddhist priests. The suppression of his opponents and the pacification of the country was completed with the capture of the fortress of Odawara outside Tokyo in 1590. For the first time for 100 years the country was at peace. But that did not satisfy Hideyoshi, who like his heirs in the 20th century, began to eye Korea. Today a statue stands in the South Korean capital, Seoul, commemorating Hideyoshi's invasion in 1597. This was the first military intrusion of the Japanese into the peninsula and the first of a series of adventures on mainland Asia that have caused so much enmity between the Japanese and their mainland cousins down the centuries. Curiously, Hideyoshi's motive for the invasion remains something of a mystery. No one is certain, but it is likely that he saw it merely as a way of keeping restive troops happy – perhaps the first example of a foreign military operation designed to deflect attention away from domestic problems. It proved a disastrous failure and the Seoul statue is a reminder of the more enduring and unhappy elements of Hideyoshi's legacy.

Slamming the door

It was an Englishman, Will Adams, the pilot of a Dutch ship wrecked off the Japanese coast in 1600, who played an important part in the next stage of Japanese history. Adams became an adviser to Hideyoshi's successor, Tokugawa Ieyasu, and warned the country's leaders that the Catholic Spanish and Portuguese planned first to convert the country to Christianity and then subvert it before finally taking control. Opinion swung sharply against all foreigners, especially after a revolt against two *daimyo* at Shimabara in 1637 in which foreigners were involved.

The revolt failed but the resistance turned its campaign into a religious crusade. Some 30,000 Christians locked themselves up in a castle to make a last stand and every one was slaughtered. Following the revolt the *sakoku*, or closed country system, was introduced by the Tokugawa shogunate and foreigners and foreign books were banned. Japanese, likewise, were forbidden to leave on pain of death. The only exception in the new relationship with foreigners was the limited trading contact permitted the Chinese and Dutch through the port of Nagasaki. For two centuries Japan was free of foreign interference, but while she slept the industrial revolution swept Europe and America.

The 'black ships'

Japan remained in self-imposed isolation till the 19th century. Then, in 1853, a squadron from the United States under Commodore Matthew Perry presented what amounted to an ultimatum to the shogun, in the form of a letter from the US president Fillmore demanding the opening of trade relations. Forced to leave without a response, the commodore warned that he would be back the following year with a much larger fleet to receive the Japanese answer.

The 'black ships' that anchored in Tokyo Bay in July 1853 had struck terror into the hearts of people on shore. The commodore was as good as his word and he appeared off the Japanese coast the following year. The majority of the power-holders recognized that the Americans could not be resisted for long and agreed to open the ports of Hakodate and Shimoda to visiting US vessels. Meanwhile Admiral Sterling of the Royal Navy won agreement for British ships to take on supplies at both Nagasaki and Hakodate. Other extraterritorial rights were extracted by the Americans against a background of competition from the British, then the dominant naval power in the East, and also the Russians. Even today, almost 150 years later, the sinister image of the 'black ships' is still invoked whenever Japanese feel that they are under unacceptable foreign pressure to yield on trade or other issues.

Townsend Harris, the first US consul, arrived to take up his post in Shimoda in 1856, ending forever the total exclusion of foreigners from Japan and opening a new era of relations with the West that would change both beyond recognition. Not surprisingly, the period immediately following the foreign intrusion saw a good deal of confusion and the gradual loss of prestige and power of the shogunate. This opened the way for the strengthening of the imperial claim to power, supported by the leading clans of the West and some of the merchant families of Osaka. Two of these, the Satsuma and the Choshu, were already beginning to exert influence nationally, which their descendants have carried into modern times.

Treaties were signed with the United States, Russia, Britain and France, without the permission of the emperor. This led to a backlash under the slogan 'Revere the emperor, expel the barbarian.' In 1862 Emperor Komei did, indeed, issue an edict to the shogun that the barbarians be expelled, starting in the summer of the following year. But even though the order went out to the foreign envoys it was immediately followed up by private signals that nothing would actually be done to carry it out. Even so, there were plenty of swordsmen around who saw it as their duty to act on the instruction. The British Legation was attacked twice and an Englishman called Richardson was cut down as he rode the Tokaido, the great highway running north–south between Tokyo and central Japan.

In June 1863, when the edict was due to be enforced, shore batteries, commanded by the Choshu family, on the Straits of Shimonoseki started to fire at US, French and Dutch ships, prompting heavy retaliation from the French and Americans. The British responded to the murder of Richardson by shelling Kagoshima from the sea. Although the Royal Navy burned much of the town to the ground in the bombardment, a mutual respect grew up between the British and Japanese navies rather than the hatred that might have been expected. The two forces went on to enjoy decades of cooperation as Japan's power grew. The incident also helped focus attention on what Japan could, and should, learn from the West if it was to become an advanced country. The first of many young clansmen left for England for periods of study.

The Meiji and modernization

The restoration of imperial power, and the accompanying drive to learn from the West, was not achieved without desperate last-ditch attempts by the shogunate to hang on to its influence. But, by 1869, the last of the great warlords had lost his power. The turning point had come in April of the previous year when the young Emperor Meiji ascended the throne at the age of 15. He moved the capital from Kyoto to Tokyo and set the seal on the future of his country with the Charter Oath: 'Knowledge shall be sought all over the world and thus shall the foundation of the imperial polity be strengthened.' There were already a number of foreign technicians in the country, but following the Charter Oath many more came. They brought instruction in everything from water-supply to finance and naval and military skills.

Thus Japan made up its collective mind, through the imperial directive, to become the equal of any Western country. That meant, in an era of robust nationalism, that Japan would seek to acquire its own overseas territories just as Russia, Britain, France and Italy were doing. In Asia the Japanese watched France annex Indochina and assume its protectorate over Cambodia in 1867. But perhaps even more important was how a weak yet arrogant China was forced to cede the coastal area between the Amur and the Korean frontier to Russia.

The example of the West's relationship with China proved most instructive. The Japanese saw how China had been treated as an economic colony by the West, and how the Europeans had run riot. They vowed that they would never be treated the same way themselves and they were concerned that there were already British infantrymen stationed in Yokohama for the protection of the business and diplomatic communities. To avoid the risk of falling under the domination of a Western power, they decided, meant rapidly absorbing everything the West had to offer.

Tentative steps to democracy

The notion of opposition, let alone an organized political opposition, was unthinkable in the era of the shoguns. Indeed, even as it drew to a close, the shogun's retainers spent much of their time trying to seek out and eliminate any show of dissent. The first 20 years the Meiji era concentrated on building up the nation while demands in the press and at public meetings for the establishment of representative institutions went unheeded. The slogan of the moment, *fukoku kyohei* – 'rich country, strong army' – left little room for what were seen as unnecessary or even frivolous Western-style institutions that had no relevance in a strongly patriarchal society.

The introduction of compulsory mass education in 1872 did not accelerate any move to democracy, as might have been expected. Instead the combination of education and conscription rapidly moulded the Japanese into a nation of patriots while fuelling the notions of expansion. This trend was reinforced by the introduction of the country's first constitution in 1889 – very much an imperial gift to the people, not the product of popular demand – and the Imperial Rescript on Education the following year.

While the constitution was heavily influenced by the German model, with a strong element of authoritarianism running through it, the education rescript owed much to Confucius in its approach. The influence of the rescript can hardly be overestimated since it set the country's moral tone for the next 50 years. It is only in the latter half of the 20th century that there has been any real effort made to reappraise the centralized way Japan runs its education system. Yet even the democratic reforms introduced after World War II have not made much impression on the way the Ministry of Education views the country's history and how it should be taught.

When, under the constitution, political parties were legalized, the government found itself without a party to represent its own view. So, with the establishment of the Diet or parliament in 1890, Japan was in the curious position of having two conservative opposition political parties matched with an equally conservative governing party. The notion of a loyal opposition is something that is still alien to the country's culture.

Testing times on the Asian mainland

Before the turn of the century, Japan made claims on Korea which were consistently opposed by China. However, Tokyo gradually strengthened its position on the Asian mainland through intrigue until it was ready to challenge Chinas openly. A revolt in Korea in 1894 provided the pretext, when Chinese troops were sent to assist the Korean king. On 25 July 1894 the Japanese sank a Chinese troop ship – without a declaration of war – and embarked on a vigorous nine-month campaign that saw them expel the Chinese from Korea, defeat a Chinese fleet and capture Port Arthur and a key peninsula in south Manchuria.

The impact of Japan's defeat of the Chinese and its ability to dictate tough terms in the peace treaty was far-reaching and dramatic. Barely a week after the signing of the Treaty of Shimonoseki, which gave Japan Formosa and the Pescadores, Port Arthur and the Liaotung Peninsula, there came the Triple Intervention by Russia, France and Germany whose envoys advised Japan to relinquish its claim to the Liaotung Peninsula along with the harbour and fortress of Port Arthur. It was the first, but not the last, gesture to show that some of the major European powers would accept only a certain level of Japanese power even in Asia. For Japan it was a classic lesson in Western hypocrisy: within five years of the Shimonoseki pact, Germany had seized territory in China, Britain had leased the New Territories north of Hong Kong, the United States had annexed Hawaii, and Russia had taken control of Port Arthur and the Liaotung Peninsula.

As the 20th century dawned, Russian claims to Manchuria and Korea provided the next test of Japanese modernization and self-confidence. That confidence was underwritten by the Anglo-Japanese Alliance of 1902, whereby Britain, then the leading maritime power, tacitly acknowledged Japan's right to undisputed influence in Korea. Russia's demands to control the economic resources of south Manchuria and form a neutral zone in Korea were the subject of long drawn-out negotiations until Japan broke off the talks on 6 February 1904. Feeling sufficient military self-confidence to strike without further warning, the Japanese attacked Port Arthur two days later, damaging two battleships and a cruiser. The following day, battle was joined once more, but it was not until the third day that war – known as the Russo-Japanese war – was actually declared. *The Times*, among others, approved: 'The Japanese Navy has opened the war by an act of daring which is destined to take a place of honour in naval annals.'

But if Japan won widespread admiration and sympathy for its rapid rise to pre-eminence at the expense of China and Russia, the Twenty-One Demands made against China in 1915, among which German interests in China would be signed over to Japan, caused alarm, particularly in the United States. From then on, Japan was recast in the role of the bully.

Overtures to world war

After World War I, Japan was given a permanent seat on the newly formed League of Nations Council. But despite its support for the Allied cause against Germany, Japan was still not recognized as on a par with the nations of the West. The Japanese delegation failed to win approval of its request for a declaration on the principle of racial equality to be written into the League's covenant. Two years later, at the Washington Naval Conference of 1921, the Japanese again felt themselves bested when a capital ship tonnage ratio of 5:5:3 between the United States, Britain and Japan was agreed despite Japanese demands for a ratio of 10:10:7. The Washington conference also ended the Anglo-Japanese Alliance, much to the delight of the Americans. However, Japanese agreement to withdraw from her concessions in China seemed to signal a more peaceful future, an impression reinforced by a highly successful exchange of visits by the respective heirs to the British and Japanese thrones in 1921 and 1922. But at home, Japan began to suffer the first of a series of political assassinations as the military began to assert itself. The Great Kanto Earthquake of 1 September 1923, which claimed the lives of 100,000 people, was a portent of even greater upheavals to come.

During the war Japan had benefited from lost production in Europe and its economy had boomed. But that was now well and truly over. The economy began to suffer and there was growing dissatisfaction with what was seen as weak government policy over China just as the Guomindang government on the mainland was trying to emulate Japan's example of asserting its national identity and modernizing China.

After a preliminary manœuvre in 1927 in which a Chinese warlord was murdered, the Japanese Kwantung Army seized the city of Mukden on 18 September 1931 as a first step towards occupying the whole of Manchuria. That period is known in Japan as the *kurai tanima* – 'dark valley' – when civilian governments were gradually reduced to powerlessness by military men in the cabinet who could impose their will through threats of army indiscipline.

Setting the Pacific ablaze

The capture of Mukden ignited the war on mainland Asia as the army pressed on with its plan to force China and the puppet state of Manchukuo, formerly Manchuria, into economic and political union with Japan. The Japanese navy was more realistic in its assessment of Japan's prospects in a broader conflict, but as outside pressure for military restraint grew, so did demands at home for bolder action. It came in July 1941 when the Japanese army occupied bases in southern Indochina, clearly threatening Thailand, Malaya and the Dutch East Indies. The army's move shocked many across the world at a time when talks with the United States over the conflict in China were at a crucial stage. The response was an economic embargo on Japan by the United States, Britain and Holland. When further

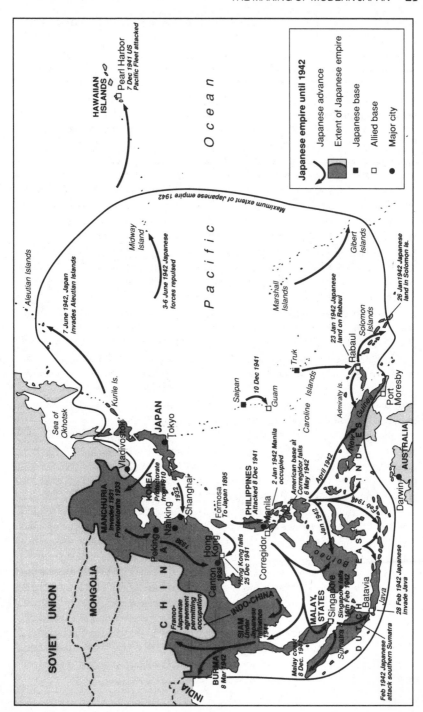

Japanese empire until 1942

Japanese advance

Extent of Japanese empire

Japanese base

Allied base

Major city

HAWAIIAN ISLANDS
Pearl Harbor
7 Dec 1941 US Pacific Fleet attacked

Ocean

Maximum extent of Japanese empire 1942

Aleutian Islands

7 June 1942, Japan invades Aleutian Islands

Midway Island

3-6 June 1942 Japanese forces repulsed

Pacific

Gilbert Islands

26 Jan 1942 Japanese land in Solomon Is.

23 Jan 1942 Japanese land on Rabaul

Marshall Islands

Solomon Islands

Rabaul

Truk

Saipan

10 Dec 1941

Guam

Caroline Islands

Admiralty Is.

Port Moresby

Kurile Is.

Sea of Okhotsk

JAPAN
Tokyo

Vladivostok

KOREA
Protectorate from 1910

1932

Shanghai

Formosa
To Japan 1895

PHILIPPINES
Attacked 8 Dec 1941

2 Jan 1942 Manila occupied

American base at Corregidor falls 6 May 1942

April 1942

NEW GUINEA

AUSTRALIA

Darwin

Feb 1942

SOVIET UNION

MONGOLIA

MANCHURIA
Invaded 1931
Protectorate 1932

Peking

Nanking

1938

C H I N A

Canton

1938

Hong Kong
Hong Kong falls 25 Dec 1941

Manila

Corregidor

Franco-Japanese agreement permitting occupation

INDO-CHINA

SIAM
Under Japanese influence 1941

BURMA
8 Mar 1942

INDIA

Malay coast
8 Dec 1941

MALAY STATES

Singapore
Singapore falls 15th Feb 1942

Sumatra

D U T C H   E A S T   I N D I E S

Borneo

Jan 1942

Batavia

Java

28 Feb 1942 Japanese invade Java

Feb 1942 Japanese attack southern Sumatra

talks with the Americans reached an impasse, the slide to war became inevitable.

Just as the navy had predicted, the early months of the Pacific war were a smashing success for the Japanese: the US Pacific Fleet was crippled by the attack on Pearl Harbor on December 7 1941, the US Air Force in the Philippines was eliminated in three days, and the fate of Malaya, and subsequently Singapore, was sealed by the loss of the British capital ships *Prince of Wales* and *Repulse*. Malaya fell in just 10 weeks, and the Japanese army quickly went on to take Hong Kong, Manila, Singapore, Batavia (Jakarta), Rangoon and Mandalay. At first, the claim by the Japanese that they were bent on freeing Asia of the white man was taken at face value by many of those whom they allegedly came to liberate. But before long they were treating their new charges far worse than the former colonial masters had done.

By June of the following year the Japanese dream of domination was looking less real. The Japanese navy suffered a severe defeat by the US Navy at the Battle of Midway, losing four aircraft carriers and two heavy cruisers. Meanwhile, after bitter fighting, the Japanese army was forced back to the north coast of New Guinea by the Australians, who destroyed the forces advancing on Port Moresby.

The emperor had spoken of the need for peace as early as the spring of 1942, but the surrender of Italy and the Cairo Declaration of 1 December 1943, which implied that Japan would have to give up all the territories it had acquired, only hardened the resolve of the military not to yield to the Allies. Indeed, despite the reverses they had suffered, the Japanese made two great offensive efforts in 1944. They advanced into south-west China and also tried to encircle and destroy British and Indian forces and break through into Bengal and Assam.

As this latter battle raged, in mid-1944 the Americans invaded the Mariana Islands in the first of their crucial island-hopping moves against Japanese occupation in the Pacific. It was a costly but vital month-long campaign, after which air bases built on Saipan put the US Air Force within striking distance of the Japanese capital.

Following the fall of the Marianas and the appearance of the dreaded US B29 bombers in the skies over Tokyo, General Hideki Tojo's cabinet resigned. The general was replaced by the moderate Admiral Mitsumasa Yonai, giving rise to hopes at home that Japan might be able to talk peace to the Allies. But the American landing on the island of Leyte in the Philippines served notice that the US war machine would grind on relentlessly to its objective. The capture of Okinawa took 10 weeks with 39,000 casualties, giving a strong hint as to the ultimate human price the Americans could expect to pay if they invaded the home islands. At the same time, the Japanese military thought that one severe reverse for the Allies would persuade them to moderate their terms for the Japanese surrender, which they feared would mean the end of imperial rule.

Allied aircraft ranged back and forth across Japan at will, causing hideous damage to the largely wooden towns and cities through incendiary bombing. But the Japanese government rejected the terms of the Potsdam Declaration which called for immediate surrender, though the Americans knew, through their clandestine monitoring of Japanese communications, how desperate some sectors of the government were to sue for peace. Nevertheless, in the early morning of 6 August 1945, the US Air Force B29 *Enola Gay* dropped an atomic bomb on the city of Hiroshima.

But even this demonstration of power did not convince some on the Japanese side, and while the Supreme Council of war leaders agonized over what to do next, a second atomic bomb devastated Nagasaki. Only then did the government seek to involve the emperor, and his advice to end the war as soon as possible was followed. The Soviet declaration of war on Japan gave the situation extra urgency, raising the possibility of invasion and the imposition of communism.

The new Japan

For Japan the postwar period started with millions homeless and starving. The occupation by the United States is regarded as having been most successful – a fully fledged cultural and political revolution that transformed Japan's institutions. But good luck played as large a part as good management, as there were times when inept economic policies imposed from Washington brought the country close to upheaval through shortages. The occupation's positive effect is seen in Japan's phenomenal economic success and its postwar stability and international status. By 1951 Japan was already achieving the industrial output that it had enjoyed 20 years earlier, boosted by the demand created by the Korean war. However, the Americans went back on some of the targets they had set themselves to be achieved under the occupation.

There could be no doubt about the import of Article 9 of the US-inspired constitution that the conquerors bequeathed to their new subjects (see Appendix 2). It renounced the country's right to maintain armed forces and ended with the words: 'The right of belligerency of the state will not be recognized.' But already in 1950, with the winds of the Cold War gusting through Asia, the Americans authorized the creation of a National Police Reserve with more than 70,000 men armed as infantry. Moreover, the need for Japan to supply US and other UN armed forces in Korea led to the release of many hundreds of Japanese interned for war crimes. The provisions breaking up the big industrial conglomerates, *zaibatsu*, were also relaxed, as the Americans saw Japan as an ally against communism and discarded notions of a new, neutral 'Switzerland of Asia'. It was but a short step to renaming those troops 'self-defence forces' and increasing their number to cover both naval and air activities.

By 1952, output was back to its prewar peak. Three years later, reconstruction was complete, with the British Austin and Hillman motor companies helping to put Japanese industry back on its feet. (Ironically, 40 years on, the situation would be reversed, with Japanese firms making hundreds of thousands of cars in Britain.) There followed a period of wholesale importation of Western technology and expertise, often at knock-down prices – American transistor technology was bought for $25,000 – which laid the foundations of later industrial success. But much of the world still looked on Japan as a third-rate nation that would never again achieve the status of a leading industrial power. Its products were of indifferent quality, and a somewhat patronizing exchange rate was fixed at 360 yen to the US dollar. The West little realized at what cost it was overlooking this new competitor.

During the 1950s Japan's gross national product almost doubled and annual growth rates verged on double figures. With twice the population, the United States' GNP was then 25 times that of Japan. The following decade, growth rates of 11 per cent helped triple Japan's GNP as its steel and shipbuilding industries became the envy of the world. By the middle of the 1960s the Japanese economy was bigger than that of Britain. By the end of that decade it had overtaken Germany and France and was third in the world behind the Soviet Union and the United States. Thus, exactly 100 years after the Meiji reforms freed Japan from feudalism, it had become the second largest economy in the free world. Moreover, less than a quarter of a century after being razed by the most devastating war the world had known, Japan, fuelled by the development boom that accompanied the Tokyo Olympics of 1964, had outstripped the economies of most of its conquerors. Tokyo was already the world's largest city, and by now Japan's potential was obvious even though its economy was only a fraction the size of that of the United States.

Still, few could have imagined that by the mid-1980s Japan would become the world's largest creditor, the owner of prime real estate such as the Rockefeller Center in New York, and part of the heart of American culture, when the Hollywood entertainment giant MCA was bought by the Osaka-based Matsushita company for $6.6 billion. Nor was there any end in sight to Japan's success. With the rest of the world seeking to co-opt Japan's power, there seemed little reason to doubt that by the turn of the century the Japanese economy could be two-thirds as large as that of the United States.

2 POLITICS
The imperatives of prosperity

Since World War II the aim of Japan has been to build an economy that is second to none, and Japanese politics has been fundamentally aligned with that aim. For the ruling party and opposition alike, this has been the primary objective to which all other considerations have taken second place. Economic growth, the maintenance of policies favourable to business, and the control of inflation mean that many of the adversarial elements found in the politics of Western countries have been either eliminated or suppressed in Japanese politics. The pursuit of a low-inflationary, low interest-rate economic policy is a given. Programmes that do not, in some way, contribute to the economic welfare or security of the country are low on the list of priorities of politicians.

The politics of growth
Arguably, Japan's primary economic goal has already been accomplished, with the country now searching for a new political matrix which will better serve the needs of a highly sophisticated world power in the 21st century. But if the consensus needed for change may take years to achieve, the defeat of the ruling Liberal Democratic Party in the July 1993 general election and its replacement by a seven-party coalition under Morihiro Hosokawa looks like the start of the process.

Given the Japanese people's experience of totalitarianism during World War II and their pragmatic nature, it is not surprising that they emerged suspicious of ideology. That, combined with the capitalist ethos that came with the US occupation, has meant that no communist or socialist party has ever had much chance of winning power. In the early postwar period the socialists might have been expected to be a strong party. That it never happened was in no small measure due to the ruling party's success in providing prosperity and security.

Ideologies suggest rigid approaches to politics and confrontation with those who hold different political beliefs. A central tenet of Japanese society and politics has always been the avoidance of conflict, or at least the management of it, and the building of consensus. This combination, amounting to almost the antithesis of Western politics, which is based on competition between ideas, has brought the development of a managerial politics aimed at maximizing the prospects for business and the economy of the country as a whole. Not surprisingly, in a society that owes much of its heritage to China, the rights and interests of the individual play a much-reduced role.

The Confucian, hierarchical heritage and the relative lack of importance of the individual have encouraged the belief that the business of government should be left to others who 'know better'. The bureaucrats have seemingly demonstrated all along that the country is safe in their hands, and the predeliction for 'pork-barrel' politics, or patronage, among the country's politicians has helped to spread the benefits of rapid economic growth and reduced the possibility of conflict between urban and rural areas. But Japanese democracy has been on a steep learning curve since the war, and nowhere is this more apparent than in the attitudes of young people, who are increasingly willing to criticize the government and its policies. The American notion that every mother's son might grow up to be president, or in this case prime minister, has not yet translated to Japan. There, an interest in politics tends to spring from the desire to achieve some, often relatively limited, goal, although it may be cloaked in such high-flown language as to sound pretentious to the Western ear. But once an individual is involved in politics it tends to become a 'family business'. There is a strong tradition of a relative 'inheriting' the following of a politician of an earlier generation, and the voting strength of local loyalists often ensures that the tradition carries on for several generations more.

Outside of election campaigns, Japanese people generally show little interest in politics on the national scale. Since the nation's domestic goals are arrived at by consensus over an extended period, there have been few sudden changes of direction and perhaps fewer arguments within the former ruling Liberal Democratic Party (LDP) than in Western democratic parties over the general direction of policy. But sharp divisions have existed within the party and fierce competition between the party's various factions for many other reasons. These often concerned the allocation of the available resources, and especially the slots in the party's line-up at election time, because of the large number of multi-seat constituencies in which up to three members of the LDP might be competing against each other.

Since the Japanese are brought up to believe that their own, individual opinions are not of great import and must be adjusted to those of the group, whether company or neighbourhood, pressure groups and factions play a large part in policy-making. But the pressure they exert is often reactive and defensive, protective of a set of interests, rather than innovative and far-sighted. This is the root of many of the problems that Japan experiences in its trading and political relations with foreign countries. Certainly, change over the long term is inevitable, as voters are becoming increasingly frustrated with what is on offer. The LDP was warned of the dissatisfaction in 1989 when it lost control of the House of Councillors for six years.

There is also anecdotal evidence that the traditional sources of the LDP's financing in business and commerce may be drying up. In the old days business would simply deliver the sort of campaign money they thought the prime minister would need. Now, conventional firms are much more careful with their money. The party has had to turn, instead, to some of the fringe service companies created by the massive overheating of real estate and land prices that has become known as the 'bubble economy'. With their brash approach and often controversial methods of doing business, these firms have often brought scandal down on the heads of the party managers.

The Diet

Although the Japanese parliament is commonly called the Diet, 'parliament' is probably a better description. The original prewar Diet was modelled on the Prussian equivalent, which could do little but suggest modifications for policies proposed by the Crown. Today the powers of Japan's lower house are quite transformed from the prewar period. However, the term has remained since the establishment of the Imperial Diet in 1890, when Japan had an authoritarian government and the Diet played merely an advisory role. The present Emperor Akihito is a symbol of state and has no powers of government.

The parliament is the highest organ of state power and has the authority to amend the constitution, approve treaties and designate the prime minister. It consists of two chambers, the House of Representatives, or lower house, with 512 seats, and the House of Councillors, or upper house, with 252 seats. Members of the House of Representatives are elected for a four-year term while those in the upper chamber are elected for six years, with half their number being elected every three years. Sessions of the two houses include ordinary, extraordinary and special sessions. The lower house has the right to pass bills rejected by the upper house by a second vote, when the bill must pass by a two-thirds majority. One of the House of Representative's key tasks is to approve the budget, which is submitted by the cabinet, each year. If the upper house fails to take action on the budget within 30 days of receiving it from the lower house, then the decision of the lower house becomes law.

The House of Representatives is also empowered to introduce non-confidence motions but the upper house has no such power. In addition, the lower house has precedence over the upper house in nominating a new prime minister and approving treaties. Officially the prime minister is appointed by the emperor, but on the recommendation of the Diet.

Under the present electoral system, members of the House of Representatives are elected from 130 small- to medium-sized constituencies, with between two and six seats allotted to each district depending on the relative size of the population. The constituency borders were last redrawn almost 20 years ago, since when shifts of population, largely from rural to urban areas, have led to a widening disparity in the number of voters represented by each member. Despite attempts to rectify this difference in the value of urban and rural votes, the October 1990 census revealed that the disparity remained as high as 3.38 to 1 in some areas.

For the House of Councillors, 100 members are elected under a nation-wide proportional representation system and 152 from electoral districts. In the national constituency, voters cast their ballots for a party and seats are allocated to each party in proportion to its share of the votes.

Reform of the constituency system to eliminate multi-seat constituencies has been mooted for some time. Many models have been examined including the British first-past-the-post system, which would reduce the number of LDP candidates to one per constituency. That would remove one of the principal rationales for the wasteful faction system which has pitted members of the former ruling party against their party colleagues, and help avoid much of the structural corruption that has plagued Japanese politics. Almost everyone is agreed that the present system has had its day and there will have to be a compromise on any future system of electoral politics.

Perhaps it has already begun. The no-confidence motion carried against the then prime minister, Kiichi Miyazawa, in June 1993 foreshadowed splits within the LDP and its defeat by the Socialists in the ensuing election. A significant section of the ruling party, led by Tstoma Hata, a former prime minister, which had supported the opposition motion, broke away to form a new conservative party, the New Life Party. Other LDP members, out of a total of 56 defections, left to form the New Party Heralds. Whether these developments will accelerate or slow down any move to a new political system remains to be seen.

The voter

The profile of a Japanese voter describes a man or woman in a 'nuclear household' of parents and two children living in one of the large conurbations. They probably live in a tiny flat owned by the husband's company and have little prospect of being able to afford their own house because of the spiralling increase in the price of land during the latter half of the 1980s. The husband's work will most likely be with a small- or medium-sized firm – they provide most of the country's employment – and the wife will most probably be in a part-time job to help out with the expenses. Although, in theory, her job is part-time, she will very likely work at least an eight-hour day. The distinction between full-time and part-time work, more often than not, concerns ancillary benefits which the employer of the part-time worker is not required to pay. The money she earns will not necessarily go to pay for extras; more often it will be used to pay for classes in a *juku*, or cramming school, where children go from the age of six or seven onwards to study, night after night, to get the grades required for the school that their parents have selected for them.

By Western standards the hours of study and work by a Japanese family are horrendously long, and the quality of life is low. But for a variety of reasons the Japanese do not blame the negative economic aspects of their lifestyle on the ruling party. Japanese people have never valued the idea of doing something with the least possible effort. The ability and the necessity to endure hardship of all kinds is expected at all times. The harder one is seen to be working, the greater one's contribution to the common good, be it for the company or the country. Conversely, the shame of a family that is not seen to be conforming to society's norms can be devastating. For the most part, Japanese voters and their families identify with the aims and the interests of the companies for which they work. This means that they may feel a little unhappy, for instance, at the way house prices are going but they do not expect government policies that favour a certain sector of the populace, such a house owners, over others. Massive anti-government protest, organized with a little help from interested politicians, may be alright for the farmers but, even if they had the organizational machinery, it is not the way that the Japanese middle-class do things. It is far more honourable to suffer in silence.

However, even before the LDP's defeat in 1993, occasionally the voters swung to the opposition as a protest against the government. For instance, in 1989 the two largest opposition parties, the Social Democratic Party and the Japan Communist Party, benefited from public disgust at the scandal of corruption in the ruling party. They won favour as the LDP's reputation sank, but not for long. The Communists soon suffered from the effects of the international discrediting of their ideology with the widespread collapse of communist regimes while the Socialists failed to capitalize on the boom that resulted from the selection of a woman party leader, Takako Doi. Voters felt that a vote for the opposition parties was not really a vote for a change of government. None of the opposition parties had the symbiotic links of the LDP to the bureaucracy – the LDP having many former bureaucrats in its ranks – and none had the LDP's unsurpassed ability to raise funds from Japanese industry to pay for local projects. There were also the allied, but no less important, points that none of the opposition parties ever put up a sufficient number of candidates to form a government at election time and none was itself free of scandal.

The Liberal Democratic Party

Until July 1993 postwar Japan had had the longest period of one-party rule in the non-communist world, the LDP having held power since its formation in 1955. Before that, with the exception of a period of 10 months in 1947–48 when conservative Socialists ruled in a coalition, the two main constituent parties that later made up the LDP ruled in similarly conservative style. But the LDP is scarcely a political party in the sense that the term is understood in the West. It is more of a coalition of interest groups allied vertically in a series of factions and horizontally in *zoku*, or 'tribes'. *Zoku* are groups of members who share the same interest in an area of policy-making or an industry such as construction – perhaps the most powerful *zoku* in the party, given its wealth of 'pork-barrel' projects. The triangular relationship between businessmen, politicians and the bureaucrats comes together in the *zoku* system. Basically, the politicians are understood to harass the bureaucrats into pursuing a given policy on behalf of the businessmen who, in turn, fund the politicians.

A young member of the former party of government, the LDP (probably male, see Out into society, chapter 3), would spend much of his time 'studying', that is attending lectures and discussion groups often with a government bureaucrat as the principal speaker. Before long he would chooose a specialization, since modern government in Japan is so complex that no one can master the legislation in all fields. Should he, for example, decide to specialize in transport, he would join the requisite committee and its subcommittees dealing with transport issues. The Ministry of Transport would brief him regularly on current issues while his contacts in transport companies would brief him on their concerns and make sure that he had the funds to function on their behalf.

After his second election to the Diet, he would aim to become parliamentary vice-minister of transport. This position would have little policy content but it enabled him to build the kind of bridges with the bureaucracy that he would need if he was to advance to the next stage of his career as chairman of the LDP transport committee or the Diet transport committee. At the pinnacle of his career, he would hope to become minister of transport for a year, after having spent five or six years in the Diet. Throughout he would associate with other members of the Diet interested in transport matters and be lobbied endlessly by the industry and by bureaucrats. He would liaise with members of other *zoku* where their interests coincided.

With the predisposition of Japanese people to distrust -*isms* of one sort and another, it is not surprising that the LDP has a conservative, pro-business, pro-American and anti-Russian credo. Loyalties to individual members of the party tend to be on a personal basis; party membership may well be a secondary consideration. Outside of election time there may be little in the way of a strictly party organization in a local area, but there will be a strong support group for the local member of the Diet. These people raise money and keep the political grass roots well nourished by never failing to mark the birthdays, weddings, funerals and other landmarks in the lives of the candidate's contacts. Between elections the actual national membership of the party may vary by as much as a million, as individuals temporarily bring in friends and relations to work towards polling day and local firms and corporations mobilize their workforces to help out. Here, as in other aspects of Japanese life, human relations rather than abstract political or economic beliefs are the key.

The rather ephemeral organization away from the party headquarters in Tokyo does not prevent the LDP, particularly its right wing, from having some strong ideas about the development of Japan's national identity at home and abroad. When the party was formed in 1955, through the coalescing of the old Liberal and Democratic parties, it set among its goals the reform of education, and of the political and administrative systems, the achievement of economic autonomy, and a diplomacy based on peace. As the American occupation had then only recently ended, there was no mention of reform of the US-written constitution. However, that has become a key goal of the right since that time, as have other issues that are seen as helping to dispel the notion that Japan is beholden to the United States on all fronts.

These reformist aims often manifest themselves through education policy and the bureaucracy of the Ministry of Education, which seems to share the view that imported ideas of democracy and individual rights have weakened traditional Japanese values. Recently, attempts have been made to reassert these values through reintroducing the raising of the national flag at schools and insisting on the singing of the *kimigayo*, the nearest thing Japan has to a national anthem. However, in many people's minds the *timigayo* is too closely associated with emperor-worship and the military government of the World War II.

The other pet hate of the right is the key clause in the constitution whereby Japan renounces the right to use force in the settlement of disputes and, indeed, to maintain armed forces of any kind. Already Japan is among the top three military spenders in the world for its curiously named army, navy and air self-defence forces. The right wing of the party wants to see this anomalous situation rectified as a badge of Japan's maturity as a nation. Such reforms require a two-thirds majority of the Diet, an unlikely prospect in the medium term.

Another display of conservative LDP lobbying power at work can be seen in agricultural policy and in the continuing, and highly effective, campaign against agricultural imports, particularly of rice. Importing of cheaper rice from California, the argument goes, would fatally undermine the country's food security. Many also contend that the home-grown rice culture is bound up with the spirituality of being Japanese and that to start eating foreign rice would be to weaken a spirituality already under siege by Western values. These last examples are illustrative of the inward-looking nature of much LDP policy. The party, up to now, has had little in the way of foreign policy, only a series of domestic policies that affect foreigners. The issue of rice imports neatly encapsulates this concept: the United States, the world's only remaining superpower, is just another pressure group when it comes to the rice issue no matter how important the Americans may feel they are. But Japan knows that if settlement of the rice issue were to jeopardize the outcome of the international GATT (General Agreement on Tariff and Trade) negotiations then there is no doubt where the country's national interest would lie.

The LDP and its parliamentary members represented the link between the bureaucracy (see chapter 4) and the public. Members of the Diet do not create legislation; that is the province of the bureaucracy, which is arguably among the finest in the world. The role of parliamentary members is to find out, on behalf of industry and the public, just what it is that the bureaucracy is up to. Hence the large sums of money channelled to members by industry groups and individual firms and so often referred to as 'corruption'. The age when the bureaucracy went entirely unchallenged, in the Chinese tradition, is now over and there are many groups with first-class policy expertise within the Diet who can match the bureaucracy in their areas of interest. Yet the bureaucracy still plays a role unsurpassed in any Western country with the possible exception of France. The LDP government offered the sort of managerial skills needed to steer Japan's primarily economic interests at home but not necessarily through the choppy waters of modern international politics. Its style of government was quite unlike the adversarial politics of Westminster or Washington. Matched to Japanese culture, it managed Japan's transition well, so well in fact that other governments, including Britain's, are adopting aspects of its managerial style.

The party leadership, which has faced few serious challenges to its dominance since the war, has always shown great skill in co-opting and absorbing opposition from within both own its ranks and those of the opposition parties. Some LDP leaders even said there was no need for opposition parties as such, since the ruling party had the ability to be all things to all people. In most other countries such hubris would get its just deserts from the electorate, and so too did eventually the LDP in 1993. Signs of discontent were already present in 1988, when a consumption tax was introduced, breaking an election campaign pledge. The following year the party got its comeuppance, losing control of the upper house in one of its worst-ever electoral reverses.

A member of the Diet

Traditionally, the role of a locally elected member of the party is to bring as much economic benefit as possible to his constituency. He does this through contacts with his own faction, the rest of the party, local business and the bureaucracy. If he is a former bureaucrat – about a quarter of all politicians fall into that category – so much the better, particularly if he was with a ministry that had the money and clout to bring public works programmes and jobs to the region.

Whether or not the member has high-flown ideas about public service is beside the point, for voters support individual personalities not ideas. Unless he belongs to the Socialist or Communist party, a member of the Diet is most unlikely to be seeking a seat in the house for ideological reasons. He is probably following in the footsteps of his father, an uncle or a relative by marriage. Some 40 per cent of all Diet members in the lower house have 'inherited' their seats from a relative, and most Japanese voters see nothing wrong in this. The sons-in-law of former prime ministers Takeo Fukuda and Zenko Suzuki both had seats in the lower house. There is little doubt that the political career of the late contender for the prime ministerial office,

Shintaro Abe, was helped by his being the former prime minister Nobusuke Kishi's son-in-law.

When a candidate adopts the role of politician for the first time, he is entering on a life that will involve him more deeply in the community than any Western politician. Vast amounts of money will be needed just to maintain a presence in his constituency let alone meet the enormous demands that will be made on him as a 'Mr Fixit' and Santa Claus figure in all aspects of local life. Even in an off-election year it will cost at least 1.5 million yen to take care of his constituency duties to say nothing of running his office in the capital. When he is seeking re-election, the five-to-win three-to-lose formula applies: that is, to succeed he will have to spend at least 500 million yen; if he spends only 300 million he will fail. This direct relationship between spending and electoral fortune is long-established.

Not for him just the short weekend trip to the constituency for a couple of hours' 'surgery': a Diet member is expected to contribute money for all local weddings, funerals and anniversaries as though he were a relative of all those involved. The size of the donation or the value of the wedding gift will be carefully scrutinized as a measure of his regard for the recipient. He must also organize all manner of dinners and excursions as well as meetings with local associations of businessmen, senior citizens and farmers or fishermen – all of which will require food, drink, gifts and tokens of esteem quite apart from the traditional seasons of gift-giving in both summer and winter. The relationships that the 'Dietman' builds up are intensely practical; often they are based on friendship between families over generations. They all create expectations and obligations encapsulated in the word *sensei*, or teacher, which describes the politician's elevated status in the community. Such expectations, which run much deeper than in Western societies, must be satisfied if the politician wishes to retain his seat.

In his official capacity he receives a generous salary that is at least twice the national average, as well as free housing, plenty of money to pay for two secretaries and research assistants at the Diet, and free rail travel. But he will need all of this, along with some good insider tips from his friends in industry, if he is to employ not two, but as many as 25 secretaries, which many members feel they need in order to manage their affairs and to attend all the necessary functions. On top of this he will need sufficient funds to live in the way to which Japanese politicians are accustomed.

The opposition
The notion of a loyal opposition is one that is relatively new to Japanese politics. For the most part the opposition parties have acted as though they did not expect to rule the country. It can be argued that the close relationship between the ruling party and the elite of the bureaucracy convinced the opposition early on in the postwar period that there was little chance of their overcoming this handicap. The other major factor that inhibited a real role for the opposition was its inability to attract funding from the major

corporations on anything like the scale that the LDP was capable of doing, not to mention the absence of policies that were attractive to the great mass of Japanese voters.

Before 1993, when it became the majority party in a new coalition government, the Social Democratic Party of Japan (SDPJ) was the principal opposition party. It is a party still heavily influenced by the early postwar period and Marxist-Leninist dogma. Its postwar persona was created from the then fashionable discussions of Marxism, and both the Socialist and Communist parties have barely advanced beyond that. Although the Socialists announced a new party platform in the mid-1980s, they, like the Communists, are still stuck in an ideological time-warp in which theory takes precedence over practical policies. Their internal debates have had little to do with what is happening in the country or the prosperity of the individual Japanese, which remains a priority for most people.

The Socialists have behaved like the Labour Party in Britain except that their positions have tended to be more extreme and have been maintained over a longer period. They have consistently opposed the very existence of the armed forces, arguing that they are unconstitutional. They are also against the centre-piece of Japanese security policy, the Japan–US Security Treaty, under which the United States, while demanding that Japan unilaterally disarm, is committed to come to Japan's assistance if required. The Socialists maintained their anti-American stance long after the protest riots against the treaty's extension in the 1960s, and long after it had become clear that Japan was getting a relatively free ride under the protection of the US nuclear umbrella while facing a potential threat from the then Soviet Union. Indeed, Russia still occupies disputed territory in the Northern Islands. Although the Socialists have now softened their line on the security arrangements with the United States, they will accept only those nuclear power stations already in place and are against the construction of any new ones. In fact, the party split on this issue. An example of the unreality of the party's policies is that, officially, the 'Great Leader' Kim Il Sung of North Korea is regarded as the head of state of the whole, divided country while the party was for a long time engaged in an agonized debate over 'recognizing' South Korea.

For many years, even in the lower house the Socialists seldom offered more than a token struggle against government policies, and hardly ever realistic policy alternatives. The kind of principled debate heard in other national parliaments was rare, even on such crucial issues as the dispatch of Japanese troops on a peace-keeping mission to Cambodia. This was an issue on which the Socialists had the backing of many Japanese who were deeply concerned about such a development, the breaking of the last great postwar taboo. It was also a major issue of principle in which the Socialists could be expected to have considerable leverage over the ruling party. In the event, they managed to delay passage of the bill for 18 months and succeeded in watering down some of its provisions, but it was a far cry from the 1960s' activism.

For all the Socialists' ineffectiveness, at the end of the 1980s it appeared that the sheer weight of disaffection with the ruling party would result in a significant shift of power to the Socialists under the first female leader of a Japanese political party, Ms Takako Doi. Confidence in the LDP had been eaten away, and for a while it seemed that the ruling party faced serious opposition, so low were its fortunes and so great its difficulties. The novelty of the new party leader and the enhanced political influence of women made it appear that things were set for a change. But it was not to be, and the Doi challenge dissolved almost as quickly as it had arisen.

At the time, there was widespread disenchantment with the LDP over the Recruit shares-for-political-favours scandal. Many leading members of the party, including two former prime ministers, benefited through the gift of shares in the Recruit group of companies. The shares were then ramped on the Tokyo Stock Exchange, yielding vast profits for their owners. But if the scandal left no part of the LDP hierarchy untouched, the opposition Komeito, 'Clean Government' party, was also implicated, leaving its leaders thoroughly compromised in their attempts to attack the ruling party despite their having the casting vote in the upper house.

The scandal revealed to the army of new Japanese holders of stocks and shares, who had come into the market with the semi-privatization of such big firms as Nippon Telegraph and Telephone, that one of the principal roles of the stock market is to help raise money for the ruling party and big corporate interests with scant regard for the rules under which the exchange is supposed to be run. Ordinary stockholders were seen to be little more than pawns in a game that was rigged to the advantage of the big players who could not lose since, if their holdings declined in value, they could look forward to compensation from their broking houses.

Fractious factions

Clans have been a central element of Japanese society from time immemorial. Regional family groupings and their struggles for power and influence make up a large part of the early history of the country. The make-up of the LDP broadly follows this tradition. The roots of the party lie in the unification of the old Liberal and Democratic parties after World War II. Subsequently, other politicians and former bureaucrats formed alliances, often based on common local, regional or industrial interests. There were usually five or six principal factions in the ruling party at any one time. They competed with each other for appointments as ministers, for the senior posts in the organization and for the right to fill the party presidency, which carries with it the office of prime minister. To the outside observer, Japanese politics appeared, for much of the time, to consist of endless rivalry between these groups – a competition that seemed to be an end in itself. In recent years one faction, led by a dominant 'kingmaker', held the major share of power, enabling it largely to dictate the make-up of the cabinet and name the prime minister.

Faction leaders wanted to attract the most capable and electable followers, while those coming into the party sought to join the faction leader who had the best *jinmyaku*, or network of connections, and access to the greatest campaign funds. The all-time king of the faction leaders was the former prime minister Kakuei Tanaka, who took 'money politics' to undreamed-of heights, or depths, depending on one's point of view. Based on the fortune he made, in somewhat dubious circumstances, supplying the Imperial Army in Korea during World War II, Mr Tanaka used his enormous wealth to build influence in the party on a scale which will most probably never be equalled.

At the height of his power, before his stroke in 1985, Mr Tanaka could count more than 120 members in his faction of the LDP as well as numerous hidden sympathizers who were not prepared to be linked to him openly. His own grouping was larger than any opposition party and he nominated three successive prime ministers, declaring that the prime minister was merely a hat worn by the ruling party to be changed with the fashion. His largesse with 'pork-barrel' politics is legendary and his constituency, Niigata No 3, boasts a level of public spending two and a half times the national average. Niigata, the 'back country' of Japan on the Japan Sea coast, was not blessed by nature – it suffers heavy snowfalls in the winter – and it had few of the economic or other attractions found on the Pacific coast. But Mr Tanaka did his best to change all that with such choice projects as a 'Bullet train' line that speeds passengers to Tokyo in two hours. At a cost of 1,000 million yen a special tunnel was built through the mountains to serve a community of only 60 households. Although no one today matches that kind of spending, such issues underpin Japanese politics and politicians on a scale unequalled in the world since the heyday of Mayor Richard Daley's Chicago.

The spending may have been over but the power lingered on. Noboru Takeshita, who inherited much of the membership of the Tanaka faction, became heir to the Tanaka political machine. Having formed a 'study group' only months before Mr Tanaka was stricken, he took over the faction when its leader became incapacitated. Even then, he was compelled to seek Mr Tanaka's blessing before he became prime minister in 1987. At its height, the Takeshita faction had some 69 members of the LDP on its roster in the lower house and 37 in the upper house. Without its support, Kiichi Miyazawa – leader of the second-strongest faction – could not have become prime minister. But perhaps more importantly, he could not have achieved that office without the, albeit reluctant, endorsement of the faction vice-president Shin Kanemaru, the 'kingmaker' who assumed that role after Mr Tanaka. Despite his being sentenced to a jail term for accepting millions of dollars in bribes from Lockheed to promote the sale of jet airliners in Japan, Mr Tanaka remains a free man because of his stroke.

But Mr Kanemaru, too, suffered an ignominious end to his political career for accepting 500 million yen and vast sums in unreported political donations from the gangster-related Tokyo Sagawa Kyubin transport company. The handling of the Kanemaru case represented a watershed in modern Japanese politics for a number of reasons, and could well have a lasting effect on the balance of power within the party. From the outset, Mr Kanemaru was ready to admit, unlike any of is predecessors, that he had broken the law. At first it looked as if he would be the most senior party figure ever to pay the supreme price for a breach of electoral law. But the plea-bargain he made with the court – a plea of guilty in return for a fine of 200,000 yen – so angered many observers that he was taken into custody.

This marked the beginning of a major upheaval within the party, as the struggle began to destroy the power of the faction leader Mr Takeshita and that of Mr Kanemaru, the *éminence grise* behind the scenes in the LDP. Just as Mr Tanaka's power in an earlier era was resented, so Mr Kanemaru caused twice as much resentment from the new, younger set of LDP members who did not want the old, machine-style politics to continue to dominate the party and the country into the 1990s. Such was the apparent damage to the party's main faction, that it looked as if its overwhelming preponderance might be reduced, allowing a more even distribution of factional power.

Political powers

A Japanese prime minister does not have the same powers as his Western counterparts. Hitherto, under the LDP, his commitments have amounted to little unless members of other factions could either directly benefit from what was being proposed or take a rain check from the party leader. In many ways, prime minister Miyazawa's rise to office was typical of the intra-party horse-trading and compromise which produces a leader who, having the full-hearted support of only a fraction of the party, must fight for every inch of whatever policy platform he may hold dear. Much of the time he can expect an easier ride from the opposition than from members of competing factions within his own party who are bent upon unseating him.

Although Mr Miyazawa led the second-strongest faction, Mr Kanemaru most probably allowed his name to go forward only because he knew that the party was facing difficult times in the economy and increasing fallout from scandals. Mr Miyazawa's tenure is a classic example of the Japanese political system at work and how it makes a virtue of expediency. Fluent in English, he was regarded with suspicion by much of the party for being 'too intellectual' and too remote from the grass roots – hardly qualifications for a man whose declared tasks included tackling controversial issues such as electoral reform and corruption. Yet he became prime minister because the most powerful factions could agree on no one else. That speaks volumes about the power and influence wielded by many Japanese prime ministers. The post is often little more than ceremonial, a situation that leads to misunderstanding by outsiders of the value of commitments given by the leaders who hold the office.

The one man who appeared an exception to this rule was Yasuhiro Nakasone, a contemporary and soul mate of the former British prime minister Mrs Thatcher. His direct manner appealed to Western listeners but he was disliked by his party for his arrogance and high-handed style of government. In an attempt to introduce certain policy reforms, such as in education, which were hard to sell to the rank and file of the party, he employed the novel device of appointing special committees of experts and academics. By choosing like-minded individuals he was able to steer their findings in advance, but had less success when it came to implementing them. However, as in the case of a key report on the economy which spelled out necessary new directions, the reports of these special bodies had the advantage of putting the debate into a format that was removed from the inevitable distortions on the floor of the parliament. Mr Nakasone's successors, with the exception of Mr Takeshita, may have shared his views but have been handicapped in their ability to implement reform. However, Mr Takeshita, a master of the political machine, succeeded in several areas where Mr Nakasone failed.

Thus, in the normal course of events, Japanese prime ministers rarely propose new policies in dealing with the West, knowing that the chances of their execution may be slim. Emollient offers are usually made before the annual summits of the seven industrialized countries in anticipation of demands that are about to be made of Tokyo. Often they are about increasing efforts to boost imports, stimulating the world economy or, lately, increasing aid to countries that have recently thrown off communism. Generally, Japanese offers do not stand up to close scrutiny, but the Japanese government knows that its Western counterparts have short memories and by the time the next summit comes around they will most probably be on a completely different tack.

Corruption at the centre

Corruption has been endemic to the Japanese political system since World War I and is intensifying as it becomes more and more expensive to meet the obligations of parliamentarians. The Recruit affair and the Sagawa Kyubin scandal, linking a former prime minister to the leader of an underworld gang whom he used as a contact with the extreme right, are just the latest in a series of scandals that have touched the majority of prime ministers since the war. Although the former prime minister Tanaka was sentenced to imprisonment, he has never actually served any of the sentence. What was true in the 1970s remains true in the 1990s, and the chances of senior politicians receiving real punishment for wrongdoing seems just as remote. But what is new and more sinister about the scandals of the 1990s is that they reach into every corner of the former ruling party and often encompass the other parties. Moreover, most of those found guilty of accepting brides, it seems, are rehabilitated even more quickly than in the past.

But whereas 20 years ago the public was less aware of the standards of acceptable behaviour of politicians in some other countries, today they know enough to make comparisons. They realize, more than ever before, that Japan may have first-class industry but it is served by a third-class political system. So far public opinion has had only a limited effect on the politicians but that could change as Japan's boom years come to an end. Political commentators are suggesting that the country adopt a system of single-member constituencies – which would effectively eliminate factions; introduce tough, enforcible laws on political funding and contributions; and cement them with anti-corruption laws similar to those implemented in Britain a century ago.

With each new scandal, the government has expressed its determination to press on with political reform to overcome corruption. But each time its resolve melts like spring snow when the realities of internal party politics reassert themselves. To the ordinary politician the more pressing requirement is for the vast sums of money needed to maintain a parliamentary seat and meet the expectations of the public. The senior politician, or faction leader with an aggressive pack of parliamentary members to service, has to find even greater sums to keep the political wheels oiled.

The scale of the financing of the LDP when it was in power can be estimated from the funds raised and publicly declared by its top five factions in 1990. This represents the tip of a vast financial iceberg. They collected a total of 7.62 billion yen (about £40 million), one and a half times more than the total raised the previous year. The sharp increase was due to the amount of money needed to fight successful general, gubernatorial and prefectural elections in that year. On the basis of its war chest and political connections, the best faction to belong to was the one led by the former foreign minister Mr Abe, which had 2.58 billion yen in the kitty. Mr Abe's faction could easily raise cash because, though he died in May 1990, he had been seen as as a · strong contender for the future leadership of the party. Any faction member could therefore look forward to a share-out of powerful ministerial and cabinet positions. It was the third consecutive year that that faction had been top fund-raiser in the party. Each member of the faction who was campaigning for a lower-house seat in the 1990 general election was given between 10 and 20 million yen for the task while the overall election spend by the faction was 1.18 billion yen.

Other factions garnering sizeable funds were those of the then prime minister, Mr Miyazawa, which took in 974 million yen, and those with prospects of providing the prime minister in future years. They included the factions of former minister Toshio Komoto and of Michio Watanabe, who ran a strong second to Mr Miyazawa for the premiership and might have been expected to win the prize in the future but for a question mark over his health. These factions gathered 1.50 billion and 1.74 billion yen respectively.

Overall donations to political parties in 1990 reached a record 185 billion yen, with the LDP topping 30 billion yen for the first time. Nearly half the LDP's total came from the National Political Association, a body constituted to receive political donations. This route is favoured by the LDP because it gets round the law that requires those making donations directly to a political party to be named, and thus avoids public scrutiny of a large part of its funding. That year the top named donors were the Petroleum Association of Japan (100 million yen), the Japan Iron and Steel Federation (98 million yen), the Japan Automobile Manufacturer's Association (95 million yen) and the Mitsubishi, Fuji and Dai-Ichi Kangyo banks, who each gave more than 90 million yen.

The laws on political corruption are quite clear, but prosecutors rarely do more than rap the knuckles of wrongdoers. Meanwhile the press, posing as the 'voice of the people', does little more than bay for blood with each new revelation, adopting a self-serving pseudo-moral stance that takes no account of its own questionable standards in the coverage of politics. What is required is a cultural sea change that would transform public attitudes to politicians and their finances, so that they are no longer seen as mere channels for economic benefits.

As with so many reforms in Japan's history, once again change may be forced on the country. The austere 1990s will most likely see companies and major corporations incapable of being as generous as they have been in the past, as sickly balance sheets take their toll. More than one senior industrialist has already expressed unhappiness with the level of political corruption and others may well do so through the size of their political donations. The new coalition government is expected to investigate political funding as part of the reform of the electoral system.

Given the broad spread of political credos represented in the coalition, policy-making is likely to prove as difficult as when the LDP reigned supreme, though some directions are already clear. In the early days of the new government, Mr Hosokawa moved to apologize for Japan's conduct during World War II. But beyond that his own philosophy, and that of his government, remained vague.

3 JAPANESE SOCIETY
The deceptive mosaic

Japanese society is an enigma to much of the world. It appears unchanged and unchanging yet underpins an economy that is vital to the world's continued economic health. In fact the surface calm of Japanese society conceals a degree of change more far-reaching than in any other industrialized country over the past 40 years. During that time the Japanese have moved away from emperor-worship to a peculiarly home-grown style of democracy today. It is remarkable that Japan has managed such traumatic change while retaining so much of its traditional culture and ethos without significant social upheaval.

Taking almost any standards by which modern societies judge themselves – education, personal wealth, longevity or crime rates – Japanese society will match or outclass many of its developed competitors. Different methods of measurement make comparisons less than ideal, but it is a fact that if you are a young Japanese growing up in the 1990s you can look forward to one of the highest standards of living in the world, in a society with relatively little crime and whose members live longer than any other nationality. Yet, paradoxically, many Japanese have a less-developed feeling of pride in their own country than do citizens of other developed countries. The reasons for that are a combination of historic memory, quality of life relative to Western countries and other less identifiable factors that may be pointers to future changes in the society.

Being Japanese
Being brought up Japanese is like being initiated into a sect that believes itself to have unique traits bound together by a language whose delicacy of expression represents an exclusive code that can be appreciated only by fellow members and defies effective translation into foreign tongues. The myth of Japanese uniqueness was promoted by the government and its agencies in the early years of contact with the West to help protect the country from rapacious colonizers and disguise the true extent of Japan's backwardness.

This Japanese self-perception has coloured foreign attitudes, greatly reinforcing the image and the reality of exclusivity, while the relative lack of Japanese-speaking foreigners reinforces the notion that ethnicity and language are inseparable. The success of Japanese industry and commerce, and in some respects the proven superiority of Japanese society over Western models, further underlines this impression of separateness despite much-increased contact over the last 30 years. Thoughtful Japanese, aware of the danger that the seemingly all-powerful, inscrutable industrial giant might evoke fear and jealousy, have attempted to try and put things into perspective.

The problem remains that where there is, or should be, compatibility in the way that Japan and the rest of the world do things, the cliches seem to be confirmed. The United States introduced Japan to baseball, but the Japanese concentration on harmony in the way they play, almost to the point of non-aggression, makes it seem like a different game. Likewise, Japan has many institutions that are superficially similar to those of the West but they function quite differently. In one sense, Japan is a victim of history, geography and its own success. An archipelago whose history has put it at odds with its Asian neighbours, as has its relative success, Japan is in Asia, but not of it.

The countries with which it now has most in common, or with which it has managed largely to overcome historical antagonisms, are all far-flung. Japan's traditions of impeccable personal behaviour and its engineering heritage owe much to Victorian England; its modern cultural model is often the United States, yet its future lies in its immediate surroundings. No wonder there is sometimes confusion even in a society which absorbs the traits of others with extraordinary aplomb.

At home

The much-maligned Japanese household – compared in the West with living in a rabbit hutch – is society in microcosm. It is a tiny replica of many close-knit units found throughout Japanese society – from factory to government department – that give it its tremendous cohesion and unanimity of purpose. These are derived, in part, from the willingness of each member to subsume his or her will in the interests of the greater good of the whole. An individual may owe allegiance to many such units whether school, university or company throughout his or her lifetime, and sometimes more than one at a time.

Originally, the farming household all worked together to bring in the harvest in the face of the elements. Today such a fundamental unifying task may be the exception rather than the rule, but the same feeling of collective purpose can be found in the company or the university, if less markedly in the home, where wealth and more living space have tended to loosen family ties. That unity rests on the willingness of Japanese to see themselves merely as part of the whole whatever their individual talents and achievements. A company man will, therefore, introduce himself as, for example, 'Suzuki of company X' whether he is doorman or director. Nor will he give his first name in his introduction unless he happens to be from the younger generation, has been educated abroad or is trying to show a foreigner that Japan is not so different after all.

Tucked away in obscure corners of Japan doing routine jobs with organizations large and small are legions of people with educational qualifications that would make them highly visible figures in Western societies. But they must remain content to be anonymous cogs helping to drive forward the whole enterprise despite outstanding abilities which may well be hampered by less-able seniors. Herein lie some of Japanese society's greatest strengths and greatest weaknesses, which are amplified by this strongly hierachical structure.

Schooling

The Meiji reformers gave the country nothing so important as an extraordinary thirst for knowledge and an emphasis on education which, along with a capacity for hard work, remain the country's greatest strengths to this day. Toddlers are encouraged to study hard even before they are launched on their educational trajectory at a preschool establishment which will be carefully chosen for its record in having pupils successfully enter selected primary schools. This first step is vital in ensuring that the child can go on through the system and be ready to enter the university of his or her choice when the time comes. Only studying at the appropriate schools in the interim will ensure that this will happen. Often pupils will be entered at birth for their schools, and mothers will queue from before dawn to complete formalities as the school year begins.

Since the end of World War II the school system has been run on the American model. Middle and high schools lead on to 514 state and private universities which provide the all-important degree without which no young Japanese can hope to gain any employment beyond menial work. All educational standards and texts in state schools are determined by the Ministry of Education, whose powers are beyond the dreams of their Western counterparts. The examinations are set from a broad-based syllabus which ensures that successful candidates are competent across a wide front and suitable material for the real shaping and moulding for working life that will take place at the company or government agency.

The education system fosters fierce competition and causes a great deal of suffering among children, many of whom miss out on the joys of childhood. But it produces well-educated citizens for Japan's excellent bureaucracy and its global corporations. The system is so rigidly ordered that, on any given day, all pupils, for example, studying English in the first year of public high schools, will be on the same page of the same textbook. Education remains geared to the passing of examinations through rote learning and not the development of individual talent. This fact, allied to the mind-numbing competition, with anything up to 300 per cent applications for certain university courses, has led to demands for reform to reduce the temperature in the educational pressure cooker in the hope of producing new generations of more creative and individually-minded Japanese. Critics of the system cite evidence of this lack of creativity in the country's Nobel Prize tally, which stands at a modest three in the sciences as against Britain's 63 and 133 for the United States. But the tide may be turning; already Japan registers more patents annually than Britain and the United States combined.

Although many parents, educators and members of government would agree that something must be done to end the ferocious competition of the 'examination hell', few are prepared to risk the future of their own children and be the first to step off the treadmill. The former prime minister, Yasu-hiro Nakasone, made a spirited attempt to get the process under way with a special committee set up to study the problem. However, it soon became clear that the idea of reform contemplated by right and left were very differ-ent. In particular, the right wanted to reintroduce more nationalist values into the education system, which they believed was short on spiritual values and too much like its American model.

Since the war, education has been a political football. In wartime it was used to support the aims of the military government, but afterwards the teachers' union took an independent, strongly Marxist line. Despite the ef-forts of the government to draw the union's teeth, it remains an important brake on attempts by some in the government and bureaucracy to revive prewar nationalism. This wartime legacy, and suspicion of the still highly centralized education bureaucracy, has resulted in years of tension between the government and the teachers' union over what the conservatives see as continuing excessive leftist influence among high-school teachers.

It is impossible to overestimate the importance of education in a society where degrees from the University of Tokyo or the University of Kyoto are indispensable for those wanting to reach the upper levels of the government and bureaucracy. Certainly, senior bureaucrats who are not alumni of the former are few and far between.

Out into society

While universities are often seen as havens of conservatism in a sea of rela-tive liberalism, for many men and women they also offer the last opportun-ity when they can mix in a carefree milieu away from social pressures. Japanese universities are generally regarded as being hard to enter, but thereafter they provide a temporary respite from the harshly competitive world of work in which people's roles become more sharply defined, with both sexes expected to marry and have a family.

It is a society with clearly marked rites of passage for citizens of all ages, but particularly for those growing up and making the all-important trans-ition to a useful and productive member of a society – one that not so very long ago rejoiced in slogans such as 'Those who don't work don't eat.' The transition to adulthood marks the beginning of the period in which the indi-vidual is expected to start paying back some of the debts he or she owes soci-ety and parents for bringing them up and providing for them. It is a time, too, when they may be expected to take on the responsibilities of caring for other, older members of the household, though this tradition is beginning to break down much as it has done in the West.

In good times, and assuming that the university graduate has a satisfactory degree, the young hopeful will already have had approaches from, or been interviewed by, several companies with job offers before graduation. When jobs are plentiful, companies compete very vigorously for the services of the new crop of graduates, so much so that, in the past, the government has had to set a date before which it is not permitted to make them offers. High-prestige firms with household names from the world of insurance and banking are among the most sought-after in the private sector while the Ministries of Finance, Foreign Affairs and International Trade and Industry are among the most prestigious government office employers.

Women graduates, unless they intend to become doctors or scientists, are generally expected to conform to the norm and spend only a brief period working before they get married, settle down and produce children. Those women who go into commerce and industry often find that their degree qualifications have no use in the type of work they are expected to do. They end up being saddled with menial tasks such as making tea and photocopying, or typing or entertaining visitors as 'OLs' – 'office ladies' or 'office flowers' – whose function is decorative rather than productive. As that implies, even the most robust blooms will begin to lose their lustre, so by the median marriage age for women, of just over 25, they are expected to be making nuptial plans. According to an old Japanese saying, the number 26 is bad for both Christmas cakes and women: the cakes are past it on 26 December and so are women by their 26th birthday.

If no suitor appears before this crucial time for a woman, then sectional or senior managers will start to bring into play one of the extraordinary social functions that are unique to Japanese companies: they will act as a go-between for the woman and possible partners of a similiar social standing, background and interest in an *omiai*, or arranged marriage. Today, the majority of marriages are 'love matches' in the Western tradition. However, because of their lower failure rate, arranged marriages still have a following in conservative and rural areas where loss of population to the great urban centres has much reduced marriage prospects, particularly for men. Indeed, in some northern rural areas of Japan, brides for farmers are imported from the Philippines and other South-East Asian countries.

Although many OLs in the cities are now delaying marriage for up to three years, often a woman who fails to contract a marriage around the median age will be asked to seek alternative employment. If she refuses, she can be sacked. Despite its assumption of certain social responsibilities, the company is still keen to keep its labour costs down. The woman leaving to get married is replaced by a younger and much cheaper 'office flower'.

It is still hard for women to carve out long-term professional careers for themselves and there remain firm expectations that women should take their place in society by marrying and producing children. So far, industry and retailing have promoted women into senior positions in only specialist areas, and while the diplomatic service has more women than in the past they rarely attain the highest ranks.

In the first flush of democracy after the war there was a rush of women into politics. Early general elections returned a considerable number of women members of the Diet, but female enthusiasm for electoral politics has since flagged and women MPs are now a rarity. In the mid-1980s there was a flurry of publicity when the Maritime Self-Defence Force appointed its first woman seagoing captain, but that has not started a noticeable trend. Indeed, the Japanese seem convinced that the growing problems of crime, juvenile deliquency and break-up of the family in Western society only confirm their belief that the woman's role is to bring up the next generation and act as household manager.

Marketing men, however, have realized what many politicians appear to have forgotten and many advertisements now focus on the woman of the house, particularly for the more expensive items for the household such as cars. The 'ad men' are merely recognizing the reality that, once you cross the threshold of a Japanese home, the lady of the house reigns supreme right down to management of the household budget. Perhaps the majority of men are given a weekly allowance out of the household budget for out-of-pocket expenses.

A middle-class country

When postwar Japan threw out its aristocracy and transformed its emperor into a mere human, it did so with such efficiency that it now believes itself to be a middle-class state through and through. Regular surveys carried out by the prime minister's office reaffirm the notion that everyone, from drivers on commuter trains to company presidents, think of themselves as middle class – just like the next-door neighbour – and they want to keep it that way.

No one knows whether these surveys reflect the views of, for example, coalminers, whose industry has been in catastrophic decline, since the government does not disclose its survey methods. But despite the reservation that must exist about the findings, the comfortable fiction that everyone is on a par is maintained. After all, unless you are a real-estate tycoon or a movie star you will face the same titanic struggle to own your own home or break out of the rat race.

Clearly, the strategy of educating the great mass of the populace to a high level across a broad front with few dizzy heights or depressing lows pays off in more than just economic terms. It creates a society whose relatively narrow income spread helps contribute to its stability. Salaries are awarded and increased according to age and experience rather than merit. Most people appear to prefer it that way; they do not stick out in a crowd, so that responsibility, rewards and blame are spread. Thus, when things go wrong, particularly in government, there are no identifiable culprits.

But with promotions handled by most firms in this fashion, the bright and ambitious have, until now, had to wait patiently for their turn at the top jobs. The general maturing of the economy has meant that fewer company men can now achieve the traditional goal of becoming a departmental section chief by the time they reach their forties. This blockage in the middle-management stage of their careers has led to more men making the break from the traditional Japanese corporate life if they are still young enough. For the older employees the surfeit of middle managers may cause them to be shunted off to a less important and less well-paid job in a subsidiary company or quietly eased out altogether. Although the word 'redundancy' may not be used, some firms have now started to lay off workers – something unheard of previously in a society that prided itself on lifetime employment.

There are sizeable areas of Tokyo and Osaka inhabited by day-labourers who subsist on minimal incomes in what have become virtually no-go areas for most people except the police and the gangsters who control the supply of such contract labour. These workers are often from the *burakumin* underclass of 'untouchables', who have traditionally been excluded from the mainstream because of their pursuit of trades deemed unsuitable for humans, such as butchery and leather work. They number about two million in the Osaka area alone, and while it is no longer possible to check the national family register for evidence of a *buraku* background, some of the larger corporations have access to such information and will avoid employing anyone with such a family history. Likewise, families will often retain private detectives to check out the prospective marriage partners of their children for similar reasons.

Most young men and women in their twenties have ambitions that vary little from the social norm: respectable, white-collar job for the men and white wedding and family for the women, with a house not too far from the workplace. Even if once, as students, they dreamed of doing more exciting things, then those dreams now seem self-centred and antisocial and are fast fading by the time they reach maturity and take their place as members of society. Society will most amply reward those who conform.

The average 'salaryman' is such a conformist and so regular in his habits that a survey of surveys shows that he has 14 ties, cuts his toenails once a week and leaves the office at 6.49 p.m. After that, he will join millions of other office workers in an evening of eating, drinking and general merry-making in one of the millions of bars across the country. This helps ease the pressures of the day and aids the bonding process that Japanese find indispensable to social harmony. The women from the office will often be asked to join their male colleagues for the early part of the evening, but will then discreetly leave before the men go on to some essentially male pursuits, generally in a bar.

But outside the big trading companies and corporations, whose exploits are so well known, there is a vast underbody of small and medium-sized companies with whom employment is a different experience. Thousands of firms fall into this category, with small numbers of employees whose hours of work and working conditions match those of the larger firms, but who receive much lower remuneration and have less-predictable careers. These firms often supply the big companies with parts and services and they are expected, year by year, to bring down their costs while maintaining their standards. In these little-known recesses of Japanese industry are the true heroes who make many of the large firms' cost-cutting exercises feasible.

But the supposed universal dream of the middle class – home ownership – is, ironically, perhaps more elusive in Japan than in any other developed country. The ballooning land prices of the 1980s ushered in the two-generation mortgage and dashed the hopes of many of acquiring a place of their own.

Law and order

Japan's low incidence of crime and high clear-up rates are impressive, though this is partly due to cultural and other reasons, which in some cases make them slightly unreal. Although the rate of cases solved in Japan is on a downward trend, both arrest and clear-up rates are better than in the West. In 1989, Japan recorded 1,308 homicides compared to the 4,596 in England and Wales, and the Japanese arrest rate was 95.9 per cent as against 78 per cent. In the resolution of robbery cases Japan had a similarly superior record of 75.9 per cent against 26.5 per cent in England and Wales.

In 1991, published statistics showed a low incidence of crime, with a little more than 137 crimes per 10,000 head of population. However, Japanese society suffers from the effects of crime in subtle ways that cannot be measured. The influence of gangsters remains widespread, and often cases of intimidation and violence against unwanted tenants or rival business premises never come to the attention of the police. Equally, police officers have an interest in reporting low levels of crime in their area. Their superiors are impressed by the low incidence of wrongdoing, not by their success rate in solving crime. Indeed, the police will often persuade a party to shelve a complaint – which then disappears from the statistics – rather than encouraging them to pursue it.

Respect for authority and the country's hierarchical structure is inculcated in Japanese children from preschool onwards. At every turn the shame of being different from others and cast out of the close-knit community – whether at home, in school or in some other group – is emphasized. The rewards of remaining in society's womb are apparent on every side and the prospect of being cast adrift through crime is too terrible to contemplate.

For the great majority of Japanese, then, their most earnest desire is to be part of the group; to do nothing that will attract attention, least of all that of the police. Rebelliousness, except in a controlled way, is not really an option. Having a police record is to cast doubt on one's reliability as a member of society and a company employee and, given the highly centralized nature of record-keeping by the Ministry of Home Affairs and the police, is to risk being branded for life. The corollary of that is to wish to remain on good terms with the authorities by informing on those who are misbehaving in some way. The willingness of members of the public to assist the police remains a strong element for the guardians of the law.

These cultural norms give the Japanese police officer a head start when dealing with his charges. Until quite recently the police offer was also aided by the relatively static nature of the population and by 'living over the shop', having an intimate relationship with an area that he or she has known since childhood. The police's regular and repeated patrolling of their area on motorcycles has earned them the affectionate nickname *omawari-san* ('Mr Going-around'). The focus of many a neighbourhood, whether in the heart of Tokyo or in some remote farming community in northern Hokkaido, is the *koban*, or local police box, which is usually occupied 24 hours a day by a duty officer. Nowadays a police officer may commute to his *koban* from some outlying dormitory town, like all the office workers around him, but his commitment remains just as great. Because of the extended hours of duty demanded during the funeral ceremonies for the late Emperor Hirohito, at least one policeman died of overwork. Knowing each household and its occupants within his area helps the police officer forsee and forestall possible difficulties, but it leaves him equipped to deal, for the most part, with only petty crime and minor misdemeanours.

Japan's somewhat cosy system of policing has worked well so far but only because the police tolerate to a large extent the real crime that infiltrates many aspects of Japanese society through the activities of gangsters (*yakuza*). They control vast areas of economic activity such as real estate, construction, gambling, sport, show business and the work of day labourers, to say nothing of their notorious links with leading politicians, which has been an important fact of Japanese life since the war. The *yakuza* also run businesses dealing in narcotics, prostitution, gambling and enforcement, which in Japan alone generate hundreds of millions of dollars, quite apart from their activities throughout the rest of Asia and in the United States.

For a long time, the police have had close relations with the *yakuza*. On numerous occasions gangsters have benefited from access to priveleges while in prison and from an unnaturally high level of police tolerance for their activities, due, in no small measure, to the gangsters' readiness to resort to violence. Currently, the police give the impression that they are not unhappy with a situation in which the criminal world is monitored and controlled by means of these relationships. How far members of the public have become disenchanted with this state of affairs can be judged from the number who have joined groups that openly monitor gangster activities in their districts or take them to court for illegal use of premises and the like. The government, too, has passed laws severely limiting gangsters activities but it remains to be seen how effective these will be in practice. The legislative branch moved after a series of gang-war shootings in the Kobe area of western Japan and growing involvement of the *yakuza* in the drugs trade.

Just as policing at the local level is changing, so reorganization will be needed to tackle crime at the national level, particularly sophisticated white-collar crime, which is on the increase. So far, the police force has been hampered by competition at the prefecture level. Solving crimes has been adversely affected by rivalry between different regional forces and their unwillingness to cooperate with each other for fear of yielding the credit for a success to another force.

The royal family

The first Japanese emperor probably took the throne about the beginning of the Christian era. Jimmu Tenno and his fellow early emperors were reputed to be robust fellows, all living to be at least 100 years' old, making a suitable beginning for what is believed to be the oldest continuous imperial line in the world.

In modern times the authority of the emperor has waxed and waned but has rarely been more controversial than during the reign of the late Emperor Hirohito, now known as the Showa Era. Coming to the throne at a young age, he oversaw Japan's aggression against the Asian mainland and the United States as a ruler with supposedly god-like powers. At the end of World War II, Hirohito offered himself as a sacrifice to the incoming US military authorities. The occupiers saw his value as a symbol round which the defeated country could be effectively rallied, but as an ordinary man not a god. Hirohito plunged into that role and, for a brief period, clearly enjoyed touring the country and meeting the people. With the decline in influence of the occupation authorities, the Imperial Household Agency once again reasserted itself, reopening the gulf between ruler and ruled. Sat astride a white charger with his military leaders or dressed in a smart American-cut suit, postwar Emperor Hirohito seemed to epitomize the belief that an emperor merely reflects the national circumstances in which he finds himself. He managed to bridge war and peace with such aplomb that for many years he was the only surviving wartime leader.

By allowing the present emperor to marry a commoner, Hirohito permitted a key step in the modernization of the monarchy. But both the imperial family and the Imperial Household Agency have taken great care not to allow popularization to proceed too far or too fast. Perhaps learning from the British experience, they have limited the number of royal appearances, and access by the press is restricted to just one highly ritualized, tightly controlled press conference a year. Even then, all the questions are vetted in advance and they receive extremely oblique answers, in keeping with the taboo on imperial intervention in politics.

The present empress, Michiko, suffered illness and trauma as a commoner entering the royal family, like Princess Diana in Britain, but the press was allowed to write little about it and she, and the institution, have survived the experience. Even so, the empress's experience as a young bride made it difficult for the future heir to the throne, Prince Naruhito, to find himself a bride. He, somewhat rashly, announced that he wanted to marry by the age of 30. When that birthday came and went without a bride in sight the speculation on his wedding prospects became so intense that the royal household imposed a moratorium on writing about the prince's predicament. (Eventually, he found an eminently suitable candidate in Masako Owada, a diplomat with the foreign ministry.) Life in the palace is still closely regulated by the Imperial Household Agency despite attempts by the new emperor to make the new regime more open and accessible. The life of any commoner coming into the palace remains very restricted and is unlikely to change in the near future.

The foreign factor

At every major juncture in Japanese history, foreigners and foreign powers have played a central role. Key reforms in domestic policy have usually been the result of outside pressure, such as the pacifist constitution dictated by the United States. Japan's late start in industrial development left it feeling insecure and distrustful of its Western counterparts, just as its inheritance of many elements of Chinese culture similarly affected its feelings towards China. The militarists bolstered the government's own efforts to build self-confidence, inculcating a feeling of superiority over less-advanced countries. This was seen at its worst in incidents such as the massacre of 100,000 Chinese at Nanjing in 1938.

Thus the Japanese people are heirs to a complex love–hate relationship with foreigners and foreign countries which, in the past, has taken extreme forms. Nowadays, Japan's obvious economic superiority over many Western industrialized countries can lead to an overweening arrogance, but it is usually no worse than the condescension Japan has suffered from the West.

In Japanese, the word *gaijin*, meaning 'outside person', distinguishes the Westerner from the local, and there are more subtle distinctions at play. But while the Caucasian foreigner will merely be amused by the children jumping up and down shouting *'gaijin, gaijin'* as he walks down the streets of some provincial town, it is preferable to the label *'Asiajin'* which the Japanese attach to other Asians in a derogatory sense. That word, which so clearly sets themselves apart from the rest of their region, has different connotations from, say, a Briton not wishing to call himself a 'European'. The latter springs from what is usually a relatively harmless political, cultural and industrial rivalry with the French and Germans whereas *Asiajin* has strongly racial overtones.

These feelings of distinction from other groups, coupled with the jealousies that such an accomplished nation attracts, have led to comparisons with the Jews and, indeed, there is a theory that the Japanese are the lost tribe of Israel. Be that as it may, the Japanese as a nation are acutely conscious that, despite the complex nature of their relationships with outsiders, they need the rest of the world more than the rest of the world needs them. Novels and films have drawn attention to this with such graphic images as Japan sinking beneath the ocean while the world looks on. Even such staples of the Japanese diet as bean curd and soya beans must be imported from the United States not to mention vast quantities of oil and various ores.

Japan's relative isolation from the rest of the world, – geographical as well as psychological – has contributed to its feeling of 'otherness'. The country receives annual visitors equivalent to 2 per cent of its native population, compared with corresponding figures of 25 per cent for Britain and 60 per cent for France. Resident foreigners number fewer than one million, less than 1 per cent of the population, the vast majority of them Koreans many of whom were born in Japan, speak the language and are, to all intents and purposes, Japanese except in how the rest of the nation views them legally and socially. This attitude stems from the large numbers of Koreans who entered Japan as slave labour during the militarist period and later as workers hired by the big corporations during their prewar expansion. Today's Korean residents still suffer the indignity of being finger-printed yet with little prospect of becoming naturalized Japanese even if they wish to do so. This alienation has caused Koreans to get involved in gambling, prostitution and other gangster-related activities, which further reinforces the prejudice against them. Their position has also been complicated by the political division of Korea into the capitalist South and communist North. Those supporting the North have found themselves in relative political isolation. Yet Koreans, whether in business, show business or sport, have made considerable contributions to the country that remains unwilling to adopt them legally. Several of Japan's greatest baseball players and team managers have been of Korean extraction, and so too was its arguably greatest-ever wrestler.

Strong policies against contraception over the years have sustained the notion that the country should have a high birth rate to keep industry and agriculture supplied with labour. This policy has been maintained despite the decline in the numbers employed in agriculture and the shift into less-labour-intensive industries. Traditionally, Japan has not been a country of immigration. Its racial exclusivity, small land area and lack of natural resources have all contributed to this state of affairs so that while others may seek to help the refugees cast adrift by war in the region, and elsewhere, Japan feels no such obligation despite its wealth. The rate of naturalization as Japanese citizens runs at a fraction of that in Western countries and the total number of refugees granted asylum since the end of the Vietnam war in 1975 amounts to only a few thousand.

Yet there is increasing pressure for Japan to open its doors to foreign workers. As the population has become more wealthy, the willingness of its workforce to do the less attractive jobs has declined. For years there has been a lively traffic in young women from other Asian countries, particularly Filipinas, to keep the bars and strip-joints supplied with new bodies. Controlled by gangsters who bring them in illegally, these women are virtual slaves of the men on whom they depend not only for their livelihood but for their continued stay in the country. In recent years; Pakistanis and

Indians have also travelled to Japan in considerable numbers to work illegally, but the biggest influx has been of Iranians. They were permitted entry by a liberal visa arrangement agreed during the time of the Shah, under which thousands now come to Japan to flee the rule of the mullahs, and many of them end up living rough in Tokyo parks. These immigrants receive a lot of publicity, but little is said about the many thousands of Chinese who have entered Japan illegally over the years, for fear of offending the Chinese government. Originally, many of them came to study but now they are just as likely to come in search of better-paid employment.

The debate about Japan's opening up to its Asian neighbours has been going on for years, but usually within those neighbouring countries. The great majority of Japanese remain firmly opposed to a policy that would permit more foreigners to take up residence or become naturalized. Most would not want a foreigner living next door or working next to them on a production line. Yet the demand for non-Japanese in tertiary-sector employment is clearly there and unlikely to decline substantially unless there is a major slow-down in economic activity. Japanese are proud of the fact that the homogeneous nature of their society is an important factor in its stability, but many are unwilling to admit that the suppression of minorities is also a strong element of that homogeneity. For instance, Koreans take Japanese names to avoid discrimination, and no name that cannot be rendered in Chinese characters may be recorded in a Japanese family register.

The sporting life

Though sumo wrestling is Japan's most prominent traditional sport, with its many subtle expressions of the national character, far and away the most popular sport is baseball, which has a following of millions. It is a markedly Japanese style of baseball, with its concentration on discipline and training, often to the exclusion of originality and spontaneity, and well-behaved fans who would no more think of rioting than they would of being rude to the boss. Both these sports are conducted with a minimum of contact with the outside world though older American baseball players are common in Japanese teams, often providing the teams' heavy hitters. But they too must conform to the Japanese way of doing things and not be seen to be too successful. Regularly games are finessed over the season so that a Japanese, rather than an American, is deemed the best player of the year.

Since the war, Hawaiians have made their mark in the world of sumo. But, in this highly-stylized ritual, they are not expected to upset the general order and a too successful sumo man may be persuaded to win a little less in the interests of 'harmony'. Akebono, a Hawaiian-born sumo wrestler, has become the first non-Japanese to achieve the rank of *yokozuna* in the sport, but it seems that he was allowed to do so because he showed sufficient humility.

For the Japanese, in international sport things have never quite been the same since the world judo championship was conceded for the first time. At each Olympics there is always a furore over why, except in the marathon, the country is consistently outclassed by its Korean and Chinese neighbours. However, there seems little chance of this situation being altered until there is greater concentration on international-level sport as a national goal, or there is more sponsorship of young hopefuls by the private sector. For the present it seems likely that Japan will continue to make world-beating sports equipment – from baseball bats to rally cars – which other nations will put to world-beating use. But there is no doubt that, with the increased stature and physical strength of young Japanese – now on a par with Europeans – the Olympics could bring a new heyday for Japanese sport once the nation puts its collective mind to it.

4 BUREAUCRACY AND THE LAW
The bureaucratic elite

Japan's bureaucracy is the envy of the world. This is not just because of its scope and size but because of the high quality of its personnel – the cream of the educational crop – and, above all, its almost seamless relationship with business and industry. The tradition of the bureaucrat is a long and prestigious one. It has its roots in the samurai who gave up their martial pursuits in the 19th century, at the time of the Meiji restoration, and took up the study of newly imported Western ways. Much as the samurai of old followed *bushido*, the way of the warrior, with its tradition of honour and self-sacrifice, so the modern Japanese bureaucrat sees himself (they are overwhelmingly male) as a supreme servant of the people and the nation, advancing their cause in the world without concern for his long hours of work or relatively low pay.

That bureaucrats are among the best-educated people in a country that sets great store by education is confirmation of their elite status. Such is the tradition of commitment that it is almost unknown for bureaucrats to leave the service before retirement age to better themselves elsewhere. Having educated and trained them, the country can be sure of retaining their expertise and experience through to the end of their civil service careers.

The elite of the elite are the personnel of the Ministry of Finance with their enormous budgetary influence. They are closely followed by the employees of the Ministry of International Trade and Industry (MITI) and the construction ministry, whose ability to allocate civil engineering and construction projects can make or break political careers, quite apart from the crucial role such projects have in local and regional development. Somewhere lower down the scale comes the Ministry of Foreign Affairs which, despite the elite nature of the calling, has little that it can dispense in the way of power on the domestic scene, and so does not rate as highly in terms of its influence.

The industrial connection
Bureaucrats are linked to industry, the government and other parts of the bureaucracy so closely that at times it is hard to tell one from the other. Sophisticated networks of cross-posting of staff between ministries and between industry and bureaucracy entail the frequent interchange of intelligence, and for much of the time the interests of the three can become

virtually identical, with the advancement of the country's interests as the overriding goal. Since the bureaucracy plays the leading role in the formulation of legislation, the role of the Diet, and thus of the democratic process, is minimized in the drafting and approval of the country's laws.

Where the interests of bureaucracy and industry do not coincide, differences can be resolved with relative ease given the symbiotic relations achieved through the system of *amakudari*, or 'descent from heaven'. This enables retiring bureaucrats immediately to find jobs in the industry that they have recently been guiding and monitoring from Kasumigaseki, an area of central Tokyo close to the imperial palace, where all the main ministry buildings are clustered. Having worked closely with the leaders of a given industry throughout his government service career, the retiring bureaucrat takes care to maintain good contacts with the industry he is about to join. He will see that it is well serviced and that there is a lucrative company post waiting for him after his retirement, at a relatively early age, from the civil service. Thus the bureaucracy gets good access to business and vice versa.

Within the bureaucracy, the interchange of staff between different ministries allows the one to be kept constantly informed of the views and interests of the other, while keeping an eye open for information in the ceaseless inter-ministry turf battles that often achieve an importance of their own. In other instances a wide range of bureaucrats from various ministries – 'diplocrats' in the phrase of Dr Barry Keehn of Cambridge University – are posted to Japanese embassies abroad.

The links begin at school and university – often the law department of Tokyo University, where most of the political and bureaucratic elite get their final polish before joining the higher echelons of 'Japan Inc'. The largest and most formidable in the field of trade is the Ministry of International Trade and Industry (MITI) which has some 15 major departments. The most important of these, at least as far as foreigners are concerned, is the Industrial Policy Bureau, which features 22 different offices alone. MITI is the direct descendant of the wartime Ministry of Munitions which managed the production side of Japan's war effort. MITI is largely responsible for having made Japan the industrial success that it is today.

It is safe to say that no major development is undertaken or decision made in Japanese industry or commerce without its coming to the attention of MITI, either in the context of domestic industrial policy or export policy. Indeed, in the early years of Japan's headlong industrial growth and rapid expansion of its export markets, MITI shaped the nation's strategy. It decided which industries were going to be developed and which allowed to decline, and how the products of industry were going to be marketed to the world.

With impressive powers to allocate resources and materials, as well as controlling what imports might be permitted and in what quantities, MITI ensures that both nascent and mature industries are protected from foreign competition. These policies are created in Tokyo but can be monitored and administered from regional headquarters throughout the country. In the early years, no company of any significance could operate outside the confines of MITI monitoring. Today, despite the partial liberalization of the economy, most companies must pay heed to the key instrument of MITI's success – *gyosei shido*, or administrative guidance. The importance of this policy tool can hardly be overestimated. Official guidance is informal, is never written down, does not have the force of law and is therefore, in theory, voluntary. But the few companies that have tried to ignore guidance have quickly been forced to back down through threats of sanctions or legal action. The system gives bureaucrats enormous flexibility and room for denial if the guidance subsequently proves wrong or politically embarrassing.

As Japan has continued to liberalize its economy, the government has made great play of the fact that companies were said to be slipping beyond MITI's control. It argued that guidance was no longer really possible and that the guidance being given was directed at increasing imports, compelling companies to buy parts from abroad and reduce exports in sensitive areas. In fact, the reverse is true. As MITI's control has become more difficult, so the bureaucrats have striven to retain their authority by issuing more and more formal decrees and instructions – almost 11,000 according to a 1993 survey by the *Nikkei Weekly*, which revealed that the number had grown by 10 per cent between 1985 and 1991. Moreover, this figure takes no account of the number of instructions issued under administrative guidance.

If a company decides to challenge guidance, the case of Lions Petroleum, a small Tokyo petrol retailer, serves as a cautionary tale. In 1984 its lively, entrepreneurial owner Taiji Sato decided to import refined petroleum from Singapore so that he could undercut the pump prices of his rivals in the ferociously competitive atmosphere of the capital's motor trade. There was nothing illegal about his plans and he succeeded in getting the first shipment into port before the MITI bureaucrats struck. Although he was a shrimp among the whales of this multitrillion-yen industry, he was upsetting MITI's carefully engineered industry cartel which, through administrative guidance, banned imports of the refined product. In so doing, the ministry believed it was protecting the national interest by retaining the capability to refine petroleum in Japan rather then letting cheaper and more efficient refining centres, like Singapore, get into that market. Not surprisingly, the ministry had the backing of other petrol retailers who did not want to see their prices undercut. But MITI was not content with merely preventing the Lions owner from landing his petrol. Through its contacts in the police and the foreign ministry, probably cross-posted bureaucrats, its officials were able to identify the financial institutions funding Lions in Singapore and make them cut off their credit so as to stop suppliers selling the company the refined product.

Had Lions risked a law suit the company would have found the courts unsympathetic. Even in cases where the courts at a lower level rule that administrative guidance is compelling a company to break the law, the verdict is normally reversed on appeal, as the courts have become increasingly reluctant to oppose bureaucratic desires. Attempts to make MITI more responsive to legal restraint through legislation have been abandoned out of fear that they might result in an increase in MITI's formal, legal powers.

The case of Sumitomo Metals in the 1960s showed that even the big corporate names have little option but to conform when MITI urges a given course of action. In their case, Sumitomo, then a relatively new producer of steel, declined to take part in MITI-engineered price-fixing for the metal and elected to go its own way with its own lower prices. After months of wrangling with both the leaders of competing steelmakers and the bureaucrats, the latter produced a trump card: Sumitomo would not be permitted to import more than the precise quantity of coking coal required for its share of the cartel cake. Sumitomo had no choice but to comply and dispatch its president on a round of humiliating apologies.

From these examples it can be seen that although Japan is labelled a liberal democracy, outsiders wishing to operate within the Japanese market should not rely on guidance from a set of laws that will govern the behaviour of all those that they will come into contact with in the bureaucracy and government. Japanese legal drafting is sparse and vague, leaving a great deal of informal, interpretive power in the hands of individuals. Because such informal guidance is never committed to paper, any such decisions are not justiciable. Rooted in an authoritative tradition in which bureaucrats were originally designated as representatives of the emperor himself, the legal system has so far not proved a viable ally in attempts to challenge their authority.

The prospects for a more open and equitable system are, however, still distant and likely to remain so, though the Japanese political system is now showing signs of being susceptible to reform. Such reform might produce a more flexible and responsive bureaucratic system, whose powers are more clearly defined through the law, and permit as much inward access to foreign business and commerce as is permitted to Japanese operating abroad.

The law

The experience of a Western woman involved in a car accident before a Tokyo court epitomized the experience of Occidental logic meeting Oriental law. To the woman the case seemed clear enough: her car had been struck from behind by a Japanese driver who did not stop in time at a set of traffic lights. The case, she was sure, would swiftly be disposed of in her favour. The judge did not see it that way. 'If you had not been there, the accident would not have happened', he told the astonished plaintiff with impeccable logic, while admonishing both drivers to take more care.

That may seem a frivolous introduction to the law in Japan but it illustrates a number of aspects that are important in understanding the cultural background to the legal system and how it works in practice. First, as in Japanese society at large, there is an abhorrence for the black-and-white analysis of situations so beloved of the Occidental. Japanese culture recognizes that things are never really that simple; life is more a series of shades of grey. And when a case comes to court the judge will very often see himself in a mediatory as much as a judgmental role.

The accepted wisdom among most Japanese is that they are not a litigious nation; that they would run a mile rather than seek restoration of a wrong through the courts. That is true up to a point, but not necessarily because they are willing to yield through selflessness. Many, perhaps, would prefer a form of redress that would not expose them to publicity. Others reach a settlement by non-judicial means such as through a contact in the police force or a senior staff member at work. But many Japanese simply recognize the sheer hopelessness of getting a judgment within a reasonable amount of time and at a cost that will not render the outcome meaningless. Recent terrorist cases have taken upwards of 20 years from initial prosecution to final resolution of appeals, and only rarely do the judgements upset the status quo. In the eyes of some people, a courtroom 'victory' is not something to be proud of since it must have been gained at someone else's expense.

Legal history

The earliest notions of Japanese law were all religious-based. The ruler was deemed to be acting as the link between the gods and the people. Here, and in the later absorption of much of the Chinese imperial code, lie the roots of the belief, deeply held by older generations, that laws are essentially a means of control by the state rather than a system open to the individual seeking redress. Many judgements, even today, appear to be made more in the interest of maintaining the authority and position of the state than in advancing the rights of the individual. The struggle between the old habits and instincts and the more liberal tendency seems likely to continue for some time to come.

Even in feudalist times there was a marked difference between Japan and Europe in the relationship of vassal and overlord. The Japanese owed his lord an absolute duty of fidelity but had no right to seek the fulfilment of the overlord's duties in return: in the words of a motto from the Tokugawa era, 'Let the people know nothing, but make them obey.' Similarly, a leading Confucianist opined:

> According to the old theory, you must not censure the writers of the country in which you live. If you do not occupy a position which gives you competence, you must not criticize state policy. It is contrary to loyalty and fidelity that an inferior should criticize his superior.

With the advent of the Meiji reformers in the late 1800s, interest in the legal systems of Europe rapidly increased. The French legal code was translated without benefit of either a French dictionary or a French lawyer and was ready for publication in 1869. The French jurist Gustave Boissonade was invited to modernize the legal system and ended up staying for 20 years. But initial plans to introduce French law in its entirety were never carried out and, later, influences came from the legal systems of Switzerland, Austria, Holland, Germany and Britain.

The first legal code was promulgated in 1880 and came into force two years later. The new constitution of 1889, solemnly granted by the emperor to his people, greatly increased the ruler's powers though it attempted a compromise between divine law and constitutionalism. It stressed that the lower-ranking samurai who made up the reformers had no intention of abandoning feudal ways, which they considered morally superior to anything Europe had to offer. At the same time, the Imperial Diet was only an organ for collaboration with the emperor and had precious little power of its own – even its control of the budget was minimal.

The new laws left a great gap between the way it was assumed that society worked and the way it actually worked. Before the laws were introduced, the Japanese had little knowledge of the concepts of rights and duties, and even afterwards judges still did not know how most people lived. A good judge was considered to be one who could dispose of contrary arguments in a few words and give his verdict succinctly. One observer of the period noted, 'Rationalism, which is the soul of modern law, was for the Japanese only a beautiful, borrowed garment which hid a traditional psychology imbued with sentimentalism.' Then, as now, the practice of law was governed more by emotional than moral factors.

The legal profession

Before World War II Japan's legal profession showed its German roots with the byword *Gesetz ist Gesetz* (Law is law), exemplifying the submissive attitude to legality that allowed military dictatorship to flourish. Postwar, a more humane and critical approach has become the norm. However, the forces of reaction have remained both alert and active as Japan has gained wealth and sought to discard elements of its US-written constitution.

Undergraduates in law face a four-year programme of study divided into two parts. The first is dedicated to humanities and the second to law studies. At the country's most famous law school, in Tokyo University, the first two years are spent at the College of General Education, so there are only two years remaining for specialization in the law. The university law school is divided into three departments: for private law, public law and political science. The majority of its graduates – about 38,000 a year – enter careers in business and the bureaucracy. A degree from the school gives ready entry to any corporation in the country, and a great number of bureaucrats at senior levels are law graduates. Thus the principal function of university law departments is not to train barristers, judges or prosecutors; only a small percentage of their graduates will enter those professions. Undergraduates in law will study a variety of academic legal theories, the legislative framework and the general interpretation of the law, but little time is spent examining the application of law in the real world.

Law graduates and others who aspire to practise law must go on to the Legal Training and Research Institute. Entry is by the national legal examination, which is legendary for its difficulty. Of the 30–50,000 candidates who sit the exam each year, less than 2 per cent, some 480–500, pass. Many of the candidates will be taking the exam for the second, third or even fourth time. The examination is, in fact, two separate examinations, the second of which is further subdivided into two sections. The first examination, from which university graduates are exempted, tests the candidate's general knowledge of history, politics, culture and the humanities. Successful candidates then sit a two-part written and oral examination dealing with constitutional law, civil law, commercial law, criminal law and criminal and civil procedure. Only those who pass in both parts are admitted to the Institute. As with other areas of education in Japan, the system of legal training has been criticized, from both those inside and outside the field, for focusing too much on the passing of exams and not enough on the creation of good, analytical legal brains. It does not, as one commentator put it, develop 'either a good legal sense or a capacity for legal thinking'.

Candidates enter the Institute for two years of study and apprenticeship divided into three terms. Instruction is by leading barristers, judges and prosecutors and the course material includes records of actual civil and criminal cases. Model trials are enacted by staff instructors and others are shown on film. There are also voluntary seminars on a wide range of topics from banking and forsenic medicine to comparative law. During the second term of 16 months, the apprentices engage in actual field training in each of the three branches of the profession. Extended periods are spent in district courts and in a district prosecutor's office, and apprentices are assigned to the office of a practising barrister. Here, they not only do legal research but participate in negotiations, draft documents and collect evidence while helping to draft briefs, pleadings and even closing arguments. After completing the course, the apprentices become barristers, assistant judges or assistant public prosecutors. Normally, about 80 graduates each year elect to join the bench while 60 enter prosecutors' offices and the remainder register with the local bar association.

With only 12,000 barristers out of a population that is twice the size of Britain's, and the misconception among foreigners that the term *bengoshi* (literally 'he who defends') is equivalent to 'lawyer' in English, Japan gives the impression that its legal profession is relatively small. In reality, per capita of population the number of legally-trained personnel turned out by centres of law education is not so different from Britain's. The difference lies in the number of legally-trained people who go into the corporate world and into pursuits that have no obvious legal connection. Many tasks undertaken by the retained law firms that advise corporations in Britain and the United States will be performed in-house in Japan by members of staff with legal training. Moreover, the legal departments in Japanese firms will probably be quite large even though they may call themselves something innocuous such as 'records department'.

Foreign lawyers

A handful of foreign lawyers are to be found practising in Japan under an arrangement that permits those working there under pre-1955 regulations to continue to do so. The more recent struggle to win access for foreign law offices has been a protracted one. The idea of foreign lawyers practising in Japan remains a contentious issue, as the domestic profession fears both competition from aggressive American attorneys and the dilution of standards. Some Japanese attorneys argue that few countries allow foreign lawyers any role in their indigenous legal system and that the regulation of such a system is, in any case, a purely internal matter. However, on 1 April 1987 a special act received approval, permitting the entry of foreign lawyers but with restrictions on their activities.

Under these restrictions, a foreign lawyer may not represent clients in connection with proceedings in Japanese courts; cases involving criminal affairs; lawsuits or administrative proceedings to be conducted by a foreign court or administrative agency; the drawing up or commissioning of a 'notarial deed'; or cases mainly relating to real estate in Japan. They may practise only under the name of the person licensed, which effectively denies them the use of their legal 'brand names,' and they may not employ Japanese lawyers or share fees with them. But perhaps the most significant restriction is that they may not advise on or interpret any laws other than those of the country where they qualified as lawyers; or in the case of American lawyers the state in which they qualified. The legislation also specifies that any lawyers aspiring to work in a Japanese branch office must have five years' experience of the profession in their country of qualification. Furthermore there must be a reciprocal arrangement for Japanese lawyers to work in the home countries of those seeking access. So far, 11 foreign legal practices have set up representative offices in Tokyo. They are Macfarlanes, Clifford Chance, McKenna, Ashurst Morris Crisp, Slaughter and May, Linklaters and Paines, Allen and Overy, Freshfields, Denton Hall, Lovell White Durrant and Charles Russell.

The people and the law

The American-imposed postwar constitution helped set up a legal system not unlike that of the United States, with the equivalent provincial and district courts, the Supreme Court at the apex, and the court of final appeal as the ultimate social and moral arbiter. At least that is how it works in the United States, where the composition of the court and its attitudes are matters of great public debate and interest. That was also how the Japanese Supreme Court started out in the early postwar years, a body of legal expertise ready to question the government's every action. Now, however, most well-informed citizens would be hard-pressed to name any of the 15 justices who sit on the Court. Generally, their appointments are made public only after they have taken place, and then only in brief newspaper reports. Even the Tokyo Bar Association, which proposes new members, cannot say with certainly who actually makes the appointments, which in theory is the duty of the emperor. Traditionally, the Court has four lawyers, six career judges, two former bureaucrats, two prosecutors and a professor of law.

In recent years the courts have become increasingly conservative. Their judgements lack clear direction and there is an unwillingness to do anything that might upset the government or the bureaucracy. One of the most celebrated cases, lasting seven years, concerned the alternative history of the war period written by Professor Saburo Ienaga. The distinguished academic complained that his book had been altered by the Ministry of Education before it was introduced in schools. After a long struggle through the courts the frail, 79-year-old professor won the case, only to have it overturned on appeal. In the final analysis the court, without warning him, pronounced on his use of the word 'reckless' to describe the conduct of the Imperial Japanese Army on the mainland of Asia during the war. Ruling against him, the court said that his right to publish was overridden by the government's right to intervene to maintain a collective harmony – something to which the constitution makes no reference.

In a society in which shame plays a large part in governing action, it is a formidable sanction against improper behaviour which comes into play almost as soon as a child is aware of what is acceptable and what is not. It is all the more potent given the Japanese need for acceptance by peers and the close feeling of community that pervades society. Behaving in any way outside the norm attracts unwelcome attention to oneself and, if it is criminal behaviour, can lead to permanent alienation. Thus, the Japanese tend to regulate their behaviour according to what will or will not attract public disapproval whether in school, in a company or in the community at large. This cultural backdrop acts as an inhibiting factor and, together with the predisposition of police officers to mediate in disputes at an early stage, helps keep crime rates low in Japan.

There is a lively debate as to whether the society is alegalistic, preferring to avoid court proceedings at all costs, or whether that reluctance has more to do with the cost, inconvenience and time consumed in taking matters to court, especially in view of the court's obvious unwillingness to find against the government. There is no doubt, also, that the much-vaunted homogeneity of the society helps to limit the number of disputes and leads to much greater conformity in behaviour than is found in more cosmopolitan societies.

Japanese laws tend to stipulate harsh punishments for offences. However, in the actual sentencing the courts, and indeed the police who bring the charges, may be relatively lenient if the accused shows contrition and apologizes or 'gives face' to the accusing officer by paying due recognition to his authority. Often, first offenders are given a conditional discharge unless the charge is serious, such as drunk driving, to which the law and society as a whole take a tough attitude. Repeat drunk driving offenders face imprisonment, but in a special kind of institution unknown outside Japan, where they are made to learn to drive all over again while constantly repenting their misdeeds. By contrast, someone committing another kind of offence under the influence of drink may be dealt with leniently – often they will be held not responsible for their actions precisely because they were drunk.

On the surface, the Japanese legal system appears geared to support the strong, given the country's relatively weak stance on human rights. In large measure it is, but over time – in many cases too much time – it works its way through some of the checks and balances familiar elsewhere. There have been frequent charges that the country has ineffective or lax legal remedies against the large corporations, who in the 1970s could apparently pollute at will without paying a notable price, or against such usurpers of public order as the ubiquitous *yakuza*, or gangsters. The use of gangster enforcers by companies to abbreviate meetings of shareholders and prevent embarrassing revelations once reached such levels that it seemed that the police were either not interested in attempting to control it or were somehow being paid off. Although the legal remedies had always been available, the laws were tightened only marginally and the new legislation was mostly targeted at the companies making the payments. The problem declined markedly, not because suddenly large numbers of people were arrested, but because the establishment as a whole had signalled obliquely through legislation that the limits of this kind of behaviour had been reached. With foreigners and the foreign media taking a much closer look at the stock market and the activities of Japanese companies, it had also become an issue of 'national face' as the rest of the world looked on – shame on an international scale.

But, to many, Japanese law still retains one of the least desirable elements of its feudal past: the death penalty. After a three-year moratorium during which public opinion and the legal authorities seemed to be moving towards its abolition, it was resumed. Immediately, three people were executed for murders that had been committed between 15 and 23 years earlier. No one knows the precise details because the authorities make no announcement, so it is doubly difficult for those outside the Ministry of Justice to keep track of the practice. Opponents of the death penalty complain not only about its use but about the way the authorities treat the relatives of the condemned. They are not told that the execution is to take place and only find out when they are summoned to pick up the deceased's personal effects. Excessive delays in the resolution of appeals, sometimes 20 years or more since they were originally lodged, also concern the many critics of the system. The only ruling that the Supreme Court makes is that the death penalty should not be 'cruel'.

Equally irksome is the courts' attitude towards the powerful – particularly politicians – who disappear into hospital as soon as they realize that the game is up. Questioning is then often delayed and eventually they are given lenient sentences that amount to little more than a slap on the wrist. A case in point was the treatment of Shin Kanemaru, the kingpin of the political world, who was fined a 200,000 yen – a week's salary for the average salaryman – for salting away hundreds of millions of yen in illegal political donations.

If that is regarded as sinister by some, then the growing tendency to take certain issues out of the power of the courts also runs counter to the norms of a democratic country. One such issue is industrial pollution. Throughout much of the 1970s firms accused of polluting the environment fought with every means at their disposal, including the use of gangster enforcers, to prevent members of the public from pursuing the case against them. The battle to bring to book the Chisso Corporation for polluting Minamata Bay with mercury raged through the courts for 20 years. Eventually, it ended with victory for those affected by the pollution, though success was so belated that many of the victims never lived so see justice done. Since it was now possible for corporate might to be defeated in the courtroom, industry decided that such disputes should be resolved in forums where it could exert more control, such as out-of-court settlement procedures. As a result, more and more disputes are now being dealt with outside the court system, especially claims against the chemicals and pharmaceuticals industries, motoring claims and claims of discrimination in the place of work.

This development is in line with the Japanese desire for conciliation between parties and the tendency to see no black-and-white solution to problems. But it is also due, in part, to the high initial costs of going to law, including a commencement fee, that have to be paid even before papers have been filed. There is also a hearing before a judge at a relatively early stage to explore the parameters of the case and the areas of dispute. Moreover, to file a complaint the plaintiff has to pay a sizeable stamp duty of up to two per cent of the amount in dispute.

Since the legal system is geared closely to the society's desire for consensus rather than confrontation, those who do not conform to this norm are sidetracked or suppressed. Railway workers who did not wish to become part of the newly privatized Japan National Railways were sent off to backwaters in the network, where they had little to do but feel the pressures of being excluded from the group until they left the industry. The Japanese Red Army members who allied themselves with farmers who opposed the construction and expansion of the international airport at Narita were dealt with more harshly. The authorities used all means to suppress them, from brutal confrontations with the police to severe treatment by the law whenever any were brought to book.

Overall, the Japanese seem content with their legal system, preferring to retain its harmonizing qualities as a means of helping to maintain a stable society. They eschew the more democratic yet self-centred, and sometimes even destructive, ethos of Western law. The Japanese attitude seems hard to equate with any increase in democracy in the country's legal or political systems, as many had expected would happen in the light of greater wealth and more individual choice.

5 THE MEDIA AND ADVERTISING
Paradox and mass circulation

From serious morning newspapers to some of the most lurid late-night television in the world, the Japanese media is in a class of its own. The daily press has the highest circulation and per capita readership in the world while the plethora of weekly magazines and cartoon books are devoured by millions throughout the country during lunch breaks or on public transport.

Modern Japanese journalism was created through the political struggles that followed the Meiji Restoration in 1867, when the Tokugawa shogunate was overthrown and national rule passed into the hands of the Japanese emperor and his warrior supporters who began the process of modernizing Japan. Members and supporters of the shogunate were an educated elite in Japanese society who despised the new government and considered its actions both ignorant and ridiculous. Former Tokugawa bureaucrats and scholars responded by founding newspapers through which they could criticize the new government and promote their own beliefs.

Today, there are five national daily newspapers, all with circulations in the millions, published in morning editions seven days a week and evening editions every day except Sunday. All would qualify as 'quality' newspapers in the same league as the leading European and American equivalents. All adopt a tone of high moral authority in their leading articles and are withering in their criticisms of politicians, despite having close links to the government. They differ from their Western counterparts in that there is a mass market for the serious material that they purvey. Top of the circulation league is the right-leaning *Yomiuri Shimbun* which sells 9.7 million copies of its morning edition and 4.6 million copies of its evening edition. The *Asahi Shimbun*, which revels in a fashionable anti-government stance, boasted an 8.2 million morning circulation in 1991 with sales of 4.7 million in the evening. An international satellite edition is printed daily in London, Heerlen (Netherlands), New York, Los Angeles and Singapore. *Asahi Shimbun* articles are translated into English each day and distributed through *The New York Times* news service. *The Asahi Evening News*, is the country's only English-language evening paper. Established in 1954, it has its own editorial staff and publishes simultaneous translations of some of the more important articles and editorials.

The Asahi publishing house is one of the oldest in the country, publishing weeklies, monthlies, annuals and between 200 and 300 book titles a year.

The weeklies include the *Shukan Asahi*, the oldest Japanese weekly of its kind, the picture-led *Asahi Graph*, *AERA*, Japan's answer to *Time* and *Newsweek*, as well as specialist titles including *Asahi Camera*, *Asahi Pasocon* (Personal Computer) and *Kagaku Asahi*, which features scientific subjects. The *Japan Quarterly* is a scholarly publication which circulates in more than 50 countries, and is found in the principal libraries around the world.

The leading economic daily newspaper is the *Nihon Keizai Shimbun*, which is required reading for the business and finance communities and has spawned a range of specialist journals, an economic and business news service and a database. The national dailies usually produce regional editions and there are also local newspapers published in all of the major provincial centres. Counting morning and evening editions as a single subscription, circulation of the major papers exceeded 52 million copies during the autumn of 1991, with an average of 1.24 subscriptions per household and 93 per cent of households taking home delivery. Each of the companies that produces the major morning papers also controls a national television network and several have diversified into baseball teams, amusement parks and retail stores. The national public broadcasting network, NHK, encompasses radio, two terrestial television channels and two satellite channels. It is modelled on the BBC and does not carry any advertising. Japan's English-language press, which has a long history, is represented by the *Japan Times*, *Mainichi*, *Yomuiri* and *The Asahi Evening News*, all of which publish daily. All except the *Japan Times* are published by firms which also print in the vernacular.

In one of the fascinating paradoxes of Japan, the media market-place, especially in newspapers, is intensely competitive journalistically and commercially, yet at the same time controlled, with clear ground rules in certain areas of editorial activity. During the illness of the late Emperor Hirohito, the papers spent millions competing with each other to get the latest news, yet late duty editors on competing titles will often confer on whether or not to run late-breaking stories.

The national dailies reflect the intensity and seriousness of Japan's commercial drive and do not shrink from leading their front pages with the most abstruse economic and political indicators. Most are extraordinarily bland, featuring near-identical front pages with the main news presented in almost exactly the same way despite constant pressure for scoops. The public are aware of this seeming lack of individual initiative and are critical of it, turning to the evening sports newspapers and weekly or monthly magazines if they want something with bite and often more than a hint of scandal. Generally it is these periodicals that break the stories of real significance; the dailies usually content themselves with whatever they are spoon-fed by the government.

The more lurid of the periodicals can happily match Western tabloids with their imaginative and garish presentation. *Friday* and *Focus* are typical examples of this weekly genre, featuring telephoto shots of cheating married couples or headless bodies, interspersed with glamour and gossip. They are produced by the publishers of newspapers and highly respectable journals, with no apparent detriment to either end of the market. Such magazines sell in the millions at the outset, but they often have a remarkably short life. As soon as there is any sign of sales flagging they disappear, to be replaced by some brightly coloured newcomer which may be equally short-lived. In 1991 alone, 165 new magazine titles were launched. There is a particularly high rate of turnover among magazines for young women and men's fashion 'glossies', which are cranked out in vast numbers. So too, are cartoon books or *manga* – paperbacks as thick as encyclopedias featuring lurid cartoon stories that are read by virtually every male commuter at one time or another. Published weekly or monthly, they sell in millions, but often last only a single train journey, as the reader becomes bored with what they have to offer. They are constantly criticized by foreigners for their infantile sexuality and escapist fantasy, but it has been argued that they play a role, as a harmless outlet, in helping keep down the number of sex offences. Whatever the truth, *manga* is now enjoying a new role as a tool of education and debate, spreading information, in an easily digestible and enjoyable form, on subjects as varied as the economy and Aids.

Inside the *Asahi*

The *Asahi Shimbun* has long been considered Japan's most influential newspaper. Like many other leading enterprises, it has its roots in Osaka but there are major facilities in Tokyo and regional bureaus in Fukuoka and Nagoya. It began in January 1879 as a four-page tabloid with a staff of about 15 journalists. The city was then Japan's largest commercial centre and the paper was a mixture of political and other news in the waterfront metropolis. But it had a special appeal with its phonetic renderings of the often obscure Chinese characters used in news stories. At this dawning of Japan's modern civilization – the paper's title means Rising Sun – people were hungry for news of the outside world after 250 years of isolation. Under its founder, Mr Ryuhei Murayama, and supported by the Kimura family, the newspaper grew rapidly, purchasing a small Tokyo newspaper to become a national publication with a circulation of 120,000 in 1897.

As the paper developed, it moved away from tabloid-style reporting and included more analytical comment on the changes taking place in the country and people's aspirations for democracy. This was a difficult task with an authoritarian government in power and the newspaper was soon in trouble. Two years after publication it was suspended for running a series of articles on the sovereignty of the people. This was to be the first of many clashes between the newspaper and the government, which continued over its opposition to military deployments in Siberia and other issues. These head-on confrontations ended only after World War II when press freedom became guaranteed in the new constitution. The wartime government had kept a tight grip on the media, but when the war was over many *Asahi* journalists and editors felt angry that the paper's leadership had not taken a tougher stand. As a result, on 22 October 1945, the board resigned, enabling a new generation of journalists to take control. The paper reopened its London and New York offices in 1952 on the signing of the San Francisco Peace Treaty.

In the postwar period the paper quickly moved to recover its reputation, joining the campaign against US nuclear testing. In the 1960s the rapid economic growth brought tensions between Japan's traditional culture and way of life and the new culture of the emerging industrial power. The paper ran a ground-breaking series of articles which featured on the front page of the evening edition for some years, serving as a model of modern Japanese journalism.

Asahi also built a reputation for its investigative journalism, starting with the Lockheed scandal in 1976 when Japanese politicians were caught taking kickbacks from the aircraft company to promote the sale of airliners in Japan. The newspaper made a significant breakthrough when it obtained the names of all the government officials involved through the files of the US Congress. More recently, a local bureau of the paper broke the first news of the Recruit scandal in 1988, which led to the resignation of Noboru Takeshita, then prime minister, and Kiichi Miyazawa who was then finance minister and later prime minister. It also caused the former prime minister, Yasuhiro Nakasone, to give up his party membership of the LDP. *Asahi* further played a prominent role in the unravelling of the Kanemaru scandal in which the 'kingmaker' of Japanese politics received some 500 million yen from gangster-related sources. The revelations forced him to retire from politics and led to renewed concern over the corrupt nature of the Japanese body politic. Fresh calls for reform eventually resulted in the historic splitting of the LDP in July 1993.

But there have been times when the *Asahi* has got things wrong as well, most notably its criticism of the Treaty of Portsmouth that ended the Russo-Japanese war in 1905. The paper said that the treaty was too lenient on Russia and severely criticized the Japanese government for accepting it. However, the newspaper was unaware of the true status of the war and the dire condition of the domestic economy. Its campaign led to riots in central Tokyo and an assault on a police station. In the mid-1960s *Asahi* called for the early normalization of relations with China, after the Japanese government, under pressure from the Americans, recognized Taiwan. But the paper was caused serious embarrassment when its efforts coincided with the Cultural Revolution and the rise of the Gang of Four. It came under heavy attack for distorting the truth of the situation and glorifying the notorious Gang.

A job with the *Asahi* is much sought after. In 1992 the editorial department received over 3,000 applications for 128 journalistic positions. Most trainee journalists join straight from university and are first assigned to one of the 299 regional or local bureaus some of which have staffs of more than

70 journalists. Between 20 and 30 places are available each year for experienced journalists and these, too, are in great demand. The *Asahi* is also building on its reputation as a paper that is willing to recruit women journalists for the news department, an area traditionally regarded as a male preserve. There are also women on the editorial board and in senior and specialized fields.

Press clubs

Every journalist working in Japan soon comes up against the notorious system of press clubs through which the government manages its information flow. Despite the huge popularity of television, and some well informed and occasionally controversial news programmes, both the bureaucracy and the public still regard the daily newspapers as the most reliable means of communicating information. Thus, each important government department ensures that it has a direct line to the media by establishing a room, or suite of rooms in its ministry for the exclusive use of newspaper journalists covering its affairs. The whole of the ministry's information output is channelled through this press club. There are regular briefings and press handouts, and club members can expect favoured treatment from the ministry. Indeed, they will be the only media people given access, since the press clubs are highly exclusive and discriminatory and even journalists from periodicals are not admitted.

Press club facilities are provided free of charge for the designated correspondents of all the major newspapers covering a ministry's activities. The Ministry of International Trade and Industry hosts its media acolytes in truly sumptuous surroundings. But only those journalists who have been assigned will have access to the information provided by the ministry, and any club member not following its, often unwritten, rules by scooping colleagues or revealing something said off the record will find themselves ostracized, cut off from the daily flow of interviews, briefings and background papers which are the lifeblood of daily journalism. That sort of penalty can be fatal to journalistic careers because, even in journalism, the Japanese must be seen to be playing the game if they are not be cast outside the clan. The result is a paternalistic spoonfeeding of the media that allows the government to control the information flow while manipulating public opinion. It also allows individual ministries to protect their own interests by being able to cut off unfavourable material at source.

Originally, the press club's stated aim was to ensure that government activities were fully communicated to the public, in an age when it was taken for granted that the government and bureaucracy knew best and when relatively few Japanese would have thought to question either. Today, in a more democratically minded Japan, it means, in practice, that government decisions, and in particular the motives behind them, are not as open to public scrutiny as they should be. Thus, there is a danger that ministries may be advocating policies that represent the interests of powerful pressure groups rather than the country as a whole. When the journalists reporting on a ministry stand to lose their press club memberships merely because the ministry does not like what they write, then the public interest is not being served. The result is a series of newspapers with near-identical stories none of which may be telling the whole truth.

Ironically, those supposed to be the most dedicated to communication of information and ideas, the journalists themselves, are among the most ardent supporters of the status quo. Even when a ministry invites in journalists from outside the magic circle of its press club, because it has something of wider importance to communicate, the visitors are usually made to feel unwelcome by the resident press club journalists. Perhaps it is for that reason that government departments are slow to call in outside journalists even when the occasion does merit it. On one famous occasion, foreign journalists were not invited to a press conference unveiling plans for the construction of an important new automobile plant in the United States. However, in June 1993 the powerful Japan Newspaper Publishers' and Editors' Association, comprising some 175 newspapers, news agencies and broadcasters, instructed its members to allow foreign journalists to join press clubs if they so wished.

Any government official confronted over the need to reform government will probably reply that a better place to start would be the press. But while many deplore the press club system, much as European and American journalists dislike lobby and confidential briefings, there are few willing to break the pattern and risk being scooped by rivals in a daily market that is just as taxed by problems as anywhere else in the world.

The press club system and the general blandness of press coverage are all the more surprising when seen against the background of intense competition between the various newspapers. They appear vastly overstaffed by Western standards, but the demand for scoops and the finest detail in company and financial reporting helps explain why there are thousands of newspaper employees. The Nihon Keizai parent company, for example, employs some 4,374 people overall, with 77 foreign correspondents in 33 bureaus abroad serving its various publications and data services.

But even the racy presentation of the tabloid evening sports newspapers is not enough to overcome the industry-wide decline brought about by the economic slow-down overall and the failure of newspapers to try and brighten their image in the face of evening competition from television news. In the 1992 business year the *Yomiuri Shimbun*, the oldest newspaper in the country, posted a pre-tax loss of 5.6 billion yen while its circulation fell by 100,000 copies. The *Asahi Shimbun* was not immune either, suffering a drop of 250,000 in its circulation over the same period, its first-ever postwar decline in sales. Market saturation, similarity of the product, falling advertisement revenues and the cost and difficulty of maintaining the home delivery system are all factors clouding the future of a mature industry faced with new challenges from data services and television. Despite these difficulties, several of the major dailies now print via satellite in Europe and the United States, copies being delivered almost simultaneously with those in the home islands.

Advertising

Among Japan's businesses, advertising epitomizes those facets of commerce and industry that are peculiarly Japanese. In the advertising business one name has dominated the scene for decades, Dentsu, now the world's largest advertising agency. It is a full-service company in a way that that expression cannot convey. Dentsu is not only involved in public relations and the marketing of products, but it will also make business connections and create new opportunities, manage business trips, research lifestyles and trends and help create government policy. So large are its billings and so close are its relations with the press and television that it can 'manage' the news about its clients who get into the media. Few marketing trends will be successful without the backing of this organization, whose influence from managing the top accounts in the country is so enormous that no new product line can go far on the mass market without Dentsu's involvement. Company personnel also play a part in government policy formulation through the activities of think-tanks and research on behalf of government. Even the rating of television programmes, which Dentsu itself is involved in making, is carried out by Dentsu.

Created out of the wartime news agency Domei, the vehicle for government propaganda from 1936 to 1945, Dentsu runs its $10 billion-a-year business from its headquarters in the Ginza area of Tokyo. There are branches throughout the country as well as 25 subsidiaries and related companies employing 34,000 people in Japan under the slogan 'Total Communications'. It reaches across the world with ambitions to become a global company and has links with some of the principal European and American concerns.

In Japan, the flagship film and video company is Dentsu PROX. The name is a typical combination of Japanese and English of the sort which the Japanese believe imparts a sense of drama to a company title. In this case, 'x' is the 'unknown' of algebra, indicating great possibilities, while the 'pro' suggests 'production' or 'professional'. Dentsu PROX's activities span an enormous range. The company is involved in expositions and conventions, theme parks, resorts, television stations, television programmes, commercial advertising, graphics and computer-games software and even the creation of audio-visual studios. Dentsu also has exclusive domestic rights on virtual-reality technology, which seems likely to ensure its position at the cutting edge of the Japanese multimedia business throughout the next century.

In the Ginza, AD Dentsu is a full-service advertisement agency for the mass media which also offers event planning, public relations, corporate identity and recruitment advertisements while Dentsu Research concentrates on market research and planning. The Dentsu Institute for Human Studies is the flagship think-tank, which monitors society and its attitudes, and Dentsu EYE specializes in marketing and public relations for companies and products directed at women. It is largely staffed by women but retains a male in overall management control. Dentsu Kosan concerns itself with real-estate services including sales, property management and insurance. For foreign firms seeking to get into the Japanese market and requiring the counselling to take them through the media and marketing minefield, there is Dentsu Burson-Marsteller, a link-up with one of the leading American firms in the field.

Despite $1.48 billion in profits for 1992, Dentsu felt the early 1990s slowdown just as much as others in the industry. But that has not dented its plans for globalization, with offices across the United States and throughout Asia as well as a spread of European offices including Dentsu UK, which has found, as have other international bureaus, that it is hard to replicate the Japanese approach in other cultures. With fully one-quarter of all advertisement billing in its home market, including the competing accounts of the three main motor manufacturers, and unequalled influence in high places, the company has found it less easy to work within the corporate culture abroad. To non-Japanese the notion of one outside company dealing with the entire marketing and public relations interests of a firm is novel, and the idea that one agency, however well compartmentalized, could handle simultaneously the advertising of Ford, Vauxhall and Rover is bizarre. In Japan it works well, with different bureaus handling the different motoring accounts and a strict ban on internal contact between the various elements – but then no Western agency has the overall clout of Dentsu.

That influence derives not least from television billings of $4.1 billion in 1992 and a close relationship with the Liberal Democratic Party, for whom it has run every electoral advertising campaign since the war. Recent campaigns for the party have included some of the oblique messages for which Japanese advertising is famous. One during the 1990 elections, when Toshiki Kaifu was the prime minister, showed him seated cross-legged on the floor with two child models. The slogan simply said, 'A vital life, a happy life'. It conveyed at once the shortage of real political ideas that the ruling party had to offer and yet maintained the smooth, untroubled facade that Japanese institutions prefer to maintain. That banal slogan, which seemed to work for Mr Kaifu, was most probably the work of Dentsu's 'ninth bureau' which handles much of the work done for the LDP and has sections corresponding to the ministries of construction, transport, agriculture, post and telecommunications, education and finance and the prime minister's office. This bureau absorbs a large share of the public relations budget of the former ruling party and of those of the various ministries and semi-privatized industries in which it has an interest. A further advantage for the LDP in its relationship with Dentsu is that the company is so profitable that it can afford to be relaxed about the size of fees its demands of the party and when the bills are paid – no small matter when viewed against the financial difficulties of political parties in other democracies.

Dentsu has managed to establish a relationship of dependence with many of the hugely popular weekly magazines. Many of them prosper because Dentsu buys up large portions of their advertising in advance. That way, the magazine is freed from the struggle of selling advertising space each week and is guaranteed regular income. It also means, however, that there is a close interest taken in the editorial content and Dentsu is in a position to 'advise' on the type and tone of the articles. In the past the company has used this power to tone down criticisms of certain corporations and to manage the news about them. Cross-shareholdings with the Kyodo and Jiji press agencies allow Dentsu to keep closely abreast of the news. Those cosy relations with news organizations also give Dentsu access to an enormous bank of intelligence, which it can draw upon to compile the influential surveys of public opinion that are published by the prime minister's office. These surveys are of great importance in telling the Japanese people what they think about themselves, their ambitions and the issues of the day. For decades it has been the prime ministerial surveys that have served to convince the population that they are all middle class, and this, in turn, has helped maintain an enviable level of public contentment and stability.

In television programming, Dentsu is behind the popular News Station, the country's highest-rated news programme, which has carved for itself a completely new style of presentation far removed from the formal, conventional approach of the Japan Broadcasting Corporation, NHK (Nippon Hoso Kyokai). Headed by a former game-show and cooking-programme host, it approaches its subject in a chatty, opinionated way, with the presenter often putting his own views into the format along with a series of studio guests who are as likely to be show-business personalities as experts on the topic at hand.

Television

It is hard to exaggerate the impact that television has made on the Japanese economy, society and culture. Just as Japan's visual culture is ideally suited to the medium, so the dexterity of its manufacturing workers proved ideal for making and precision-welding the tiny electronic parts that go into television sets. The manufacture and worldwide sale of Japanese-made TVs and related technology helped build the country's strong base in electronics and provided the foundation for its legendary success in other fields.

There are now television sets in 97 per cent of Japanese homes. A 1992 Ministry of International Trade and Industry (MITI) survey shows that the average set is running for eight hours a day, most people watch for about three hours and 32 per cent of homes have three or more sets. As with so many other things, Japan has gone that little bit further – television, with the notable exception of NHK news and documentaries, is unashamedly entertainment, and for sheer banality the endless round of game shows and quizzes are hard to equal. Cocktails of youth, novelty, fame and money, they bring relief and diversion to some of the most demanding urban lifestyles in the world. There is also a wealth of economic information broadcast as part of the general output, and no news bulletin would be complete without the latest yen–dollar exchange rate. But for the most part it is the printed media that provide the serious information and news stories.

NHK socio-dramas, often with important points to make about the society, are required viewing for much of the population. Shown in 15 minute segments every morning and repeated in the afternoon, these slice-of-life *homu-drama* generally focus on a peculiarly Japanese aspect of living. One recent series, *Onna wa Dokyo*, ('Women gotta have Guts'), centred on an unfortunate married woman and her nasty in-laws. The difficulties of married women oppressed by their live-in mothers-in-law are a real social problem: one-sixth of divorcing couples cite conflicts with in-laws as the reason for the breakdown of their marriage. Watched by anything up to six million people, for the morning segment, series such as *Onna* have more than a hint of the morality play about them. The sufferings of another woman, if only in TV drama, brings relief to the frustrated housewife and helps persuade her that life with a thoughtless husband, selfish children and unpleasant in-laws is not necessarily so bad after all. An earlier series, called *Oshin*, about a young girl surviving the traumas of postwar Japan in the aftermath of defeat, was a smash hit and in 1984 became popular in translation all over Asia. But relatively few attempts are made to export this type of material which gets to the heart of Japanese life.

Television broadcasting began in February 1953, when 866 proud owners of TV sets tuned in to watch four hours of black and white programmes. But the medium really came to life in the 1960s when the economy took off and a television set became as important a status symbol as washing machines had been earlier. National income levels rose, fuelling consumer demand which saw 20 million households equipped with sets by 1962. Only six years later, another five million homes had them. With the introduction of colour broadcasting in 1960 by both NHK and the commercial stations, colour sets became an important part of the scramble to 'keep up with the Suzukis' next door – as important as home air-conditioning and cars. By 1969, 7.6 million households boasted colour televisions and by 1988, 30 million of the country's 40 million homes had one.

NHK, with its solid base of funding through monthly fees from the public, had been the first to develop Japanese television, a full decade before the commercial stations were set up. It was only after NHK had established the popularity of the medium that the commercial stations were able to move in and attract sufficient advertising to fund the production of more entertaining programmes across a broader range. In the peak year of 1970, the country spent the equivalent of 0.54 per cent of its gross national product on TV sets, and that rapid growth generated the profits which enabled the development of the products that have kept the industry booming into the 1990s –

video-cassette recorders and video cameras. The electronics industry began the large-scale export of TV sets as early as the 1960s. It quickly eclipsed the American industry before going on to dominate other markets, with domestic production running at about 13 million sets a year. Since the Plaza Accord of 1985 raised the value of the yen against the dollar, exports have decreased sharply and there has been a shift to production abroad, with the establishment of plants such as Sony's in Wales.

Now, Japan appears to be losing the historic impetus that propelled its electronics industry forward. The next technological jump to high-definition television, and its coming to the market-place, happens to have coincided with the worldwide economic slow-down. Despite a strong government campaign aimed at helping an industry headed for lean times, even the wealthy Japanese have been reluctant to pay the prices being demanded for the new sets, especially as the hours of broadcasting in the new format remain relatively limited. Satellite channels, too, have had a relatively slow start, partly because terrestrial television signals can reach most parts of the archipelago but also because the programmes offered were initially limited and focused more on foreign interests and sports.

As an instrument for moulding public opinion and taste, television broadcasting is second to none. There is clear evidence that the medium's concentration helped sustain the 'bubble economy' of the 1980s, by focusing on wealthy individuals and giving extended air time to the opinions of economists who have achieved a status that economists enjoy nowhere else. The economic clout of television is borne out by the MITI survey which showed that there is a direct relationship between an obsession with making money and long hours of watching TV. The 1992 study found that, paradoxically, the less free time people had at their disposal, the more TV they watched. Thus, the more time people spend earning or making money, the more commercials they watch and the more they become active consumers.

Japan Broadcasting Corporation (Nippon Hoso Kyokai)

The corporation, usually known by its initials NHK, is modelled largely on the BBC and is financed through the contributions of 34.2 million households who subscribe to its terrestrial and satellite services. The broadcaster receives no assistance from government or the private sector except for a 1.5 billion yen subsidy, about 0.3 per cent of its budget, for its overseas short-wave programming. The two terrestrial television channels feature general programming on the one and educational broadcasts, including nine different language programmes for more than 20 hours a week, on the other. Multiplex sound – transmitting more than one message on the same channel – permits bilingual news and films to be shown. A satellite television channel provides news bulletins from 17 broadcasters in 10 countries and Hong Kong as well as domestic and foreign sports. A second satellite channel relays entertainment and cultural items, but is used mainly to improve reception in areas where the signal is weakest. Two medium-wave radio stations provide the same mix as the two terrestrial TV channels while FM radio is dedicated to music. Radio Japan is the country's only short-wave overseas service, with 60 hours of weekly broadcasting in 22 languages.

NHK pioneered the development of high-definition television in Japan and has promoted it to a wide viewing public. Through its satellite channels it is beginning to realize multichannel, multi-interest TV broadcasting, which offers the potential for a considerable expansion of choice for viewers in the future. In addition, NHK is seeking to expand and develop its coverage of Asian affairs. New bureaus have been established in Vladivostok, in Russia, and Phnom Penh, in Cambodia, while others have been expanded.

6 BUSINESS AND INDUSTRY
The nail that sticks up

Armed with briefcase, business cards and schedule book, a small metal company badge winking from the lapel of his charcoal grey suit, the Japanese 'salaryman,' or white-collar businessman, sets off from home each morning for an hour-long journey to work, crammed into a commuter train with hundreds of other charcoal grey suits. The uniform is absolutely predefined, for a client's first impression of a company starts with the salaryman and he knows that he must therefore look reliable and trustworthy. A clean white shirt is the standard; a coloured or striped one would be an unnecessary risk, betraying a strain of unreliability and a lack of commitment to corporate harmony. Like going to work with sideburns, a moustache or long hair, it would also stop him from achieving that desirable anonymity to be found in blending with the millions of other white-collar workers seen every morning but Sundays, flooding the trains, pavements and offices of Tokyo. To succeed in a Japanese company, a salaryman must be prepared to think and act as one tiny and purely functional cog in a vast, well-oiled corporate machine. Japan's most famous aphorism, 'The nail that sticks up must be hammered down', is applicable to many facets of Japanese life, but not least to life as a company man.

Working hours, working styles, the physical layout of the office and staff hierarchies all take account of the common desire for harmony and consensus, a desire that is often unspoken but must become intuitive to those office workers who are to succeed. Office hours are officially from 9 a.m. until 5.30 or 6 p.m., but senior executives come in earlier, at around 8 a.m. and expect subordinates to do the same. In the evenings, time spent entertaining clients, or drinking or playing mahjong with a superior or colleagues until close to midnight, is all considered to be part of a normal day's work. Going home on the dot of 6 p.m. is still generally frowned upon as betraying excessive individuality and threatening to rupture the precious group working spirit, a discipline originated hundreds of years ago in the cooperative work ethic required for rice cultivation, when every adult member of every family was expected to lend a hand to feed the community.

A 12-hour day on the job for today's salaryman is no less strenuous than that of his rice-cultivating forbears. The working day requires tact, sensitivity, stamina and a high degree of commitment. The morning may begin with a series of physical exercises performed by senior and junior staff alike, to a company song which is piped electronically into the office. Open-plan offices of up to 200 desks cater for the ranks of junior employees, as well as middle and often senior management, all working elbow to elbow and regularly consulting with each other at desk meetings to maintain consensus and a free flow of ideas. For the Japanese salaryman, hours spent bent over the desk or in the company of clients or senior employees are generally longer than those of his Western counterpart and it is easy to see how Japan's businessmen have acquired a reputation abroad for being workaholics.

The reputation is not undeserved. Government offices and companies with high proportions of administrative personnel have been reluctant to cut down from a six- to a five-day working week, although the idea is slowly being accepted among the biggest companies. Employees, nevertheless, still manage to put in longer average hours in the day than their foreign counterparts, because corporate philosophy teaches that serious contributions to the company should be made through working long hours and that this is a prerequisite to advancement. Employees who do not work overtime and who take their full share of alloted paid holidays tend to be evaluated less highly than those who do work extra hours and waive their holidays. On average, Japanese salarymen take only 50 per cent of the holidays to which they are entitled.

In 1991, Japan's white-collar workers put in an average of 2,080 hours on the job compared to 1,943 in the United States and 1,902 in Britain. As a result of claims by foreign trading partners that Japan's long working hours constitute an unfair 'trade impediment', the government set itself a target of reducing average working hours to 1,800 by 31 March 1992. This has not been met. But foreign criticism has been partly allayed by the introduction, in the late 1980s, of a clutch of new national holidays and the legal enforcement of a five-day week for financial institutions and some government offices. Ostensibly, the strategy was designed to encourage salarymen to learn how to take it easy, but some Japanese workers concede that in practice they feel no freer to relax than before, and that the strategy's purpose was largely to mollify American trade negotiators. In any case, adaptation to the changes has not been as smooth as one might have expected. Cultural and social problems were immediately thrown up by the new plans to shut down offices on Saturdays. Many middle-aged and older employees, who had never experienced a two-day weekend, were initially reluctant to observe the new rules and persisted in coming to work on Saturday mornings. Administrative staff, perplexed by their unusual problem, then turned to offering lecture courses designed to teach industrious salarymen what could be done with a Saturday off – instruction on how to spend time with the family, where to go for a weekend trip out of town or how to enjoy a day of sports with friends. Some companies, while officially honouring the new regime of two-day weekends, also stepped up pressure to create longer working weekdays, expecting employees to put in extra overtime to make up for the hours lost on Saturdays. At one of the country's leading city banks, salarymen gained 4.00 hours from their Saturdays off, but had to spend longer hours in the office during the week. All in all, they made a net gain of roughly five minutes per week in which to practise their golf swings.

But while foreigners may consider the salaryman's long working hours – often spent merely passing the time and developing connections with clients or waiting for the boss to go home first – to be unproductive in the short term, they are an essential part of his painstakingly slow and patient progression up the corporate ladder. From the age of 22, when the university graduate symbolically folds away the blue jeans that represent his past four years of freedom, and buttons up his crisp grey suit for the recruitment ceremony on his first day at work as a salaryman, he is imbued with a philosophy encouraging him to think every day of his future with his chosen company: of how he can demonstrate his trustworthiness, his loyalty and his responsibility as primarily a company man and only secondly as an individual. His loyalty and devotion will be rewarded with the support of his superiors, sometimes taken to a level of virtual parental support, and an egalitarian approach by the company, as a whole, to the welfare of all employees and their families.

Giving the impression of a high performance rate is essential at every level in corporate Japan, as hierarchy is central to Japanese thinking. Individuals, the teams they are part of and the companies they work for, are forever being ranked and judged on their ranking. The concept of a meritocracy is still rare, and seniority of rank is normally assigned according to seniority of age. The chairman is the company's figurehead (he is often a past president) and the president is the chief executive. Middle management makes up the important centre of the Japanese personnel pyramid and it is in this sector that new ideas must win acceptance before they can be implemented.

Consensus-building, known as *nemawashi* (literally 'wrapping around, or binding, the roots'), is a crucial part of business in Japan (see also page 133). Within a company it typically occurs from the bottom upwards, and often in informal meetings either in the office or after work in a bar or restaurant. Middle-management members spend much of their time laying the groundwork for a full understanding and support of strategy, before openly formulating and launching a new plan in the form of a draft to senior management. Once comments have been gathered from on high, adjustments made and the plan is sanctioned, it is then possible to implement it at high speed, as staff at all levels are already briefed.

Business structures

The *keiretsu* system – the networks of company alliances commonly built up around one large manufacturing or trading company or around a bank – demonstrates the exclusive and binding quality of relationships in Japanese business, a quality that makes some sectors of the domestic market extremely difficult for foreigners to penetrate. These networks, which often derive from the links between suppliers or subcontractors and the central manufacturer, are cemented over years of cooperation by cross-shareholdings and centralized labour supplies, training operations and information exchange. Toyota Motor, for example, has a network of tens of thousands of subcontractors and suppliers, most of which do not work exclusively for Toyota but rival each other to provide parts and services to the company. Toyota maintains a discipline down the lines of its network by making periodic agreements to divide up demand between its fixed number of suppliers in pre-agreed proportions and at prearranged prices. Interests are entrenched and suppliers that fall outside the *keiretsu* have scant chance of winning contracts.

The *sogo shosha*, or general trading company, provides another example of the octopus-like growth of Japanese business interests. The nine dominant *sogo shosha* – Mitsubishi Corporation, Itoh Chu, Marubeni Corporation, Mitsui Corporation, Sumitomo Corporation, Nissho Iwai Corporation, Tomen Corporation, Nichimen and Kanematsu Gosho – were built up in the late 19th century as the original trading companies that spearheaded the development of Japan's commercial interests with the rest of the world, following two-and-a-half centuries of self-imposed isolation. Japan's dependency on foreign supplies of raw materials provided the *sogo shosha* with their central trading role, one which continues today, of importing resources for sale to domestic manufacturers and then buying back the finished product for sale to export markets.

The financial might of the nine leading *sogo shosha* is enormous and their combined business activities account for over half of all of Japan's domestic and international trade. Their function as suppliers of natural resources gives the *sogo shosha* a crucial role as the vanguard of corporate Japan's progress into new and developing markets, and the intelligence they gather on economic developments has proved invaluable in the past for both the private and the public sector as strategic information tends to trickle through from the big corporations to their guardians at the ministries. The nature of their business as go-betweens means that the *sogo shosha* have each developed vast domestic alliances of their own 'relationship' buyers and sellers, alliances which are cemented by equity cross-shareholdings and which provide the benefit of loyalty offered by exclusivity and collusion.

Employment systems

The *keiretsu* style of inter-company alliance offers many advantages in times of economic growth but also plays an important complementary role in times of economic downturn. With each economic crisis that has hit Japan in the last two decades or so – the two oil shocks of the 1970s, the appreciation of the yen in the 1980s, and the collapse of the 'bubble economy' and domestic economic slow-down in the early 1990s, combined with recessions in important export markets – pressure has been placed on Japan's lifetime employment system. In many cases, the *keiretsu* corporate alliance has come to the rescue, allowing companies under threat to avoid lay-off's by reallocating workers to other *keiretsu* member companies which are under less pressure.

Japan's lifetime employment system has worked wonders for labour relations. Employers tend to invest heavily in the training and welfare of their employees, and they expect – and receive – loyalty in return. They are therefore reluctant to sack them at the first signs of trouble. A flexible wage system has been partly responsible for the kind of room for manœuvre that Japanese employers have, a flexibility which their counterparts in foreign countries can only dream of.

Workers in large, high-technology and high-production firms of over 500 employees, which account for roughly 30 per cent of the workforce, are normally contracted into long-term if not lifetime employment. They receive a substantial part of their annual remuneration in the form of two annual cash bonuses paid in June and December. Originally introduced as an incentive, the bonus has come to be regarded as an entitlement and usually accounts for between two and four times the worker's basic monthly wage, a figure which varies depending on the size and the profitability of the company. The bonus system allows employers to avoid higher basic wages. When profitability falls, the bonus can be squeezed, costs are contained and the policy of avoiding lay-offs at any price does not, theoretically at least, cripple the company.

Corporate Japan's preference and ability to regulate output through overtime work rather than through changes in personnel numbers has offered another cushion against lay-offs. During times of high economic growth, workloads inevitably increase and overtime pay becomes a substantial part of a worker's income. Conversely, during economic slow-down, workloads decrease, overtime is cut back and net incomes shrink.

Such a system would, of course, be impossible without the compliance of a willing workforce. However, that willingness appears, in some cases, to have been taken to extremes during both the economic boom of the 'bubble era' (see chapter 7) and the '*endaka* years' of the mid-1980s, when the yen appreciated against the dollar and forced export-oriented companies to redouble their efforts to survive. Many companies forced enormous quantities of overtime work on employees, partly, as mentioned earlier, to offset the effects of the newly instituted two-day weekend, and partly to avoid setting a precedent for hiring new personnel. In a few isolated and highly publicized cases, tragedy ensued. Between 1985 and 1990, dozens of white-collar workers collapsed and died on the job. Investigations of their working habits carried out prior to their deaths indicate that many died from symptoms triggered by overwork, though in subsequent court cases the judicial authorities have tended to dismiss lawyers' claims that the deaths were related to the Japanese phenomenon of *karoshi* ('death from overwork').

The sanctity of Japan's lifetime employment contract has been tried and tested in the past, but never so much as during the economic downturn of the early 1990s. Large companies have been forced to compromise and adapt in order to retain their key employment policy of providing workers with jobs for life. Although the policy is currently under unprecedented pressure, it is still being honoured by most large firms. Nippon Steel's case demonstrates the gravity associated with laying off workers in Japan and the extent to which a company will go to avoid it. When Nippon Steel, the world's largest steel-maker, closed down two blast furnaces in the early 1980s in the Tohoku town of Kamaishi, north-east of Tokyo, the company had been employing one in every four local workers. The shutdown threatened to turn the isolated community into a ghost town. Nippon Steel had already kept the steelworks operating long after it had become unprofitable and closed it only gradually, transferring workers to other Nippon Steel plants around the country. When it could no longer transfer workers, the company turned to creating new businesses in Kamaishi to employ its former steel workers.

A combination of government subsidies, industrial promotion plans and the imagination of local Nippon Steel management teams started new businesses employing the remaining workforce in enterprises ranging from mushroom-growing and miniature Brazilian orchid cultivation to office furniture-making and soya meat-substitute production. Today, the new businesses are struggling but they still employ 700 former steelworkers and, as local Nippon Steel managers point out, immediate profts are not considered necessary because their primary objective is to keep employees on the payroll come what may.

The experience of Nippon Steel's Kamaishi plant has been instructive for other large companies facing the pressures of plant closures and staff lay-offs in the early 1990s slump. Nissan Motor announced, in February 1993, that it would close down its automobile assembly line in Zama, south-west of Tokyo, by 1995. The closure announcement attracted widespread domestic and international attention because Zama had once been the company's flagship assembly line, visited by foreign leaders including Prince Charles and former prime minister Margaret Thatcher. More sensational, however, for Japan's car manufacturing rivals overseas was the fact that the closure announcement involved Japan's seemingly invincible car industry.

Dramatic as they may sound, Nissan's closure plans, when subjected to closer scrutiny, do not actually anticipate any job losses at all. The company has offered transfers for 2,500 workers to two other Nissan plants in Tokyo and in the southern island of Kyushu. The remaining 1,500 will continue to work in Zama in administration, distribution, design and specialist-part manufacture. Nissan plans to reduce its 48,000 workforce by 5,000 by 1996, mainly through restricting recruitment and through natural wastage. The brunt of the Nissan reshuffles and reduction in capacity will probably be born by the subcontractors, suppliers and other supporting entities that had grown up to service the fully operating Zama plant. The threat of lay-offs has not only affected blue-collar workers. Significantly, 80 per cent of the staff reductions announced by Nissan in 1993 will be in white-collar jobs (about 32,000 of Nissan's workforce are office or administrative staff).

Japan's vast trading companies, electronics companies and other multi-national concerns, which employ tens of thousands of administrative and managerial office staff, have also been forced to review their employment policies, and many of them to confront the problems of bloated management departments built up during the bubble years. Several companies announced early-retirement incentive schemes in 1993, offering what American or European workers might regard as the ultimate dream pink slip. The magnetic tape manufacturer TDK, for example, offered to managers of 40 years' old and over, who are deemed to be underproductive, a continuation of full salary payments until retirement age if they promised not to come to the office any more. Those taking up the offer would be free to pursue any activity of their choice including entering the employment of another company (provided it is not a rival to TDK). The company reckoned that the savings made in telephone charges, entertainment expenses and other office overheads for these employees would exceed the cost of continued full salary payments, although adverse publicity following the scheme's announcement has forced TDK to reconsider its application.

Measures such as these to support employees, come what may, through bad as well as good times, offer evidence of the long-term thinking of Japan's large companies. Historically, Japan's manufacturing companies have had scant natural resources to rely on their prosperity, and have always therefore depended on their human resources, placing high priority on cultivating loyalty and developing what Western observers might view as a sense of self-sacrifice. Evidence of the success of those policies can be seen today in employment stability.

Trade unions

The character of the nation's unions offers further clues as to why employment has remained so stable in postwar Japan. Roughly 12.4 million of Japan's workforce of 49 milion belong to over 72,000 unions throughout Japan. However, their consistently lacklustre performance in winning significant pay increases or other improvements has meant that membership rates have fallen steadily in the last 30 years. In the late 1960s, when Japan's unions were arguably at their most mililtant (but much less militant than their European or American counterparts, with whom they cannot be compared), membership rates rose to over 35 per cent. By 1991 they were down to 24 per cent and are still falling.

The vast majority of union members (some 90 per cent) belong to company unions as opposed to industry unions and negotiate locally on company-specific terms. Japan's canny corporate managers have long maintained the tradition of dangling juicy rewards before union leaders, encouraging them to lean in favour of agreement with their paymasters. The union top brass learn to keep one eye on their future prospects and expect to be given a management position as a reward for keeping union action to a minimum and doing their bit to maintain the nation's much vaunted ideal of corporate harmony. Some unions even go so far as to name the company president as the top union representative, doing away with the fiction that labour and management are permitted the luxury of real confrontation.

Every April brings a performance of *shunto*, or 'the spring labour offensive', which foreign observers often liken to a choreographed and pre-scripted kabuki play because of its utterly predictable nature. For several months prior to the *shunto* season, industry representatives, interested academics and government economists pontificate on the current economic situation and the effects it will have on management assessments of wage negotiations for the year. Clear signals are sent to union leaders as to the range within which they will be expected to keep in the coming round of pay bargaining. This elaborate form of indirect *nemawashi*, or consensus building, results in remarkably harmonious negotiations once unions sit down with management.

The effects and future ramifications of the economic slow-down of the last three years have clearly been impressed on the union leadership, which has accepted average wage increases – as offered by management – of 5.9 per cent in 1990, 5.7 per cent in 1991 and 4.9 per cent in 1992. As severe economic slow-down appeared to have set in in 1993, the unions, like lambs, accepted the 3.9 per cent offered. Symbolic outbursts of industrial action still take place for unions to save face, but these typically last no more than an hour during the lunchbreak and involve polite and immaculately well behaved sit-ins where union members wear red headbands and chant a few slogans to clear the air and restore pride. After lunch the same workers can usually be seen trooping back to their desks, headbands put away and hair neatly brushed as if nothing had happened. Numbers of days lost annually to union action in Japan are among the lowest in the industrial world. According to the latest figures available for 1990 showing 1,000 man-days lost in labour disputes, the United States clocked up 5,926, Italy 5,181, Britain 1,093, Germany 364 and Japan just 140.

Underscoring the cooperative nature of Japan's unions, quite apart from the carrots so blantantly offered to their leaders, is the thinking, skilfully exploited by management, that personal prosperity in the long term depends on the profitability of the company. Accepted wisdom holds that, if unions were to demand 'unreasonably' high pay increases in bad times, the company's competitiveness would suffer and so, eventually, would the individuals who work for it. It is a philosophy that makes good sense in a country where lifetime employment is to all appearances still the norm, but would be anathema to a society where workers hop from job to job in search of short-term reward.

An aging population

Despite the new phenomenon that has appeared in the early 1990s in the form of recession-driven job cuts, and the new emphasis on austerity, there seems to be no evidence of change in the traditionally harmonious labour–management relations. What is forcing a wrenching reassessment of traditional company values, structure and performance, however, is demographic change. The relative increase in the number of old people, now regularly referred to rather whimsically in the local media as 'the silvering of Japanese society', will mean, according to accepted predictions, that at the turn of the century the proportion of the Japanese population aged 65 and over will be 16 per cent, compared with 15 per cent in Britain and 13 per cent in the United States. That in itself would not be too much to worry about, but long-distance forecasters reckon that by 2025, 65 year-olds and their seniors will account for 24 per cent of the total as opposed to 19 per cent in Britain and 20 per cent in America.

Quite apart from the implications this has for the future of Japan's already stretched state-pension and state-run health insurance systems, the demographic upset is likely to have a major effect on savings patterns, with long-term effects on the economy. Given Japanese inclinations to anguish about problems and changes long before they occur, the population is already being encouraged to prepare for its own silvering. Middle-aged salaried workers and their families are putting money aside in anticipation of a future Japan in which care for the elderly will be harder to come by than it is now. Eventually, as the silver bulge arrives, there will be relatively fewer potential savers (salaried workers) and larger numbers of spenders (retired people), so the net effect will probably be a fall in the national savings rate. If it is a large fall, its impact will be felt in investment rates and the cost of capital, and the outlook for economic growth will be less rosy.

The younger generations

There are other reasons to believe that savings patterns may be changing. One is the emergence, at the margins of Japanese society, of a supposedly new breed of younger-generation Japanese known as the *shinjinrui*, literally 'new humans'. The term was coined in 1985 by a weekly magazine which identified a new set of motivations and desires catching on among Japan's 20–30 year-olds, a generation brought up in an era of affluence and high technology, with fewer financial anxieties than their parents and grandparents. However, the *shinjinrui* have not suddenly abandoned their parents' basic values in life: of being hard-working, apolitical, materialistic, long-termist and needful of security in a job with a large stable company. The change that is being slowly, and perhaps only temporarily, wrought on Japanese consumption and savings patterns by this 'new breed' is incremental. But it is nevertheless identifiable. In 1991, research by the advertising industry found that young people do still save, but their motivations for saving are different from those of their elders. While their parents might be saving for the eventual purchase of a house or for their futures as the silver generation, the *shinjinrui* are saving to buy consumer goods to facilitate their alleged new desires to be leisured and pleasured. Assiduous followers of the fashions and trends presented in mass-circulation glossy magazines such as *Brutus*, *Marco Polo*, *Croissant* and *Big Tomorrow*, the *shinjinrui* spend their savings on the best and newest ski wear, surf boards and computer toys – expensive brand-name articles designed to be flaunted every weekend among teeming crowds of young people clutching the latest in ski wear, surf boards and computer toys.

Attitudes to jobs have also begun a partial evolution. While most young people would, ideally, like to work for large established 'name companies' like Mitsubishi Corporation or Toyota Motor, many are more willing to make compromises and to risk changing companies in mid-career. Smaller, younger and more entrepreneurial companies hold new attractions for a generation less willing to be bound by the traditions and the perceived conformity of their parents. Design, fashion and computer software-related companies have become popular among university graduates, although many of them are aware that jobs with younger, less-established companies do not have the cachet and social standing that positions in bigger and older concerns offer. Nor can they usually provide the job-for-life security or the extra allowances, paid by big established firms on top of the basic wage, that come in the form of subsidized housing, commuting expenses and other extras relating to personal circumstances such as marriage and educational costs, sports and recreational facilities, holidays at company resorts, cheap loans and private medical insurance.

Job-hopping is another new, if still relatively marginal, development in the metamorphosis of Japan's business society. It is a trend which has been given new impetus by the latest dark threats of job cuts issuing from Japan's leading companies, casting doubt on the inviolability of the lifetime employment system. Moving to a new company mid-career is no longer considered to be the sign of failure that it was a decade ago. Sony, for example, has introduced a policy of actively taking on mid-career staff into its management teams in order to promote the creation of new ideas and to encourage greater flexibility in a managerial and development team that depends for its future on the continuous flow of fresh ideas.

The arrival of large numbers of foreign financial companies in Tokyo, following the relaxation of restrictions on membership of the Tokyo Stock Exchange in the late 1980s, lent new credibility to the concept of job-hopping. American securities firms, in particular, lured crowds of Japanese financial specialists through their doors as the bubble economy began to inflate and huge profits made on the stock market encouraged them to expand their trading rooms. But Western style job-hopping suddenly looked much less attractive when the bubble burst a few years later and foreign securities companies reacted by instituting what the locals considered to be typically Western short-term policies of rapid-result cost cuts in the form of redundancies.

Some of the Japanese high-fliers who were tempted to join foreign firms now find that their pay-packets, some of which were commission-related, are not as glamorous as they once appeared. Still more galling for many of those aware that they may not be spared the chop of the cost-cutters, is that their conservative Japanese former employers are reluctant to take them back once they have been 'tainted with the brush of foreign values'. Reactionary views such as these, which discriminate against Japanese who have experience of foreign environments, are not new. They date back centuries, but were perhaps at their peak during the 1630s, when Japan entered a 250-year period of self-imposed isolation (see chapter 1). The government of the time, believing it should attempt to arrest the spread of dangerous and corrupting foreign ideas, declared that any Japanese re-entering the country from abroad would be executed. Punitive measures are obviously not so drastic today, but the concern that high-performance young employees, the corporate leaders of the future, may jump ship to join younger and less hierarchically-structured competitors, is likely to force a change for the better in Japan's notoriously conservative and tradition-bound corporate giants. As with many aspects of a Japan that is gradually opening itself up to the world, change is often accelerated and is occasionally initiated as a result of foreign pressure.

Joanna Pitman

7 FINANCIAL SERVICES
A world force

Japan's financial services industry is one of the most potent influences on financial markets and economies in the world. The five biggest banks in the world, ranked on total assets, are all Japanese. Most of the world's most influential investment banks are Japanese. Japan has the biggest insurance companies in the world, some of the wealthiest institutional investors and a stock market whose total value exceeds that of New York, London and Frankfurt combined. Decisions made in Tokyo by fund managers, equity salesmen, foreign-exchange dealers and Japan's financial authorities influence not only the world's bankers and brokers, but also politicians, bureaucrats, businessmen and individuals from Hanoi to Hamburg.

However, an enduring strength in Japan's financial services industry is not the impression given by the bulk of reports that have appeared in the domestic and foreign business press during the last four years. These have charted the dramatic slow-down in annual economic growth rates, the plummeting prices on the Tokyo stock exchange, the collapse of the property market and the two years of debilitating financial scandals in the banking and securities industries.

A welter of statistics have supported the impression of impending disaster. Almost 8 trillion yen (US $59.2 billion) in corporate bankruptcies were recorded in fiscal 1991, up 122 per cent over the previous year. Japanese banks have an estimated 50 trillion yen (US $467 billion) in non-performing loans. Some three trillion dollars of wealth have been wiped out in the past three and a half years because of the 60 per cent decline in the stock market, and between US $2.5 and US $3.5 trillion have been lost through the 50 per cent drop in residential real-estate prices.

Forecasts of Japan's financial collapse have made dramatic headlines and been the subject of books. They may, of course, prove to be accurate, though this looks improbable. Not that Japan's recession has been a trifling matter: there is no doubt that the Japanese financial community has a lot more to worry about today than it did four years ago. Business sentiment and earnings prospects are worse now than they have been for 20 years, and the economy's ability to grow is likely to be both delayed and weakened if stock-market turnover and prices remain at their current low levels. But when judged on a scale that embraces recessions in all developed economies in the early 1990s, Japan's was only ever relatively small.

Prospects for fundamental economic growth still appear to be sound, if not good. Even at the worst depths of the 'recession', annual GNP growth rates never dipped below 1.5 per cent. The governor of the Bank of Japan, Yasushi Mieno, has dismissed suggestions that the Japanese may have to get used to a slower-growing economy. 'I am optimistic for the longer term', he declared in June 1993. 'The idea that we should learn to live under low economic growth is a pathetic notion. It will not happen.' Financial Japan's sources of strength lie, to a large degree, in its institutions and its methods. To date, both of these have remained more or less intact. The case for optimism can therefore be built on the combination of the sound foundations of the industry and the willingness of the financial authorities to recognize the need to rationalize many constituent parts of their empire.

Pressures for change in the industry have been building since long before Japan's economic slow-down set in four years ago, and there is reason to believe that the recession has created the very conditions necessary to carry through long-overdue changes. The tight monetary policies introduced by the Bank of Japan in 1990, which resulted in the collapse of overvalued asset prices, commonly referred to as 'the bubble economy', should perhaps be interpreted as a victory for the Bank and the foundation of a stronger financial sector rather than its death knell. Japan's international financial competitors would be wise to prepare for the possible emergence, out of what looks like near chaos, of a Japanese financial system that is leaner, more efficient and more competitive than before. Purged of the excesses of the 1980s, and stung into action by the pain of that purge, a powerful force of restructured financial institutions could be at the vanguard of a renascent and more confident Japan.

Financial reform

Japan is in the process of trying to reform its entire financial system to make it into a more 'modern' and market-oriented operation. That Japan's banks, securities houses and other financial institutions have been able to grow so strong in domestic markets and become such formidable competitors in the international market-place begs the question: why is reform perceived to be necessary? The answer is that the basis of competitiveness in Japanese finance is very different from that of financial systems in other financial centres, and the growing pace of emerging international compatability requirements is gradually putting pressure on Japan to fall into line. Securities houses as well as banks are now expected to meet international capital-adequacy requirements. The slow progress towards the full internationalization of the yen, the pressure from overseas firms to dismantle barriers to inward investment, the call from foreign shareholders for foreign-style dividend returns, the demands on Japanese firms to adopt internationally compatible accounting standards – all these pressures, and many others, are building inexorably towards a fundamental revamp of Japan's financial services sector.

It will not necessarily be foreign parties who reap all the advantages. Japan's leading banks, for example, stand to gain power, size and prestige from a reorganization of the banking sector that could lead to a reduction in the number of licensed banks from the current 6,000 to a mere handful. Their profitability rates will also come under examination, for Japan's biggest banks may lead the world field when ranked in terms of total assets, but when judged by rates of profit on their assets they do not even appear in the world's top 500. Some have argued that this is due to special (and therefore unfair) advantages handed to Japanese banks by their protectors at the Ministry of Finance, such as low interest rates for depositors and restrictions on the activities of foreign banks in Japan. The Japanese government's concern to build up a strong and internationally competitive financial industry after World War II is evident in the degree of direct intervention, which is greater than in most Western countries. However, the precise contribution of specially protective domestic arrangements to the extraordinary success of Japan's financial institutions on the international stage remains the subject of much debate.

The history of Japan's banking sector

The origins of Japan's modern banking system are to be found in the government policies of the early 20th century. In 1927, a financial crash led to a reduction in the number of banks and set the scene for the consolidation of the industry in a small number of financial institutions with growing power, many of them operating within influential industrial conglomerates known at the time as *zaibatsu*. The increased domination of the economy by the military during the 1930s and World War II led to greater government control over the banks and the forging of alliances between banks and manufacturing companies, particularly those involved in munitions production. After the war, the Allied occupation forces abolished the *zaibatsu* holding companies but left intact much of the structure of relationships between banks, the government and big manufacturing companies. Banks continued to handle most individual and institutional savings and corporate fund-raising functions, thereby no longer requiring borrowers and savers to tap the capital markets directly. This system of encouraging indirect financing via banks as intermediaries rather than participating in the capital markets is still in place. It offers some explanation for the rapid growth and vast asset accumulation of Japan's banks.

From the end of the war until the beginning of the 1970s, bank borrowing was rigorously promoted as the preferred method of financing through a combined policy of maintaining low interest rates and strictly limiting direct access to the capital markets by potential borrowers. The types of borrowers, the amounts of capital, and the terms and conditions on which it could be raised in the stock market and bond markets were subject to government control. The dual shocks, in the early 1970s, of a breakdown in the world's currency arrangements and the enormous rise in oil prices are identified as major factors in the structural reorganization of the Japanese economy over the last two decades. Japan's annual economic growth rate fell from an average of 10 per cent to around 5 per cent, causing manufacturing companies to reduce their levels of investment in new plants and equipment and therefore their borrowing requirements. Simultaneously, the government was faced for the first time with the need to finance large budget deficits.

The development of new markets

The banks, still operating within the old and restrictive rules, were unwilling to purchase government debt in the required quantities, so the authorities were obliged to make a number of reforms, including the creation of a secondary market in government bonds and the liberalization of short-term money markets. More new instruments were permitted, interest rates were freed and financial markets of various sorts began to replace the old system of close relationships between borrowers and lenders that had depended on a segmented industry. Japanese-style 'relationship banking' had become so intimate that most corporate clients were clustered around a main bank which owned their shares (up to a legal limit of 5 per cent) and maintained a close watch on their activities, often helping to reorganize firms in financial difficulty to prevent bankruptcy. During the years of rapid industrial growth up to the 1970s, almost half of all bank lending was to manufacturing industry, with another 30 per cent to the distribution industry. Individuals got just 4 per cent.

By the mid-1980s, the Japanese financial system had been considerably liberalized, causing a fundamental reorganization of domestic capital flows. The banks' traditional relationships began to weaken and manufacturing firms, given more direct access to capital markets, began to reduce their share of indirect financing through bank borrowing in favour of issues of equity or equity-linked instruments. Innovative new markets in 'samurai', 'sushi' and 'shogun' bonds were created, giving corporations of all nationalities greater flexibility in raising finances directly through the markets. (Sushi bonds are issued by Japanese companies in dollars, samurai bonds are issued by foreign companies in yen and shogun bonds are issued in dollars on the Japanese market by overseas borrowers.)

New commodities and futures markets were also established. In 1984, commodities trading was restructured with the creation of TOCOM (the Tokyo Commodity Exchange for Industry), which trades platinum, gold and silver contracts. In 1985, the Tokyo stock exchange began trading 10-year government bond futures, and in 1988, 20-year government bond futures. In 1989, TIFFE (the Tokyo International Financial Futures Exchange) opened for business, trading yen futures and three-month Euro-yen and Euro-dollar contracts. The proliferation of new markets and instruments had a powerful effect on the banking sector. During the first half of the 1980s, manufacturing industry's issues of equities and other instruments such as equity warrants or convertible bonds accounted for a quarter of their total funding. By 1989 this had risen to over 70 per cent. The share of bank loans that went to industry therefore shrunk from about half in 1970 to just 16 per cent in 1990 while loans to individuals rose to 16 per cent, those to the service industry rose from 5 to 15 per cent and those to real estate companies increased from 4 to 12 per cent over the same period.

The inflation of 'the bubble economy'

Other sectors of the financial services industry also went through a terrific change in the latter half of the 1980s, when the inflationary asset boom known as 'the bubble' took place. A combination of partial financial deregulation, an accommodating Bank of Japan monetary policy of low interest rates (aimed partly at restraining the rising yen), and a rising stock market encouraged manufacturing companies to raise large amounts of funds, through equity and equity-related issues, to be used not only for investing in new plants and machinery but also for buying more financial assets.

Having spent the first half of the 1980s investing over 70 per cent of funds raised in fixed investments, manufacturing industry had reduced that figure to less than 50 per cent by 1989 and had increased investments in financial assets from 25 per cent to 40 per cent. A new investment concept known as *zaitech*, most often translated as 'financial engineering', was created which encouraged industrial firms to play a new role as financial intermediaries for themselves, setting up dealing rooms from which to command their financial investment strategies. The cost of financing became so low, and in some cases even turned negative through the use of ingenious new funding techniques, that many manufacturers came to regard financial investments as a more important source of profit than their core industrial production. While the rapid expansion of financial activity fuelled the rise of asset prices, rising asset prices also fuelled further financial activity. Corporate, institutional and individual investors watched as the stock market and the real estate market rose at unprecedented rates, and borrowed more to invest in them so that their expectations for further rises eventually became self-fulfilling.

As the access to cheap funds widened and industry began doing much of its 'banking' for itself (Toyota Motor's treasury department even became known as 'The Toyota Bank'), banks and other financial institutions were struggling to retain their traditional business and their relationships. The banks priced their loans at artificially low rates to encourage investors to borrow cash to put into equities or land. The banks' fight to continue their lending business led at times to suspect deals and outright corruption, and to an increase in loans to speculative borrowers, particularly real-estate-related companies, whose collateral derived from artificially high stock and land prices. Securities houses, too, fought to retain their corporate relationships by offering illicit guarantees of return on stock investment for certain favoured clients. The details of such corrupt dealings have since been exposed in a welter of banking and broking scandals which reveal the desperate lengths to which banks and brokers were obliged to go during the bubble years to retain the loyalty of their newly enriched corporate clients.

Suddenly, in 1989, the market psychology changed. Fears that the bubble had expanded beyond the capacity of the real economy to sustain it, and that asset inflation might lead to general inflation, prompted the Bank of Japan to institute a high-interest-rate policy in 1990. Land values suddenly dropped and stock prices went into a steep decline. The Nikkei 225 average lost 60 per cent of its value in the space of two years and residential property prices fell by a half. Because so many outstanding loans were tied to property development and a rising stock market, the end of the bubble also meant that Japanese banks found themselves sitting on a mountain of bad debt.

It is difficult to predict the long-term implications of the bubble and its bursting for Japan's financial services industry, but the immediate aftermath is clear: a drastic contraction of household and corporate wealth. Money supply stopped growing, consumer demand fell and many companies found that, having borrowed heavily to gamble in the markets, now that these had collapsed they were no longer able to service their debts. The financial authorities' intention to stamp out the speculative bubble was made clear with their imposition of tight new monetary policies. In eradicating the corporate sector's new love affair with *zaitech*, and preventing stock manipulators from pursuing their own brand of speculation, they sought to stem their own loss of control over the markets. The authorities' success quickly became evident in the rash of bankruptcies which began to appear from 1990 onwards.

Corporate bankruptcies

The April 1992 bankruptcy of Mitsuhiro Kotani's speculative investment firm illustrates the success of the authorities' attempts to regain control. Kotani went down with debts of 122.5 billion yen, becoming the second-largest individual insolvency in Japan after the 410 billion yen demise, in October 1990, of Nui Onoue. Ms Onoue was a restaurant owner and Buddhist mystic stock-tipper whose speculative investments had been fuelled by huge loans from Japan's most high-minded and prestigious lending institution, Industrial Bank of Japan, evidently desperate to prop up its dwindling lending business. But the Kotani bankruptcy was perhaps more symbolic for the Ministry of Finance. Mr Kotani had been at the centre of an illegal loan scandal which forced the chairman of Sumitomo Bank, Ichiro Isoda, to resign in October 1990 and triggered a succession of long-running scandals in the financial industry which led to the resignation of senior industry figures.

The shock caused by the Bank of Japan's successful bursting of the bubble forced a new sobriety on the industry and a reassessment of business practices and industry strength. The true extent of the banks' non-performing loans – many of which are related to the deflation of the real es-

tate market – has been difficult to gauge because there is no standard definition of what constitutes a non-performing loan and Japan's accounting
standards, which are generally considered permissive by Western standards, do not oblige banks to release the details publicly. Estimates of total
bank debts vary enormously – anything from 5 trillion to 50 trillion yen –
and year-end results tend to disguise such weaknesses by inflating profits
with the proceeds from securities' sales.

All but two of the country's 11 leading commercial banks announced
drastic reductions in profits in the fiscal year 1992. Total unconsolidated net
profits shrank by 43 per cent, marking the fourth consecutive year of falling
profits. However, analysts note that the Ministry of Finance is giving the industry plenty of time to nurse its problem loans, by maintaining its traditional reluctance to allow banks to write-off debts with the risk of
undermining public confidence in the banking sector. Prior approval from
the Ministry is required for loan write-offs, and if the bank still holds property, for example, as collateral which even nominally covers the loan, the
bank cannot usually write-off the loan.

The informal control which the powerful Ministry of Finance maintains
over its banking constituents will probably guarantee their survival in some
form and the industry's overall stability. A control structure still pertains today in which no bank would ever wish to be put in a position of having to ignore a directive from either the Ministry of Finance or the Bank of Japan. The
firmness of the authorities' guiding hand has led to the very careful development of the industry: not one Japanese bank has been allowed to go bank-
rupt in the last 70 years. Those who understand the pride that the Ministry
of Finance takes in this record are convinced that no bank will be allowed to
fail now.

This is not to say that they will flourish, given their debt burdens and
their inability to create new loan business as a result of Bank of International
Settlements capital adequacy restraints. But now that the stock market's
meteoric rise has ended, for the time being at least, and the industry's ever-
dependable hidden reserves of the past have been radically depleted, a ra-
tional restructuring of the bloated banking sector looks possible. With more
than 6,000 institutions licensed to take deposits in Japan, and more than 20
major international banks duplicating services and expenses throughout
the world, a restructuring through deregulation has become long overdue.

Deregulation

As in most other powerful economies, the process of innovation and deregulation in Japan was originally set in train back in the 1970s. An economic
upset of partly foreign origins, combined with subsequent internal stresses
and strains on the market system, has begun to partially undermine a highly
controlled structure. The various conflicts between the demands of the different market participants – the borrowers, the lenders, the intermediaries,
the savers – have been complicated and have moved the process of deregu-

lation at a faster pace than the authorities might have wished. Today the functional boundaries between different types of institutions have become blurred. The key conflict over vanishing boundaries has been between the banks and the securities houses. Under postwar legislation, banks have not been permitted to engage in securities business in Japan. The first significant change in this area came with the Banking Law of 1982, which allowed banks for the first time to sell their large holdings of government bonds 'over the counter' without having to deal with securities houses as intermediaries.

Numerous government advisory reports since then have edged the authorities closer to permitting open competition between banks and securities houses. An amendment introduced in June 1993 to Article 65 of the 1928 Banking Law, which separates commercial banking from investment banking, has allowed trust banks and long-term credit banks to begin operations in some investment banking fields for the first time. They are allowed to establish securities subsidiaries to issue, but not market, convertible and warrant bonds and to deal in straight bonds. No final formula for the full abolition of Article 65, however, has been agreed. Nor has it been made clear what effect this might have on the future strength of Japan's hitherto protected and highly territorial banks and brokers.

The issue of dismantling the barriers between commercial and investment banking is only one example of the conflict and debate going on within the Japanese financial system. Its slow and, to date, only partial resolution is representative of almost all of the Ministry of Finance's planned reforms, designed to widen its markets and make them more international and more transparent. So far, neither the banks nor the securities houses are content. The banks argue that the authorities have kept them out of the securities market for too long and are still protecting brokers weakened by the collapse of stock prices and market turnover. The brokers, on the other hand, complain that their cherished access to trust banking is still unnecessarily restricted and in other areas, such as corporate bonds, trading remains weighed down by government regulation.

Most market participants agree, however, that the government should push ahead with reforms because without them there is the risk of a long-term weakening of Tokyo's position in the world financial system. Professor Kazuo Ueda, coordinator of the Committee to Make Tokyo Markets More Transparent and International (CTTI), an industry body with Japanese and foreign representation, argues that continued regulation in Tokyo will limit Japan's ability to profit from value-added financial instruments which are more freely available abroad. Of the 25 major financial instruments freely available in US and European markets, the CTTI estimates that 23 are also freely or partly available in London, 19 in Frankfurt, but only 12 in Tokyo. The committee has also noted that in US and European markets, an action is allowed unless specifically prohibited. In Japan, on the other hand, an action is forbidden unless it is specifically permitted. Given the general trend towards internationalization of markets, methods and instruments, it is becoming increasingly difficult for Japan's financial authorities to ignore the views and requirements of foreign financial institutions operating or intending to operate in Japan.

Foreign financial institutions in Japan

Significant foreign participation in the Japanese financial markets dates back only a few decades. In the 1960s and 1970s foreign commercial banks rushed to set up representation in Japan in order lend money to the rapidly growing economy. However, operating restrictions, such as the number of branches they were allowed to open, meant that they were prevented from having market access equal to that of domestic banks. But foreign banks did have exclusive rights to make foreign currency loans, which were encoraged by the authorities because of the positive impact they had on the country's balance of payments. In 1980, however, that right was taken away as exchange controls were suspended and Japanese banks ploughed into the foreign currency lending market, swamping it and effectively pushing foreign banks out. The foreigners were left with tiny shares of the lending and deposit markets. By 1983, the 103 foreign bank branches in Japan had less than 3.5 per cent of loans and only 1 per cent of deposits.

Foreign investment banks and securities subsidiaries of foreign commercial banks were not making much progress, either, in penetrating the vast Japanese financial markets. Searching for new sources of profit, they decided they wanted to deal in and underwrite Japanese securities. In 1983 no foreign firm was a member of the Tokyo stock exchange (in fact foreign firms were not yet allowed to be members of the London stock exchange either). With powerful American investment banks such as Salomon Brothers and Goldman Sachs yet to open representative offices in Japan and being forced to cover Tokyo markets from Hong Kong, the US Treasury decided it was time to go into battle on behalf of free markets and foreign firms against Japan's Ministry of Finance. In partial response to this and other foreign government pressure, but more significantly in response to the growing domestic need for change, the Japanese government put together a programme for financial reform and liberalization by the mid-1980s. New markets developed in newly liberalized foreign exchange, bond futures, swaps, offshore banking and Euroyen bonds. Foreign firms moved rapidly into Japan to tap these new markets and, as the growth of the Tokyo stock market began to pick up pace, more foreign securities firms demanded access to the stock exchange.

By 1989, 22 foreign firms had been permitted to buy – at great expense – membership of the Tokyo stock exchange and three more were clamouring, through their governments as intermidiaries, to be admitted. By 1990, 25 foreign firms were members. Many of them moved into expensive central Tokyo offices, hired large numbers of local staff and brought over teams of expatriates on high salaries to exploit what appeared to be a perpetually rising market. For many, the high profits in Tokyo were only ever an illusion, due in part to the astronomically high cost of having a representative office there, but also to the monopolistic hold the Japanese securities firms had on the securities market. The better foreign securities firms did make a lot of money out of the market's rapid ascent while it lasted; but when it crashed, profits also crashed and scores of less prudent foreign firms in Tokyo have been left with vast overcapacity.

With stock-market turnover and prices languishing at their lowest levels since the mid-1980s, and the income from brokerage commissions (which are fixed at 0.25–1.25 per cent) dramatically squeezed, some foreign brokerage firms have been forced to retrench. Business practices in the 1990s stand in stark contrast to those of the bubble days of the late 1980s, when the more flamboyant foreign securities houses were competing head-on with Japanese brokerages in lavish entertainment expenses, wining and dining their clients at hotel reception parties, complete with geisha hostesses and ice sculptures, at a cost of US $20,000. Expenses have now been brutally slashed, some of the expensive expatriates have been sent back to head office or let go altogether and a few firms have moved into more modest office accommodation. One British firm, County NatWest Securities, has decided that the costs of continuing to maintain a presence in Tokyo outweigh the potential gains. In the spring of 1993, it sold its seat on the exchange and pulled out. Others are also said to be questioning the wisdom of staying on in Tokyo. However, several foreign securities firms, notably the large American investment banks, have made large profits from stock index arbitrage trading, an important profit source when the Nikkei 225 was at its most volatile, allowing traders to make good margins using sophisticated computer programs to anticipate the market's movements.

Foreign banks too have seen their fortunes rise and fall in Japan. The 80 foreign banks doing business today, one-quarter of which are American, account for only 3 per cent of the lending market between them. Most have taken the decision to concentrate on fund management and corporate finance, though one American bank, Citibank, has obtained the licence to set up a small retail network in the large cities and is said to have further ambitions in the retail banking sector. Ministry of Finance restrictions still keep foreign fund managers out of parts of the trust banking market, however, and forbid them access to government pension fund management. In February 1992, a British investment management company, MIM Asset Management, became the first foreign firm to be retained by a Japanese corporation to manage part of its pension assets. Other investment management companies are hoping for new openings to what is considered to be an extremely lucrative niche in Japan's financial markets. Fixed costs nevertheless remain high and profits are still small. But in a country where appearances count for much, the virtues of maintaining an image of continuity and long-term commitment still seem to take priority for most foreign financial companies in Tokyo. This, combined with the desire, common to large investment banks the world over, for maintaining at least the appearance of a truly global operation, makes Tokyo a market in which it is hard for a foreign financial firm to admit defeat.

Japanese securities companies

Like their foreign visitors, the Japanese 'Big Four' securities companies (Nomura, Daiwa, Nikko and Yamaichi Securities) have been forced by adverse market conditions to adopt a new philosophy of humility after half a decade of hubris and, in many cases, profligacy. It is a far cry from the dominant position they held during the years of the bubble economy. Then, the Big Four between them accounted for between 50 and 70 per cent of all share trading on the Tokyo stock exchange and 80 per cent of bond trading. The Tokyo market at the time was almost entirely speculative, with share prices bearing only a passing resemblance to the economic fundamentals of their issuing companies.

In such bullish days of the late 1980s, Nomura Securities, the securities industry's acknowledged leader, moved through the market like a bulldozer, ramping the stock of its choice for the day and instructing its 5,000-strong, nationwide army of salesmen to fan out across the archipelago, pushing the chosen stock onto institutional and individual clients. Nomura Securities dominated Tokyo's financial markets like a collossus. Insiders began to let it be known that the company had 100 dollar millionaires on its staff, and youthful employees swaggered to work in Armani suits and drove expensive foreign sports cars. Corporate pride swelled to new heights when Yoshihisa Tabuchi, the former president, was paid the compliment of being pictured on the front of *Time* magazine. Then, when the market turned, Nomura's status, image and enormous profits all shrivelled. The company was found to have been involved in three major financial scandals: offering illicit compensation to institutional clients, laundering money for *yakuza* (gangsters) and encouraging 'excessive trading' (Japan's euphemism for 'ramping') in the shares of a railway company called Tokyu Corporation.

From its peak business year in 1987, when Nomura made pre-tax profits of 493.7 billion yen (US $4.6 billion), the company's profits have shrunk to 3.6 billion yen (US $34 million) for fiscal 1992. Nomura has not been the only one of the Big Four shamed and humiliated by market collapse. All four dominant players have been tainted by scandal and are suffering from the fall of the Nikkei Average. With a market that is run on the basis of fixed commissions, Tokyo's shrinking trading volume – which has dwindled from a peak of 2 billion yen a day to roughly 3–400 million yen – has hurt profits. In fiscal 1992 Daiwa Securities lost 13.29 billion yen, Nikko Securities 8.09 billion and Yamaichi Securities 42.27 billion.

Many industry executives agree that the shock of the burst bubble has, in general terms, had a beneficial effect on securities industry ethics and on its efficiency, resulting in drastic curbs on the unrealistic spending excesses of the bull market period. Small Japanese securities firms have yet to demonstrate their ability to pull through the lean period, but the Big Four can survive on their vast reserves. Nomura Securities is reported to have stashed away more than 1.5 trillion yen (US $14 billion) in cash, securities and other assets during the bull market, and had built up shareholders' equity worth roughly the same amount. In fiscal 1991, the company made 142 billion yen (US $1 billion) net from interest and dividends on its cash and securities holdings. While it has implemented plans to pare down its staff, cut costs and rationalize along more efficient lines, the company is believed to be capable of remaining technically in operation – covering all overheads for 10 years – without doing one yen's worth of business.

The stock market

The Tokyo stock market's volumes, prices and appeal to investors may have shrunk dramatically in the 1990s, but its fundamental structure remains more or less unaltered. Ever since the war, Japan's leading banks, insurance companies and corporations have built up and maintained interlocking shareholdings with each other. These shareholdings are understood to be 'stable', meaning the holder will hang on to them for capital appreciation and not sell. The system is designed to prevent hostile take-overs. An estimated 60 per cent of the total shares on the market are believed to be such 'stable' shares which are never traded.

Individual shareholders account for 23 per cent of the total market holdings. Japanese investors have traditionally favoured capital gain over dividends, which are extremely small compared to Western stock dividends (some leading bank shares yield only 1 per cent a year, for example). With the economic growth rate much reduced and corporate profits under pressure, demands from institutional investors for better short-term returns on equity investments are growing. Many Japanese financiers predict a reassessment of investment philosophies, which could lead to the import of more Western-style investment habits such as demands for higher dividends.

As with many areas of the industry designated for eventual reorganization and rationalization, the voice of the foreigner, from both the public and the private sectors, appears to be acting as a catalyst for progress. But the ultimate incentive for Japan's powerful monetary authorities comes from the recognition that the financial industry under their charge cannot hope to continue its dominating march over the world's financial markets unless its own house is up-to-date and in order. A fully deregulated and liberalized Japanese domestic industry could produce a more formidable challenge to the world than ever before.

Joanna Pitman

8 JAPAN INC
The success of corporate Japan

For more than two decades, Japanese corporations have been admired and feared in roughly equal measure by their competitors in overseas markets. The awe in which they are held derives from the speed and efficacy of Japan's postwar economic growth. This surge of wealth – often dismissed by envious observers as 'a miracle' – has transformed, in the space of less than 50 years, a war-torn and starving nation into the world's strongest economic power on a per capita basis.

Japan's economic growth has not been miraculous. Its derivations are tangible, numerous and also highly contentious. Postwar economic build-up occurred under the diplomatic, political and military protection and encouragement of the United States, a strategy designed by the US occupation authorities to bolster Japan as a bulwark against the spread of communism in Asia. With a high degree of Japanese government support and coordination, a fierce level of domestic competition and a fastidious control over foreign competition, Japanese industry was nurtured and strengthened at home so that by the 1970s, when it was ready to tackle overseas markets, it was able to launch a formidable assault on targeted sectors.

Western competitiors were unprepared for the onslaught and Japan's concentration on a limited, albeit fast-changing, range of products. Protectionist restrictions were quickly implemented, first in the textiles sector, then in the car and heavy-industry sectors and subsequently in the electronics sector, each time forcing Japanese industry to diversify into new markets and new industries and to pioneer new technological developments which spurred them on to fresh conquests abroad. One of the sectors which has begun attracting attention most recently among Japan's industrial competitors is aerospace and the high-technology telecommunications and satellite industries. Both are fields which Japanese industry is showing signs of targeting with the next century in mind.

Japanese industry has been fortunate for many reasons, not least the United States' strategically motivated postwar devotion to its development. In addition, it has benefited from sound and far-sighted government guidance which has kept inflation low and promoted economic policies to support long-term growth. Domestic protection of growing industries has been extremely effective. In the past this was achieved through the implementation of tariffs and quotas on potentially competitive foreign products, although these have since been drastically reduced and the Japanese market is today one of the most open in the world in these respects. Market penetration difficulties are caused, rather, by non-tariff barriers such as industrial standards and measurements, a complex and expensive distribution system that favours indigenous producers, government procurement policies that discriminate against foreign companies, and other circumstances. These include the high savings rate and high land prices, which reduce the purchasing power of the consumer, and the existence of huge industrial conglomerates with preferential systems of lending and cross-shareholding which favour intra-group dealing.

Industry has also been fortunate to have had access to a well-educated and highly industrious workforce, and it has traditionally nurtured a high level of cooperation between unions and management. As a result, in part, of government encouragement, industry has made sustained and judicious investments in technology and maintained high levels of expenditure on research and development in comparison to its overseas counterparts. NEC, for example, a world leader in three of the fastest-moving technological fields – semiconductors, computers and telecommunications – spends over 10 per cent of its sales income on R&D. Indeed, the key characteristic of Japan's technical research in the second half of the 20th century has been the input of the private sector. In 1989, for example, only 19.9 per cent of Japan's research was state-funded, compared with 48.3 per cent in the United States, 38.7 per cent in Britain and 35.3 per cent in Germany.

Industry has also reaped the benefits of a far-sighted management that has encouraged policies of cost-cutting, reducing break-even prices for products through the introduction of new technology and the automation and relocation of production facilities to low-cost centres. Beneficial financing arrangements, too, have fuelled high-speed growth and cushioned the strains it causes. Because Japan's economic policies have traditionally encouraged its people to forgo consumption, to save their yen and deposit them at low returns in banks and other intermediaries, companies have been able to borrow on unusually favourable terms. Shareholders, too, have been encouraged to seek long-term capital gain in their investments, taking the pressure off management to produce the high dividends and short-term gains that Western shareholders have traditionally demanded.

But the picture has not always been so rosy for industry, for it suffers from two fundamental disadvantages. First, it depends almost entirely on natural resources from abroad, making it vulnerable to the vicissitudes of foreign commodities prices, and second, it depends on foreign markets for its exports, making it susceptible to politically motivated protectionist forces. But 'Japan Inc', as the formidable might of Japanese industry came to be known in the 1980s, has time and again demonstrated an impressive capacity to reinvent itself and to remake its structure to cope with economic crises of both external and internal derivation.

The two oil shocks of the 1970s caused a dramatic restructuring of heavy industry, pushing manufacturing companies to seek new, light-industry technology and high-value product development to carry them into the

1980s. As a result, manufacturing companies emerged more competitive in world markets. Again, in the mid-1980s the appreciation of the yen, marked in 1985 by the Plaza Accord which officially devalued the US dollar against the yen, forced another tough rationalization upon industry, which led to new international strategies based on the relocation of labour-intensive manufacturing in low-cost centres overseas. Japanese industry had again demonstrated the capacity to adapt in order to overcome difficult circumstances, in this case effectively insulating itself against the dangers of currency fluctuations. Once more, manufacturers emerged stronger than they had been before.

The next threat came with the emergence of the 'bubble economy' in the second half of the 1980s. Prices of assets, such as real estate and stocks, became artificially inflated and encouraged a period of perilous overextension in the manufacturing sector among others. Even the most conservative Japanese industrial companies were lured into the belief that *zaitech* (a form of financial engineering designed to create profit purely from financial market investments) was an important 'profit centre'. As the Tokyo stock market's Nikkel Average moved steadily upwards, approaching its December 1989 peak and fuelled by investors' self-fufilling expectations of ever higher prices, companies had access to unusually cheap capital, which they used to make heavy investments in new plants and machinery. In overseas markets too, domestic asset price-inflation was transformed into purchasing power over real foreign assets, and free-spending Japanese companies unleashed a wave of mergers and acquisitions at vastly inflated prices.

But, at the beginning of the 1990s, the Japanese financial authorities, led by the newly-appointed Bank of Japan governor Yasushi Mieno, instigated harsh deflationary policies designed to burst the bubble. Economic growth quickly slowed and industry found itself lumbered with huge overcapacity. The stock market readjusted itself to more realistic levels, falling more than 50 per cent in two and a half years, and the cost of capital rose sharply, undermining one of corporate Japan's main advantages. The bursting of the bubble marked an end to the era of ever-expanding markets for manufactured goods at home and abroad. Characteristically, corporate Japan is forcing itself to remake its structure to adapt to the new climate of austerity. Companies are retreating from much of the gospel of profligacy of the 1980s. Product ranges are being thinned out, and product life-cycles are being extended. Supplier and distribution networks are being rationalized. Employment contracts are being reworked to allow greater mobility within a shrinking supply of labour. Early retirements among older workers and increased investments in automation, combined with widespread staff cuts, are part of a new and compelling philosophy of controlling costs and expanding profit margins.

While the balance sheets of Japanese companies have been weakened considerably by the fall in asset values, the larger companies have retained deep financial reserves, built up and safeguarded during previous eras of high profit. Toyota Motor, for example, is believed to be riding out the 'recession' with 2 trillion yen in cash assets. Most of Japan's large concerns have retained reasonably good access to global capital whereas smaller companies with weaker balance sheets have not. The large number of bankruptcies, which have particularly affected the speculative elements of the economy, supports the theory that Japan's economic slow-down will, in the long run, result in a shake-out of smaller and less robust companies, leaving the bigger concerns more dominant.

There is growing evidence that, at least in the near term, there will no return to the free-spending philosophy of the bubble years as the economy begins its slow recovery. Many companies will never again experience the glories of the 1980s and most will enjoy fewer advantages than they did then. Corporate Japan's advantages may be narrowing, but they are still there and it would be unwise for Western competitors to assume that the Japanese challenge has faded. Past performance suggests that corporate Japan could emerge from the 1990s recession both leaner and stronger than ever before.

Sony corporation

More than any other sector of world industry, the Japanese can be said to have made consumer electronics their own. And of all the Japanese companies that churn out everything from video-cassette recorders and cameras to electronic bread-makers and waterproof stereo systems, it is perhaps Sony that has imprinted its name most firmly on the minds of the Western consumer.

Before long, the charms of the Sony Walkman will make themselves known to rice farmers in Mongolia and to goatherds in Kenya, such is the mass appeal of Sony's technologies. But in addition to its flair for marketing and brand name promotion, Sony is unusual among Japanese manufacturing companies for being 'a company with a face'. The vision of Akio Morita, Sony's flamboyant and outspoken chairman and co-founder, had been responsible for driving the company's rapid overseas development and establishing its overseas manufacturing subsidiaries, making Sony one of the few Japanese companies to be approaching true multinational status. An assiduous pursuit of publicity for the Sony name has spurred Morita to take on a role of grand theorist and interpreter for the outside world of corporate Japan. This is an unusual role in a country where business leaders typically strive to remain anonymous, or 'faceless' as the Japanese say. As a result of Morita's enduring philosophy of promoting the trademark as the lifeblood of an enterprise, the Sony name, 47 years after the company's foundation, is emblazoned on a vast array of electronic and entertainment-related products.

In the electronics field Sony is a formidable player in three main areas. Its video production lines include laser disc players, home-use videotape recorders, video equipment for broadcast and professional use and high-definition TV-related equipment and videotapes. In the audio sector, Sony produces CD players, mini-component stereos, hi-fi components, radio-cassette tape recorders, car stereos and ultra-small digital microrecorders. In the television sector, Sony makes colour televisions, satellite-broadcast reception systems, projectors and large colour video display systems for professional use. Other electronic products pouring out of Sony's factories all over the world include semiconductors, electronic components, telecommunications equipment, computers and other information-related equipment. Multimedia systems, which integrate computers with audiovisual equipment, are one of Sony's targets as products for future expansion in the consumer electronics sector, and in industrial electronics the company will be focusing on new developments in the field of semiconductors, recording media and telecommunications-related equipment.

Music and entertainment operations form the second pillar of Sony's international activities. A relatively new departure, Sony first ventured into this field in 1988 with the acquisition of CBS Records, now known as Sony Music Entertainment Inc and then hit international headlines in 1989 when it bought Columbia Pictures Entertainment, now renamed Sony Pictures Entertainment. The high-profile acquisition sparked enormous controversy in the United States, coming as it did at a time when Japanese overseas direct investment in the United States and elsewhere was nearing a peak, fuelled by the heavily inflated asset prices of the 'bubble economy'.

The music and entertainment arm, designed to team up Japanese hardware with American software, has been an expensive experiment in cross-border cooperation. Sony's ready chequebook has attracted some big names. In 1991, for example, Michael Jackson signed a multi-record, multi-media contract with Sony Music Entertainment, reputedly worth several hundred million dollars. Sony's motion picture business boasted a number-one finish in the US box office in 1991 and Sony money has been behind several American blockbuster films.

But while Sony's investments in new entertainment products have been substantial, its returns have yet to bear full fruit. Music and entertainment-related products represent 11 per cent of total net sales, and film-related sales account for 8.6 per cent. Consistent with Morita's original desire to produce consumer electronics for the homes of the masses, it is still video and audio equipment that dominate Sony's sales balance sheet. Audio sales bring in 24.8 per cent of the total net sales and video another 23.5 per cent. Televisions account for 15.5 per cent and other electronic products for 16.1 per cent. Morita's drive to make Sony into a truly multinational company reached a landmark in 1991, when net sales in the United States and in Europe each outstripped net sales in Japan, a trend that continued in 1992 and allowed Sony America to notch up 29 per cent of sales and Sony Europe, 28.3 per cent. Sales in Japan accounted for 25.3 per cent of the total that year.

The maturity – some would say saturation – of the Japanese consumer electronics market is a fundamental factor in this trend. Today, over 99 per cent of Japanese homes have at least one colour television, more than 98 per cent have electric refrigerators and washing machines and almost as many have stereo systems. The market has changed dramatically from the days when Sony produced its first 'pocketable transistorized radio' in 1958, when only 1 per cent of Japanese homes had a television, just 5 per cent had washing machines and only 0.2 per cent had a refrigerator.

As the markets of the United States and Western European countries also approach levels of maturity, Sony is faced with an enormous challenge. Given the potent combination of largely saturated markets, the slow-down of national economies in all three market areas and the shrinkage of consumer spending, the maintenance of existing sales levels will depend to a large degree on the production of radically new and innovative 'hit products'. Sony has a strong history of innovation behind it. Originally established in 1946 under the name of Tokyo Tsushin Kogyo, the telecommunications manufacturer had a paid-in capital of 190,000 yen. In 1955, it produced Japan's first transistor radio and in 1958, the year the company listed its shares on the Tokyo stock exchange, it changed its name to Sony. In 1960, the first transistor TV was launched and Sony established its first overseas subsidiary, Sony America. Eight years later, Sony UK was founded and in 1974 the first British Sony manufacturing operation began at a colour television assembly plant in Bridgend, Wales.

Developments of videotape recorders were progressing apace in the mid-1970s, and in 1979 Sony's first headphone stereo Walkman was launched. With rising labour costs and an appreciating yen, Sony fell into line with other Japanese manufacturers in setting up new overseas manufacturing subsidiaries in the United States and in several European countries including Germany, France and the Netherlands. In 1982, Sony's first compact disc player was marketed and CD production plants were opened in France and Austria. Sony's forays into music and entertainment began with the CBS purchase in 1988, but the new geographical focus of attention in the electronics sector was South-East Asia. Sony established new offshore manufacturing plants in Malaysia and Thailand in 1988, built to take advantage of some of the lowest labour costs in the world and to lay the foundations for the servicing of what promises to be the world's most dynamic consumer market of the foreseeable future.

Today, Sony has 40 overseas manufacturing subsidiaries, 15 of which are in Asia (in Indonesia, South Korea, Singapore, Taiwan, Thailand and Malaysia), 14 in Europe (in Britain, Germany, France, Austria, the Netherlands, Italy and Spain) and the remainder spread across the United States. Sony's strategy in Europe, in common with that of many major Japanese manufacturing companies, was to ensure the establishment of a sufficient manufacturing presence before 1992, a date which, in the minds of many Japanese businessmen, conjured up visions of fresh protectionist sentiments and a 'fortress Europe'. Japan's leading manufacturers, Sony included, appear now to have completed the bulk of their new plant investment plans designed to deal with a post-1992 unified Europe and, in many of their host countries, have won the desired status of classification as local producers.

The localization of activities is one of Sony's primary targets in Europe, where product planning and engineering, component procurement, production, marketing and sales are expected eventually to be totally integrated and totally localized. The establishment of local R&D facilities is the latest phase of a trend that has seen Sony's original distribution operations of the early 1970s transformed into substantially autonomous entities, responsible for their own operations from R&D right the way through to marketing and sales networks. Development and production aside, the localization of personnel has proven to be one of the most difficult hurdles for Japanese companies to cross, but one which must be crossed if they are to achieve full multilateral status. Rigidly hierarchical and devoted to the Confucianist principle that seniority in years equates with high rank, many conservative Japanese firms have difficulty accepting Western concepts of meritocracy and individuality in their Western subsidiaries.

Sony has, perhaps more than most, adopted a flexible approach. Wary of local reactions to the volume of trade, Sony realized that it would be both logical and prudent to create employment in the places it was selling its products. Sony has also identified advantages in promoting local employees to high ranks. A Swiss national, Jacob Schmuckli, for example, is chairman of Sony's European operations and is a member of the parent company's board. As such, he has considerable autonomy in relation to Sony's European activities, which now span the continent from Dublin to Athens. In the last 10 years, Sony's management has been deliberately decentralized in response to the company's diversification. The company now has 689 subsidiaries and affiliates and 120,000 employees worldwide.

Like the rest of corporate Japan, Sony's wave of rapid overseas expansion through direct investment and mergers and acquisitions beginning in the mid-1970s and, rising to a peak in the late 1980s, tapered off from 1990 onwards as Japan's 'bubble' burst and asset prices came tumbling down. The economy has slowed, profits have fallen dramatically and Japanese companies have been forced to call a halt to their overseas expansion. A few have even reduced their overseas presence to reflect local economic conditions.

Sony has proven to be no exception. With talk of recession prominent, Japanese consumers went into hibernation, and Sony's domestic sales have suffered a major setback. Profits in fiscal 1992 fell to 36 billion yen from 166 billion yen the previous year. Rationalization and ruthless cost-cutting programmes have been implemented. Product ranges have been slimmed down. Recruitment has been cut and middle managment has been pruned. But Sony appears to have escaped the fate of several other manufacturers which were forced, in 1993, to close plants and reallocate labour in subsidiaries or affiliates.

Sony's future prosperity lies in its continuing ability to innovate. If there appears to have been a dearth of radically new 'hit products' since the CD, Sony would have it otherwise, claiming its short-term future lies in the success of the mini-disc (a miniature version of the CD with a recording capacity) and in the very competitive HDTV market. In the long term, Sony plans to concentrate particularly on the telecommunications and computer sectors while acquiring further expertise in the development of key components and technology. Sony has a long tradition of leading corporate Japan in its devotion to R&D investments. In 1992, Sony spent 6.3 per cent of its net sales income on R&D.

When Japan's former prime minster Hayato Ikeda made his first trip to Europe in 1962, he was described by the more irreverent members of the local press as 'a mere travelling transistor-salesman'. As Japan has shown the world, transistor sales can become the foundations of vast national wealth. Sony is proud of its own contribution to Japan's economic success in polishing the image of the words 'made in Japan'.

Honda motor

If the 1980s was the decade in which the Japanese car-manufacturing industry pressed ahead with a fully-fledged expansion programme to establish itself as a global force and double its penetration of Western overseas markets, then the 1990s began as the decade for reassessment, for the consolidation of overseas interests and the reorganization of management capabilities both at home and abroad. Now that Japanese makers have more or less achieved international dominance in the mass-production passenger car lines, they are moving up-market with an emphasis on sophisticated and stylish luxury designs, to tackle the custom-built performance cars of the United States and Europe in their own markets.

Of Japan's 11 leading car manufacturers, Honda, its youngest and third-largest in sales terms, has a reputation as the industry's most nimble, most adaptable and most instinctively internationally-minded producer. Honda was the first Japanese company of any sort to make a direct investment in a manufacturing plant in Europe – a motor-cycle assembly factory in Belgium established in 1962. It was the first car maker to introduce reverse imports into Japan from overseas plants, and it was the pioneer of the separate marque for overseas car models, a move designed to spearhead its overseas drive up-market.

It has taken less than 50 years for Japan's car industry to reach its position of international pre-eminence. Motor car production in Japan was still in its infancy at the end of the World War II, when it was targeted by the government as a strategic sector for careful nurturing and became one of the beneficiaries of heavy government protection. In the 10 years from 1956, annual production was forced up from 32,000 vehicles to 900,000, and by 1986 had reached over 12 million. Against this background, Honda Motor was founded in 1946, originally as a motor-cycle manufacturer, by a bicycle repairer's son, Soichiro Honda. His fascination with machinery began, according to the Honda legend, at the age of four, when he developed a habit of spending hours every day watching a gasoline-powered engine operate a rice-polishing mill near his home.

At the age of 25 he patented a new iron wheel and at 31 invented an innovative new piston ring. In October 1946, the Honda Technical Research Institute opened its doors in Shizuoka prefecture and, a year later, production began on the first 50-cc motor-cycle. By 1955, a 350-cc scooter was on the market and the renamed Honda Motor had taken the lead in domestic annual motor-cycle production. Honda's first car, the sports S-360, was introduced in 1962, and over the next 10 years new Honda overseas manufacturing plants began operations in Taiwan, Thailand and Mexico, and distribution centres were set up across Europe and the United States. Production at Honda's Ohio plant began in 1978 and, the following year, Honda established its relationship with the British firm Rover, a link that has become the key to Honda's Europe strategy.

Today, Honda is the world's leading motor-cycle maker. Honda is also fighting it out with Mitsubishi Motors for the number-three spot in Japan's ferociously competitive domestic market and Honda America ranks third after General Motors and Ford in terms of car sales in the United States. The Honda Accord, built in Ohio, first became the US's best-selling car in 1989. In fiscal year 1992, Honda made worldwide sales of US $36 billion. Honda now builds over 2 million cars a year and employs 85,500 people internationally of whom some 40,000 are non-Japanese.

Like other Japanese manufacturers with overseas production interests, Honda is giving the concept of local integration, and therefore true 'globalization', a new primacy in the 1990s. In Honda's case, a reassessment of management structure was initiated in the late 1980s and plans were implemented to develop a new pattern of self-reliance for its three key operations: Japan, the United States and Europe. The company is moving away from a one-way export approach that is typical of most Japanese companies, to a world headquarters function. Honda Japan is now referred to by local company executives as just one of Honda's three main geographical interests. Already, R&D, product development, manufacturing and engineering, sales and marketing and export operations are, as far as possible, performed locally. Honda has embraced the idea that while the car industry has become global, each major market is becoming more distinct and increasingly more segmented, making a world car concept difficult to apply. Honda considers the development of car models specific to the local market to be important in creating a corporate culture that will be compatible with each market's distinct requirements.

Honda's partnership with Rover has become the central pillar of a Europe strategy designed not only to survive the creation of the single European market but to profit from it. Rover holds a 20 per cent stake in Honda UK and vice versa, and the collaboration has already led to economies for Honda on the components supply side and in the sharing of common parts, enabling Honda UK to achieve higher local content and lower costs. The Rover link has also provided advantages in sales and distribution in a European market that is considered by the Japanese to be considerably more complicated and competitive than the US market. Honda UK opened a new production plant in Swindon in 1992 to build a four-door Honda Accord designed specifically for the European market. The company plans to sell 270,000 units a year in Europe by the mid-1990s of which 100,000 are expected to come from the Swindon plant, 150,000 will be exported from Japan, and the rest from Honda America.

With such a high-profile presence in overseas markets, Honda now faces new challenges in its overseas centres in the social, political, environmental and safety fields. Manufacturers can no longer focus only on styling and performance, and an increasing amount of time and investment is having to be spent on the development of new technological solutions to the world's growing environmental and safety concerns. Issues of improved fuel economy, lower emissions and recyclable parts as well as safety measures such as traction control and anti-lock brakes must be addressed. As Nobuhiko Kawamoto, Honda's president and chief executive, likes to remind his colleagues, one of the most important new focuses for Honda in the 1990s will be to change the way the company is managed in order to be able to overcome unforeseen social challenges ahead.

Consistent with its reputation in Japan as a nimble, entrepreneurial company relatively free of the bureaucratic strictures and paralysis that tend to plague the older and larger industrial conglomerates, Honda claims to have foreseen and taken evasive action to avoid, some of the effects of the four-year economic slow-down that began in earnest in early 1990. One year earlier, as Japanese stock and real estate prices approached their historic heights, Honda began to adjust for slower economic growth, anticipating the gravity of the US and European recessions.

Huge investments in new plant and equipment had been the hallmark of the 1980s, and Honda like its competitors had committed large sums to this end, leaving it with vast overcapacity and rapidly depreciating assets. Kawamoto, the chief executive, took stock and made a decision in 1989, for the first time in a decade, to plan no new automobile plants. He forecast that there would be no need for new manufacturing facilities until the mid-1990s at the earliest. A new strategy of rationalized management and radical cost-cutting was introduced. New personnel hires were cut by one-third, product development systems were reviewed and assembly lines in some domestic plants were reduced.

Honda's market assessment for cars in Western industrial economies does not make happy reading. It shows that the US market has long matured, reaching a stage of little or no growth in new sales, that the Japanese market matured in 1992 and that the Western European market has entered a period of slow growth which will lead to maturity in the mid-1990s. For all Japanese car makers, therefore, the South-East Asian market has assumed a vital importance for future prosperity. But they expect to have to wait until the next century before seeing the broadly defined patterns of strong consumption, as developing economies institute more stable and consistent growth trends. Isolated markets, however, are already showing their colours. China, for example, is expected to have overtaken India as the world's largest car market by the end of 1993. And Vietnam, a future low-cost manufacturing centre for Japanese industry as well as a promising market of 73 million consumers, holds out excellent prospects for car producers. Honda already has a head start, as the word for 'motor cycle' in Vietnam is 'Honda'.

As far as its domestic future is concerned, Honda has stated its intention to avoid the trap of overextension and of attempting to cover all facets of a car market that is increasingly having to rely on a luxury, leisure-driven business where new cars are likely to be sold on the strength of fashionable accoutrements. Certainly, most of Japan's leading car makers will come out of the current world recession deprived of many of the advantages, such as low costs of capital, which they enjoyed in the 1980s. But past performance in times of economic downturn would suggest that the challenge of continued fierce domestic competition will spur Japanese car makers to new sources of prosperity both at home and abroad.

Mitsubishi

A visitor to Japan arriving at Tokyo's Narita International Airport can drive into the city in a car made by Mitsubishi Motors, on roads built by Mitsubishi Construction, to a hotel owned by Mitsubishi Estate. Transported by a Mitsubishi elevator to their hotel room, furnished by Mitsubishi Corporation, they might use a telephone made by Mitsubishi Electric and open a cold beer made by Mitsubishi's Kirin Brewery. The Mitsubishi group, which rests upon 41 central pillar companies, appears on paper, like Japan's eight other powerful industrial conglomerates, as a vast and sprawling industrial octopus, its tentacles engaged in enterprises as diverse as life insurance and glass-making, but united in the centre under the Mitsubishi name.

Yataro Iwasaki, a rice trader from Osaka, founded the 'Three Diamonds' (*Mitsu-bishi*) steamship company in 1870, as Japan was opening up to international trade after 250 years of self-imposed isolation. Mitsubishi quickly expanded into shipbuilding and then metal-and coalmining. Following Iwasaki's death, in 1885, the company began a wholesale expansion which took it into virtually every sector of the economy – heavy industry, oil refining, chemicals, banking, real estate, insurance, telecommunications and aerospace. By the early 1940s Mitsubishi, like its rivals the Sumitomo and Mitsui groups, had become a huge conglomerate, or *zaibatsu*, and became responsible for powering much of the production of the hardware for Japan's war effort. In 1946 the US occupation administration dissolved the *zaibatsu*, splitting up the groups into independent entities formed by their constituent companies.

Strict government direction, low wages and a judicious use of scarce capital were the key to the development of the Japanese economy in the 1940s and 1950s. By the 1960s, fierce domestic competition had recreated such prewar industrial giants as Mitsubishi Heavy Industries, which in the 1970s were ready to unleash their might in overseas markets. By reducing product variety, targeting niches and applying more efficient production techniques, Japanese exporters pushed into overseas markets, entering industry after industry and forcing a retreat by Western firms in their home markets. Since the mid-1980s, however, the giant industrial conglomerates have been shedding capacity and going through a period of major rationalization and restructuring. Buffeted by lower-cost competition from newly industralized economies such as South Korea and Taiwan, and hit by the pressures of falling world demand and protectionism in export markets, they have been forced to cut back radically in their old export mainstays such as steel, shipbuilding and chemicals and diversify into new high-technology speciality industries.

Today, the Mitsubishi group's 41 major companies are engaged in activities that range from brewing and glass-making to atomic power production and semiconductor manufacturing. Hundreds of affiliates and susidiaries all over the world support and complement the main core constituent companies. The group has also branched out into cultural and social activities, including the renovation of historical buildings and gardens as well as a matchmaking club and 'pre-nuptial counselling service' for employees of Mitsubishi companies, which boasts a success rate of almost 2,000 Mitsubishi weddings to date.

The Mitsubishi group companies are no longer subject to central control but are linked by cross-shareholdings and share much in the form of resources, information and technology. Mitsubishi Heavy Industries (MHI) remains one of the biggest central pillars of the group, though it has been going through a radical restructuring period since the start of the worldwide shipbuilding slump in the late 1980s. MHI diversified into production of power-generating equipment and managed to maintain a competitive measure of profitability as a result of the steady stream of defence-related orders from the government Defence Agency.

MHI is Japan's largest defence contractor. In 1992, 17 per cent of the company's total sales of US $20 billion went to the Defence Agency through the production of tanks, surface-to-ship guided missiles, F-15 fighter aircraft and Patriot surface-to-air guided missiles. But the company's dependence on defence-related demand to support its private-sector shipbuilding and heavy industrial operations now puts it in an uncertain position following defence spending cuts at the end of the Cold War. The Society of Japanese Aerospace companies predicts a 35 per cent reduction in aerospace-related demand as a result of the contraction in defence spending and the worldwide recession in the airline industry. The necessity for a conversion to meet more civilian demand has prompted MHI to move into new aircraft ventures. These include plans for the joint development, with Sikorsky Aircraft of the United States, of a new 20-seat twin-engine helicopter which is expected to begin production in 1996. MHI has also joined a consortium of three Japanese subcontractors to produce body parts for Boeing's intended new 777, 350-seat jet airliner – the latest evidence of MHI's plans to expand its non-military business from 10 to 20 per cent of its aerospace operations by 1998.

Mitsubishi Corporation, another of the group's core business, is one of the country's nine leading *sogo shosha*, or trading companies, which are a major force in Japanese industry and commerce, handling between them more than half of Japan's internal and external trade. Mitsubishi Corporation is a US $130 billion giant with heavy investments in oil and natural gas, having grown, almost unrecognizably, from its original role as a matchmaker and partner in business deals. With its geographically vast and financially powerful global network, Mitsubishi Corporation does still act as a go-between, buying raw materials from abroad and selling them on to manufacturers, and buying back the manufactured products and selling them on to the distribution chains. Its huge international representation, which includes some 5,000 employees abroad in 182 overseas offices, has made Mitsubishi Corporation's intelligence-gathering facility one of the strongest in Japan. According to most informal estimates, the collective information-gathering powers of the nine *sogo shosha* eclipse those of the government, reinforcing the traditional role of corporate Japan as the eyes and ears of the Ministry of International Trade and Industry.

But the vast overseas presence does not suit all economic and political climates. Since the contraction of recession-hit Western markets and the hardening of protectionist attitudes among political and business figures in Europe and the United States, Mitsubishi Corporation has been forced to move away from high-volume trade and is looking for higher value-added business in technology-intensive sectors such as communications and space development. For example, in 1985 Mitsubishi Corporation became the leading investor, along with 29 other Mitsubishi group companies, in setting up a satellite communications operator, Space Communications Corporation, which now has two fully-operating satellites. Japan's spending on space and rocket development programmes is rising – it stood at US $1 billion in 1989 – but it still lags behind those of the United States and Europe by almost a decade. Companies like Mitsubishi Corporation are now gearing up to push Japan into a new era of high-technology space exploration.

Its traditional business styles are also in for a change, as foreign political and environmental pressures have pushed the company into a new phase. It is now attempting to turn itself into a more internationally sentient and adaptable operation – less the cumbersome and conservative grey lady of Tokyo's blue chip trading companies. The appointment, in March 1992, of Minoru Makihara as the company's new president is perhaps symbolic of the desire for change. Makihara was born in England in 1930, educated at

Harvard University and was stationed overseas for 22 years before being invited into Japan's corporate ruling elite. His pedigree is impeccable: his father was a Mitsubishi man and his wife is a great-granddaughter of Iwasaki, Mitsubishi's founder. But it is his cosmopolitan flavour that appears to have come to the fore in his dealing with corporate Japan's new challenges. These are presenting themselves not only in the international market but also at home, where a restive and affluent younger generation is growing up, less swayed by the country's postwar dream of a single-minded and cooperative pursuit of industrial and economic growth.

Makihara, who can slip as comfortably into the banter of an American businessman's club as he does into the rarefied atmosphere of a traditional Japanese gathering of business and industrial elite, believes that his thinking patterns are still very Japanese but that his international background will assist effective communication with Japan's international partners. Such communicaton is becoming ever more important as Japan finds itself left to its own devices in international politics and diplomacy now that the United States is withdrawing its protective shield of the Cold War.

Given their long history and vast scale of operations, Mitsubishi group companies attract criticism for their staid, conservative approach to business and their unwieldy giantism. With young and nimble postwar companies springing up and creating new markets in industries such as electronic games, which did not exist 10 years ago, the older components of the Mitsubishi empire must force themselves towards a new fitness and adaptability if they are to face the growing and unfamiliar challenges of the contemporary international business environment.

Joanna Pitman

9 THE MARKET AND THE JAPANESE CONSUMER
Consumer trends, 1950–2000

An account of the changing tastes of the Japanese consumer since the end of World War II offers a vivid backdrop to Japan's economic history in the second half of the 20th century. Demographic trends have influenced consumer behaviour while new consumer markets, such as 'office ladies' or 'new breed salarymen', which emerged in the 1980s, reflect social and psychological changes and new living patterns, such as the nuclear household or the single lifestyle, have directed consumer preference. Japanese inventiveness and the rapid succession of booms and trends have in turn moulded and reflected the behaviour of Japan's 120 million consumers.

Economic growth and consumer tastes, 1950 to 1985
Changes in the macro-economic backdrop and the developing tastes of Japanese consumers are graphically illustrated by the progression of status symbols from the 1950s to the early 1990s. In the dark days of despondency and deprivation in the early years of peace (after 1945) and independence (from 1952) the main target was survival: to get enough to eat, to afford clothes and to buy books and other educational needs for one's children. Later, status symbols which set a Japanese household well above the herd were an electric iron (1952) and an electric fan (1954).

From about 1956, the Japanese 'calmed down', as they themselves explain. There began to be time left over, after the struggle to earn a livelihood, to reassess the many indigenous values dumped unceremoniously after they had failed Japan during the war. From this re-evaluation, there emerged a synthesis of restored indigenous and newly introduced elements with which an increasing proportion of Japanese consumers could happily identify. Perhaps the most impressive status symbol of the day was: black-and-white television (1956).

Incomes increased rapidly during the 1960s. The Ikeda Cabinet early in the decade set an income-doubling programme and reached the target long before schedule. The Japanese consumer responded with the behaviour of the economic animal. Status symbols followed each other in rapid succession, most of them linked closely with home improvement and the expansion of leisure patterns.

It was during the 1960s that the Japanese consumer coined the term 'tools of culture' for consumer durables, particularly electrical and electronic household durables. The more they consumed, the higher the level of 'culture' Japanese consumers attained. Status symbols of the 1960s included a tape recorder, record player, washing machine, refrigerator, piano and colour television.

Emboldened by success, for nothing succeeds as well as success in Japan, the Japanese launched themselves into developing, producing and using a range of consumer durables of ever increasing value. First there were the '3Cs': a car, a colour television and a cooler (some form of air-conditioning). By the early 1970s, 97 per cent of households owned a television set (86 per cent had colour).

The early 1970s saw the emergence of more lavish tastes. At the outset of the decade, those who led the Japanese Joneses aimed for the '3 Vs': a visa, a villa and a visit.

A visa meant foreign travel. Ordinary Japanese were allowed passports for overseas travel in 1964, and in 1970, 663,000 overseas tourists left Japan's shores. A villa was a second home, in the hills or by the sea. A visit was a novel phenomenon, a visit *en famille* to the home of a business colleague or shopfloor mate, now that it was more spacious, and better equipped (with culture tools). Shortages of construction materials and a land price 'bubble' put an early brake on the villa boom. Then came the succession of 'shocks' of the first half of the 1970s – Nixon shock, dollar shock and oil shock – which cramped the Japanese consumer's style.

Even so, by 1975, a wide range of consumer durables had reached a diffusion level of 75 per cent or more of all Japanese households, which totalled 32.14 million in that year. Among them (with household diffusion rates) were washing machines (97.6%); refrigerators (96.7%); electric fans (94.3%); electric *kotatsus*[1] (91.3%); vacuum cleaners (91.2%); colour televisions (90.3%).

In the same period, among rising stars were stainless steel sink units (72.8%); gas water heaters (67.2%); extractor fans (59.2%); passenger cars (41.2%). True 'tools of culture' included electric organs (22.9%) and pianos (11.8%).

Bubble consumers, 1985 to 1991

There were new key words for the tone and themes of consumption as it matched the dramatic pace of asset appreciation during the economic bubble years of the second half of the 1980s. Factors and themes included:

Strong yen	enabling the Japanese consumer 'to step into what had been a dream world'
Domestic demand	officially stimulated, leading to
Investment and travel overseas	

[1] A traditional, heated well in the living-room floor, over which a table is placed and in which you dangle your feet, hips tucked into a quilt.

Spread of five-day week	and a slow reduction in working hours stimulated weekend travel and resort condominium development
Quality of life	selective and individualized consumer tastes
Convenience	handy, time- and space-saving, portable and miniaturized
Natural	health and sport
Personal investment	self-realization
Affluence	traditional, genuine, luxury, global, enabling 'the combination of the elegance of Japanese tradition with the opulence of the present'
High function	and high performance, upgrading with new concepts and technologies

Many of these themes appear in:

Housing development and home enhancement	two- and three-storey structure basements system bathrooms, kitchens, bedrooms multi-function bathrooms (with warm-water bidet) bay windows with built-in air-conditioning air purifiers new range of 'fuzzy' household appliances exclusive high-tech, large-scale durables, including
	larger fully automated washing machines (39.8%)[2]
	large capacity refrigerators (72.4%)
	high-definition television (HDTV) automatic breadmakers exclusive imported furniture, tableware
Convenience	prepaid cards nationwide house-to-house deliveries networking services microwave ovens (69.7%) portable and cordless telephones (39.6%)
Upgrading	CD players (34.3%) CDs (95% of the music market in 1990) satellite broadcasting

[2] figures in brackets denote household diffusion rates in 1990

Affluence	luxury leisure patterns
	high-class cars, domestic and imported
	luxury cruises
	leisure-oriented recreational vehicles
	'aesthetic' (beauty) clubs
Health and sport	natural
	household water purifiers
	oxygen business
	mineral water, imported and domestic
	nutrition-fortified and sugar-free drinks
	high fibre-content foods
	anti-germ, anti-odour blouses
	jogging
	cycling
	sports clubs
Personal investment	early morning and 24-hour classes for business people
	seminars for entrepreneurs
	colour consulting, using colour to make a personal statement
	manners seminars for young ladies
	bridegroom charm schools, to mould the man to the modern woman's personal tastes
Miniaturization	passport-sized video-cassette recorder
	laptop personal computer
	book-sized computer
	memo-sized word processor
	personal facsimile
	card-sized photocopier
	card-sized voice recorder

Post-bubble consumers, 1991 to 1993

With the bursting of the bubble early in 1991, consumer wariness was generated by the reverse assets effect – the rapid fall in the worth of assets inherited, such as land or property, or acquired in the heady 1980s. This caution was reinforced by anxiety about other aspects of Japan's economy. There was stark evidence of the stunting of growth as the effects worked through to the consumer in the form of lower wage increases, reduced bonus payments, a lowering of overtime and even the unthinkable 'employment adjustment', a euphemism for lay-offs. Post-bubble consumers reassessed values and preferred personalized and authentic tastes. Although there was a marked slow-down in the luxury item boom, consumers continued to opt for quality lifestyle products and services.

Major themes of consumption were:

Nature	natural water for drinking, cooking, skin care household water purifier natural cosmetics recycled products
Health	beauty care, of the whole body 'aesthetic' salons nutritional drinks
Enjoyment	recreational vehicles domestic travel overseas travel, in small parties, to historic towns, staying in moderately priced hotels and eating in restaurants patronized by the locals
Personalization and 'homification'	cellular telephones personal facsimile home banking, travel, security two-storey home parking

Characteristics of Japanese consumers

Since at least the early 1960s, when incomes doubled within a few years, over 90 per cent of Japanese have ranked themselves as middle class, when polled for the prime minister's office annual *Survey of Living Standards*. Judging themselves as identical with others, the Japanese have, until quite recently, shared the same preferences and similar aspirations. As a result, there is an identifiable, usually predictable, vogue or trend, boom or craze, for a particular product or product family or for a specific form of service, leisure activity or lifestyle. Everyone climbs on to the bandwagon: all aspire to own the status symbol of the year.

So those who manufacture for the Japanese, or offer them services, are in a position to plan well ahead and corral consumers safely into the appropriate pen. Household diffusion rates of consumer durable items surge dramatically; queues for restaurants or leisure facilities in vogue grow longer. There was, for example, a dramatic rise in the number of households with colour televisions, from 0.3 per cent in 1965 to 90.3 per cent in 1975. Households with videos rose from 2.4 per cent in 1980 to 66.8 per cent in 1990.

Yet although they have moved with the herd, Japanese consumers have always been discerning and demanding, knowledgably seeking out quality and value-for-money, 'high-sense' products and top-level service. Even though most Japanese are still unable to escape from regarding themselves as poor, they demand luxury level products at standard class prices.

The later 1980s saw the start of changes in consumer behaviour which will become more prominent and will create new patterns in the later 1990s.

One of these changes was the end of showy displays of opulence when the economic bubble burst early in 1991. The Japanese consumer 'took one step down' – and then carried on consuming. Business persons travelling by air moved from first to business class or from business class to economy. Office ladies (OLs) took one less trip overseas or to Japanese resorts each year. During Japan's recession, business-related expenditure on entertainment plummeted (with the Ginza bars and entertainment spots suffering). But personal consumption, on the whole, remained healthy, although on a lower plane, 'one step down'.

Another well-marked trend is the move away from the herd in the direction of individual preference. This tendency can be seen in all areas of consumption, and is particularly evident in overseas travel. Overseas holiday-makers in several consumer segments are choosing to travel as individuals or in as small a group as is feasible. They will map out or request their own individual tour. The flag-carrying two-hundred strong group is an increasingly rare sight.

Consumer segments

There are 125 million Japanese, every one of them an eager yet discerning consumer. Men live to be 76 years, women live to be 82 years, dramatic rises from the life expectancy figures of 60 years for men and 63 years for women in the early 1950s.

Sophisticated consumer segmentation techniques have been developed by the Japanese media, by advertising agencies such as Dentsu and Hakuhodo, by those whose business is to service consumers, such as Japan Rail, Japan Travel Bureau, Japan Air Lines and All Nippon Airways, and by research organs such as Nikko Research Center and Nomura Research Institute. The main consumer segments are:

teens, aged 11–19
young adults, aged 20–29
adults, aged 30–49
mature adults, aged 50–59
'silver' citizens, aged 60 and over.

Within these broad groupings there are several important subsectors which have their own distinctive consumer behaviour. Among specific consumer subgroup targets identified by Dentsu, Japan's leading advertising corporation, are:

office ladies (OLs) aged 20 to 24
Hanako, the model OL, aged 25 to 29
working men in their 20s
'Trente Ans', working single women or DINKS in their 30s
mothers in their 30s
men in their 30s
baby boomers

men in their 50s

Interesting segments or subsectors are:
the 'silver generation'
the baby boom subgroup
the new generation of salarymen in their 30s
office ladies (OLs) in their 20s and early 30s students

The 'silver' generation

The title the Japanese give to their over 60s reflects an attitude to this generation far more positive than the drab 'grey' or cold 'pensioners' used in the UK. There are silver seats on trains, buses and subways; old people move into silver homes. In 1990 there were 21.55 million silver citizens, aged 60 or above, constituting over 17 per cent of the total population. By the end of the decade, the segment is expected to grow to 28.98 million, 21 per cent of the total population. The 'active silver' group, now in their 60s and nearing retirement in the first half of the decade, are part of the workaholic generation which was in its teens and starting work at the end of the war. An important element in the team which built Japan's recovery, they were in their 30s as Japan entered the years of double-digit growth in the 1960s. As they assumed managerial roles in their 40s, Japan was buffeted by the 1970s shocks. In their mid-to-late 50s, they lived through the boom and bubble of the later 1980s. Members of the silver generation have never managed to bring themselves to relax. As they enter their active silver decade, they are expected to remain vigorous, consuming with mature yet well-heeled values and sensibilities.

There are markets specific to silver-generation consumers, in housing and the home, food and drink, clothing, health and hygiene, and especially in leisure and travel, where active silver Japanese have a particularly high propensity to consume services. Favourite destinations for domestic travel are thermal spring resorts. Travel operators offer a wide variety of specifically targeted special-interest overseas tours.

Japan's silver segment will grow steadily to the year 2020. Silver citizens have firmly held and well-defined tastes and preferences. During the 1990s, as these tastes are accommodated, Japan bids fair to build and make profitable the world's most comprehensive silver industry.

The baby boomers

The Japanese born in the immediate postwar years form a distinctive subgroup, departing significantly in character and behaviour from their immediate predecessors, the silver generation. The new tendencies of this subgroup can be observed most clearly in the baby boom salarymen, whose leaders are now, or may soon become, members of the *bucho* (head of department) class.

Baby boom managers are assertive. They are competitive, having been born into deprivation and lived in their early years with shortages. They have had to fight all the way, to get into good middle and high schools, top universities and leading corporations or public institutions. Now they compete for promotion against a large cohort of contemporaries. They are well educated. The educational norm for high-flying baby boomers became a university or college qualification, a major step-up from the middle or high school standard of the segment whose place they are taking. They are more resourceful and independent than their predecessors and there is a tendency to be less devoted to consensus and more receptive to personal and individual preferences and challenges than their elders. They are sometimes disillusioned and bitter – at not being able to afford a home of their own, for instance – and some of them are beginning to ask themselves 'Why sacrifice yourself for the company?' These traits appear not only among salarymen in offices and shopfloor workers: they also affect the behaviour of this subgroup as female as well as male consumers.

New generation salarymen in their 30s

The background and values of this subgroup are different again. Born in the late 1950s and the first half of the 1960s, they have grown up with plenty and have never been forced to compete against shortage – in the home, in school or in college. This subgroup were members of the first generation of Japanese children to have their own bedroom.

As salarymen, they are apt to draw a clear line between the demands of the company and the claims of private life: to older generations, they seem more interested in leisure than in what is happening in the office. Older Japanese appear to find it difficult to make up their minds about the character and capabilities of the 'new breed salaryman' generation in their 30s. On the one hand, a reputable research institute attached to a leading advertising corporation (Hakuhodo Institute of Life and Living, HILL) traces unattractive, by traditional assessment, traits back to their being pampered, and implies weakness of character. Yet some industrial and business leaders hold high opinions of employees in this age group. The then senior managing director of Honda Motor, aged 54 years and a former head of Honda's R&D operations, said in 1990, 'In the future, more ideas and concepts will be born in Japan. Our young engineers have a different culture from my generation. We thought that hard work had a value by itself, and that satisfied us. They don't work so long, but they are more able than we were. I have high hopes for them.'[3]

Again, this generation is very near in age and background to the older OL segment – the model Hanako, born in 1964 (see below). And whatever else in Hanako may be found to be at fault, she has never been criticized for being pampered and lacking drive and resourcefulness.

---

[3] quoted in *Fortune*, 26 March 1990

Office ladies (OLs)

OLs are 'office ladies', female office workers. There is no pejorative element in the term. According to the widest definition, the total segment comprises single women woking in offices of an age range of 18 to 44.

Japan Travel Bureau Foundation splits the OL segment into two: OL I comprises single working women aged 18 to 29; OL II comprises the age range 30 to 44. A Nikkei survey divides the segment into three. OL I is aged 20 to 24: OL II is aged 25 to 29; and OL III is aged 30 to 34. The Nikkei sample is 1,000 single OLs employed in 70 leading companies in the Tokyo metropolitan area. Thirty-three of the companies are manufacturing and 37 are non-manufacturing. The affectionate nickname given by the media to the stereotype OL is Hanako.

The Hanako depicted in the survey is fun-loving and free-spending, yet serious and responsible, often under stress, planning for the future and concerned to cultivate and invest in herself. Above all, Hanako has an astonishing propensity to consume. It is widely anticipated that Hanako will retain this habit as she marries, becomes a mother and passes through subsequent consumer segments.

Hanako's chief interests are:

- travel (48%)
- her future (47%)
- marriage (34%)
- fashion (30%)
- cultural events, music, cinema, theatre (28%)
- love (27%)
- sports (25%)
- savings and 'financial technology' (11%)
- current affairs, social, economic and political issues (8%).

Twenty-five per cent of OLs regard themselves as upper class or upper-middle class: 16 per cent rank themselves as lower class or lower-middle class. The remaining 59 per cent are self-styled middle-middle. The higher the level of disposable income, the greater the percentage judging themselves as upper or upper-middle: only 18 per cent of those with up to 70,000 yen monthly disposable income allocate themselves to the upper level, while 40 per cent of those with over 100,000 yen disposable monthly income regard themselves as belonging to the upper categories. More than half of the OLs in the Nikkei sample are satisfied with their circumstances. The higher the level of disposable income, the greater the satisfaction rate.

One of Hanako's favourite phrases is '*ima dake*' – literally, 'only now'. 'If it's only now that I can do such and such, buy this and that or visit so and so', then I should make the most of the present. Given the choice between enjoying life today or providing for the future, 61 per cent of the sample opts for today, with only 14 per cent looking to tomorrow.

Hanako also thinks:

it's only now that there are so many happy things in life (78%)
it's only now that I have so much money to spend on myself (66%)

but also:

it's only now that there are so many misgivings and anxieties (77%).

Hanako has a high level of confidence in her own talents. She is capable of performing tasks given to her in the office. She is understanding and sympathetic. She can cope with human relations and she knows what she wants. Hanako is keen to improve and invest in herself. The sample was asked to select from 10 items on which to spend money. The top choice, with a score of 56 per cent, was cultural interests and hobbies: next came travel – a form of broadening experience. Following these were fashion, eating and drinking, and developing friendships. Sixth came 'enriching the future'.

Hanako is very interested in fashion wear. She has her own idiosyncratic views and will not blindly follow vogues. She looks for quality and 'how it feels' rather than 'how it looks'. She is not a brand worshipper. She is something of a gourmet. She will 'hunt down a good restaurant which people don't know about' and she often eats in places which she has read of in newspapers or magazines. She follows her own inclinations in choosing from the menu and is likely to know which wine will go well with her choice.

Hanako loves to window shop, even when she is not really interested in buying. Before she buys something, she likes to hold it and 'feel' its quality. As a shopper she is a highly discriminating individual. 'I lose interest if lots of people have the same thing.' This trend leads her to steer clear of top brand items.

Hanako's office is likely to be working a five-day week, with a regular two-day weekend. Every year she will probably take two holidays of four or more days. Hanako's life is stressful. The principal areas of stress are linked to her job: they include interpersonal relations in the office, the trivial nature and the volume of her work and the weight of the responsibility she is given. Other stress areas include her own personal human relations and problems connected with marriage and the home.

Hanako has no sense of lifetime loyalty to her employer. Eight per cent of the sample are actively planning to move jobs. Sixty-eight per cent would change jobs if there was an attractive opening.

Hanako 'feels tired'. She is likely to spend leisure time in sedentary and recuperative activities, such as watching television or video and reading newspapers and magazines. As a traveller, she will choose a restful and relaxing holiday, rather than one filled with restless roving round shops and sightseeing highlights. Her favourite sports are skiing, tennis and golf.

The level of Hanako's disposable income is affected by her residential circumstances. Of the sample:

29% have between 50,000 yen and 70,000 yen monthly disposable income

25% have between 70,000 yen and 100,000 yen

22% have more than 100,000 yen

In spite of her propensity to consume, Hanako is an enthusiastic saver. In the sample:

23% of OL I (aged 20 to 24) have savings between 500,000 and 1 million yen

25% of OL II (aged 25 to 29) have savings between 1 and 2 million yen

21% of OL III (aged 30 to 34) have savings between 3 and 5 million yen

Hanako's ideal boyfriend is a handsome hunk. Her ideal husband is a man with economic power and potential. With her boyfriend she likes to eat out or go for a drink, visit the cinema or shops, take a drive in the city or to the sea, ski or play golf and tennis. She likes the idea of a holiday overseas, a skiing trip or a weekend away from it all somewhere in Japan.

Her ideal is to marry and have children. Of the sample, 83 per cent want to marry and have children, while 11 per cent will be happy with a childless marriage. Three per cent want to stay single. From 25 to 26 is the ideal age to marry, with a luxury hotel as the favourite honeymoon venue for over 50 per cent of the sample. The dream ideal for one in eight OLs is a quiet wedding – just the couple – in Hawaii or some other resort overseas.

Students

Students form an important subgroup in the teens and young adults segments, if only for its size and spending power. In 1955, only just over a half of middle-school graduates entered high school, and only 10 per cent of high-school leavers entered three-year colleges and four-year universities. By 1975, over 90 per cent of middle-school leavers were entering high school and 37.8 per cent of high-school graduates went on to college or university. These figures have stayed fairly constant, so over 90 per cent of Japanese have high-school standard education and just over one-third are college or university graduates. A further development is the rapid emergence of special training schools, usually called 'academies' by their proprietors. These are alternatives to colleges or universities in the tertiary sector. Examples are computer 'academies', language colleges and calligraphy institutes. In recent years, just over one-third of high-school graduates have entered employment, just over 30 per cent have entered colleges or universities and just over 30 per cent have entered special training establishments.

There are 499 four-year universities, with 2.07 million students, 584 three-year colleges, with 460,000 students, and 3,254 special training establishments, with 740,000 students. The total number of Japanese in tertiary education is 3.27 million – a significant consumer market.

The wan and shabby, poverty-stricken student is a figure of the past. The student's average income – 70 per cent from parents, 25 per cent from *arbeit* (side job) – is just over 200,000 yen per month, well above the average starting wage for a male graduate. The main targets of students' disposable income are travel related, study abroad and computer software. For overseas travel, recent favourite student destinations include Greece, Spain (Seville and Barcelona in 1992), France and the UK, followed by the US West Coast and Mid-West and Central and South America. A prominent feature in student overseas travel is the 'graduation trip', squeezed into the interval between the end of study in February and the start of work in April. Typically lasting three weeks or more, the 'graduation trip' is a present from parents or grandparents, or is part paid for by the student's savings from *arbeit* income or a bank loan.

The Japanese consumer 1993

Real economic growth for 1993 is forecast at 2.6 per cent, 1.4 per cent in the first half and 3.7 per cent in the second half.[4] Private consumption is forecast to pick up in the second half, spurred by the expectation of income tax cuts of 3 trillion yen in the autumn. It was estimated at the start of 1993 that there were still 900,000 excess employees in the manufacturing sector.[5] To rectify this, 'employment adjustment' will have to continue for some time.

Although the spring 1993 wage increase was lower than that of the previous year (3.8 per cent in 1993, down from 4.95 per cent in 1992), there is a growing propensity to consume, based on the expectation of a falling inflation rate and a smaller decrease in the amount of overtime worked. The year is expected to see replacement demand for consumer durables bought in the later 1980s, led by a pick-up in passenger car registrations and in sales of white goods (particularly refrigerators and washing machines). This recovery is helped by the launch of low-price, high-quality products, some based on new developments in fuzzy and semiconductor technologies.

On a volume basis, private consumption hit bottom in the April–June 1993 quarter. As land and stock prices appreciate, inventory adjustment is completed and increases in capacity utilization translate into growth in overtime payments, there is likely to be less uncertainty about the economy and less anxiety about unemployment. These improvements are expected to result in consumption on a value basis turning positive from the autumn of 1993.

Ten -izations and -fications affecting Japanese consumers in the 1990s

1 Rich-ization

The watchword for the 1990s will be enrichment through self-realization after the cash-richness of consumption in the bubble years of the 1980s. Consumers will seek value for money.

2 Information-ization

There will be a growth in the complexity of information. With a personal computer for every office worker, networking – LAN, ISDN – will be the

---

[4] April 1993 forecast by Nikko Research Center (NRC).
[5] also by NRC

theme. The home and the individual will be automated, with the 'homification' of computer, word processor and facsimile.

3 International-ization

There will be further steps in globalization and internationalization, through imports, exports, two-way investment and movement of people, media, telephone and mail.

4 Age-ization

Longer life expectancy and lower birth rates will quicken demographic change. With fewer productive members of society to support the rapidly growing 'silver' segment, the social cost burdens of the over-60s will increase sharply. New employment patterns will retain 'silver' citizens in the labour force.

5 Female-ization

The pace of women becoming actively involved in society will increase. There will be new jobs and better conditions for women in work, who will want new and improved forms of leisure. A higher percentage of women will go to university, college and other forms of tertiary education. Women will continue to be the engine of faster growth in the practice of the polite arts, in community and leisure activities.

6 Leisure-ization

The spread of the five-day working week pattern will slowly lead to a fall in hours worked. Coupled with a reduction in the time given to housework, this trend will stimulate swift growth in the leisure market, from 68,124 billion yen in 1990 to a forecast 149,670 billion yen in the year 2000. There will be a growing variety of forms of leisure.

7 City-fication

Cities are expected to retain their appeal. Improvements in transportation facilities will increase the capital zone radius from 30–50 km to 70–100 km. Major conurbation lifestyles will be copied in regional towns and cities.

8 Single-ization

Women in work are expected to delay further the age at which they marry. Because of differences in life expectancy between male and female, more old people will live alone. Relocated male workers will continue to live alone.

9 Higher-ization of education

More students will proceed to graduate school, enter a second undergraduate university or study abroad, in order to create a 'super CV' to combat the fall in the value of the graduate. Demand for a full life in old age will stimulate the growth of knowledge-seeking leisure and lifelong learning facilities.

10 Service-ization

The service-ization of the Japanese economy will be a long-term trend. There will be an increasing variety of services targeted at the individual.

Geoffrey Bownas

10 DOING BUSINESS WITH THE JAPANESE
The etiquette of success

The Japanese can be found doing business anywhere in the world, while their business and management practices have become global phenomena that are emulated from Mexico to Manchuria. Japanese business may be the financing of a joint venture in Europe or car-parts manufacture in the Midlands of England, but their chosen forms of business management may be found anywhere that modern production methods are in use. From car manufacture to insurance, jewellery shops to home removals, they are part and parcel of business life and anyone looking for new opportunities must be ready to compete with them or meet their needs.

If the requirements of a Japanese firm or individual client seem unreasonable today, they will probably be the norm tomorrow, so fast have Japanese standards of quality, finish and service been adopted in manufacturing and other fields. Almost without exception, where Japanese manufacturing interests have set up factories in Europe or the United States, they have pushed local competitors and suppliers to new levels of achievement, compelling them to demand more of themselves, to the ultimate benefit of both and of the consumer.

The principal requirements for success in doing business with the Japanese are in reality no different from those needed to do business with anyone else: good preparation, hard work, attention to detail and determination. But there is one additional requirement – patience.

The first-time visitor
For all but the least well-off, it is advisable to choose a hotel with a high reputation and status because your Japanese contacts may well base some initial judgements of you and your company on your choice of hotel. The leading hotels in Tokyo and Osaka, such as the Imperial and Okura in Tokyo and the Royal in Osaka, also have excellent business centres. Appearances and presentation may not be everything, but they are very important for potential Japanese partners when they are judging whether you are a man or woman with whom they can do business. It is also important to have somewhere pleasant and tasteful where they can be entertained. Often, for the first-time visitor, it is better to do the entertaining on the 'home ground' of an international hotel rather than venturing out to restaurants of un-

known quality and cost, unless the host company or individual has a particular one in mind.

Also important is the timing of your visit. Make sure that it does not coincide with national holidays (see Appendix 1) or the 29 April to 5 May 'Golden Week', and be sure to have your appointments set up well in advance. Key executives in Japan have the busiest schedules imaginable with all the in-company meetings and conferences they must attend. A firm will also need time to prepare for your visit. It may seem an inordinately long time, but it could be vital in allowing you to get the most out of your meetings. Remember, they may have to consult with each other and reach an agreement beforehand that you know nothing about. On the other hand, it can seem that, once your visit has started, they are very flexible in their scheduling. If so, that may not necessarily be the result of instant changes, but rather of well-laid contingency plans. But do not count on being able to make appointments at short notice after your arrival.

When setting up any meeting it is important to check whether or not an interpreter will be required. Often, a firm which is already interested or involved in international business will have a staff member who can act as interpreter. But, if not, it is essential to have an interpreter who comes recommended by your embassy or a professional body. When discussing preparations over the telephone, make your English clear and speak at a speed that, while not insulting the person on the other end of the line, will permit easy understanding. A foreign language spoken over the telephone, without the aid of visual reinforcement, can lead to misunderstanding. Indeed, most Japanese not like to do business that way with someone whom they do not know very well, and, face-to-face contact is much preferred. The object, very often, is first to build a relationship of trust, with the business following on at a later date. Friendship, trust and long association are often the motivations behind long-term Japanese business arrangements, which could probably be conducted with more immediate financial return by other means. But, doing business with friends is generally considered the best way.

Wherever there are opportunities to use local Japanese agents or contacts to arrange itineraries they should be taken up. Although the European Community representative offices, chambers of commerce and commercial sections of embassies are usually only too willing to give advice, they may not be in a position to give such detailed assistance. A good starting point for any trip would be the Japan External Trade Organization (JETRO), the Exports to Japan Unit of the Department of Trade and Industry, or the Japan Chamber of Commerce and Industry, all of whom have offices in London and other European capitals (see Appendix 3 for addresses).

Welcome to Japan

The greeting on meeting someone for the first time is '*Hajimemashite*'. This is usually followed by '*Dozo yoroshiku*', literally 'a request to be treated with consideration'. A modest attempt to use the Japanese language will go down well at your first meeting with any new potential business partners.

But before your first contact there are a number of key points to remember. Appearance to the Japanese is very important. Men should dress smartly but not flashily, with neatly trimmed hair and clean shoes. Women executives should be modestly dressed without too much make-up or perfume, and should not wear high heels that make them tower over their hosts. For their part, the subtle inspection of such points will confirm that, if you have paid attention to such detail, then you will probably make the sort of partner they can do business with.

Bring with you lots of pamphlets and detailed information about your company, preferably in Japanese. Failing that, at least have summaries of the material in the vernacular. The Japanese read English much better than they speak it, so English information is acceptable, but the extra cachet of some text in Japanese will undoubtedly go down well. But if you do decide to have Japanese material prepared, arrange to have it done by a consultancy well in advance of your departure. That way, there will be plenty of time for a proof stage to eliminate errors. Error-free translation is one argument for having the material produced in Japan, after your arrival, but there may not be time and it will cost much more. Visual aids such as videos or slides are always acceptable but make sure beforehand that your hosts have the right equipment to show them.

Crucially important is that you go to that first meeting fully prepared, with as much knowledge about your new partners as possible and with sufficient knowledge of your own company to be able to answer any questions. You may be asked detailed questions about your company's products, its finances, the workforce or the company's affiliations and competitors. Be ready to provide accurate information on production capacity and delivery dates and never promise anything unless you are certain that you can honour that promise. Trustworthiness and reliability are the two cornerstones of business in Japan; other shortcomings may be forgiven but not these two. But however well you prepare for your meeting, it is likely that your Japanese hosts will have prepared even better.

To create the right atmosphere from the start, make sure that you arrive on time for the appointment and have enough business cards to hand out to everyone of significance that you meet. Business cards, or *meishi*, are of a standard size, usually 90 mm × 55 mm, and include on one side, in English, the company logo, with the person's name and title displayed in larger type, and on the other side the same information in Japanese. Qualifications and other detail are sometimes also included on the English side. Nowadays some Japanese use more elaborate business cards that include a colour photograph of themselves, but for the present, foreign business people should stay with the more conventional style.

To avoid arriving late, check out what route to take in advance, unless a car is being sent to pick you up. As you will probably be using the underground railway, it will not be difficult to work out your itinerary (see page 156). All the major stations are marked with English language signs and routes are colour-coded. Using the subway is certainly quicker than taking a taxi and risking getting stuck in a traffic jam. The Japanese have worked hard to find their way in the world without the benefit of a universal language, so they are unlikely to be impressed by unpunctuality caused by linguistic ignorance or bad planning.

Officially, the appointment will probably be with someone of equivalent rank, but it is unlikely that he will be alone. Representatives from other departments concerned may attend, so the visitor might like to be accompanied for moral support. The visitor will be greeted by his or her contact in the company and then introduced to the staff by their family name in order of seniority, each name being suffixed with the honorific '-san'. First names are not used and it is not advisable to start using your own and request that others do so; this smacks of a false camaraderie which is inappropriate. You may be greeted by an extended hand which you should shake without too much pressure while slightly bowing from the waist. Some Japanese content themselves with just a bow from the waist, in which case do the same. Immediately afterwards proffer your business card with the English side away from you so that it can be read straight away by your hosts. You will receive a card in return which you should hold with both hands, studying it with obvious interest, as a mark of respect, to fix that person's name and rank in your mind. Lay the cards in front of you in the order in which the people are seated so that you can easily keep track of who is who.

Whenever possible, have your business cards printed before you leave on your trip. If, for some reason, this has not been done you can order them at short notice through the hotel, but that is a special service which will be reflected in the price you are charged. At the first meeting, it is likely that tea will be served and the discussion may be so oblique as to appear to have nothing to do with the matter at hand. Sports, food and your impressions of Japan may be covered at some length and often with quite lengthy silences. The golden rule 'never fill a silence' applies. At best, you may say something inappropriate or silly, at worst you may make an unnecessary concession. Japanese men are expected to be the strong, silent type and there is suspicion of anyone who is too loquacious. It implies a lack of seriousness or too much of an effort to impress. To conform to the convention that the British and Japanese have similar qualities of reserve is much better. The intention on the part of the Japanese, in any event, is to begin to get to know their putative partners before the real stuff of the relationship begins.

All this is likely to be rather formal, but if you are invited to accompany your hosts for an evening meal and some drinking, accept the offer with alacrity, for nowhere else is there a better chance to get to know the Japanese in a more relaxed, frank atmosphere. Here more than anywhere else, with the possible exception of the golf course, will it be possible to found a relationship that will last. Britons in the Far East have something of a reputation for not being able to let their hair down, in short, for being a bit stuffy. But do not try to compensate by telling jokes: they may not sound funny to the Japanese. If their sense of humour seems a bit juvenile or singing karaoke has you dying with embarrassment, just go with the flow and your efforts are likely to be rewarded. One of the most successful British stockbrokers in Tokyo made his name not through his ability to make deals but because he could wow a night-time audience of tipsy Japanese punters with his karaoke singing.

Spotting the signals

Do not expect that all your questions will be answered by the time you are boarding your plane for home. Japanese firms are notorious for taking a long time to make up their minds, particularly where foreigners are concerned. This is because the whole of top management, and probably also those managers much lower down the corporate tree, have to approve any deal. Probably, even before your first visit, the process of *nemawashi* will have taken place – the word literally means 'binding the roots'. This is a general consultation within the company from which a consensus emerges – the decision to invite the foreign firm for exploratory talks. It has to be agreed by all sections of the company, a process that may take weeks or even months, involving numerous consultations and much horse-trading between various individuals and departments. Once agreed, the decision must be confirmed by the circulation of a *ringi* document containing the final version of the agreement, for everyone of managerial rank to sign. It is sent out by the department that initiated the proposal and will eventually return there. Then, and only then, does the new project, joint venture or sales relationship really begin. To the outsider, things apparently move at a snail's pace with nothing concrete taking place for months, but then things can suddenly develop with surprising speed. This highlights a major difference between Japanese and Western companies: the Japanese will never move till everyone is behind a given decision, whereas the Western company may move quickly at first, making all sorts of promises which it later finds cannot be honoured, because too few of the people concerned have been canvassed on its feasibility.

There is thus no reason to worry if the Japanese take some time to respond to proposals. But it is important to realize that if they do not want to pursue the matter, they will probably not respond with a straight 'no'. Signs of a lack of real interest will become apparent in meetings. They include flagging questions and short, cryptic answers where once they were full and enthusiastic. They will search for any possible way of dressing up the bad news so as to let potential partners down gradually. Spotting the disguised 'no' at an early stage is, therefore, an important time-saver. Any talk of 'difficulties' is a bad sign since the use of the word *muzukashi* – normally translated as 'difficult' – really means 'not possible, don't press me on it'.

Unless there is an urgent need to launch your new project, because of swift changes in technology or competitors about to take quick advantage, you may have to wait a considerable time before you receive a definitive answer to your proposals. If they entail a major commitment on the Japanese side it could all take several years. However, there is no reason why you should not keep in touch by letter or fax in the meantime, nor does it rule out subsequent visits, which are essential once the relationship is established.

After hours

In some respects, perhaps more important than what happens in the boardroom is the after-hours entertainment. Most business lunches are normally brief, with little alcohol consumed. The real 'getting to know you' entertainment takes place in the evening. It will most likely begin at a small bar close to the office or your hotel, then move to a restaurant for dinner and finally end up in a hostess bar, where the drinks on offer will be beer (*biru*), sake (*o sake*) and whisky and water (*mizuwari*).

For the first-timer it is probably better to allow your host to order dinner for you. It is in keeping with the occasion and you can be sure that no Japanese host will embarrass you with a dish you cannot handle, provided that you have signalled any special need before accepting the invitation. Skill with chopsticks is a bonus if you have already mastered them, but there is no harm in being seen to give it a try, even if knife and fork have been set out, provided that your antics do not intrude into the conversation or hinder the progress of the meal unduly. As in so many things Japanese, smoothness and calm, at least on the surface, are considered essential.

During the meal, many older Japanese still conform to the custom that you eat first and talk afterwards, so you may find everyone taking their food in silence. There is no need to feel compelled to break the silence. Younger people do not follow this rather old convention and are quite happy to chat away. It is polite to taste the food first before adding any seasoning. To splash on soya sauce before trying it implies that the chef has got it wrong. Equally, it is not polite to add soya sauce to rice in the belief that it will give it some 'taste'. Rice has a subtle taste all of its own which may not be easily detected by the western palate, but it is none the less there. Desserts are not often taken by Japanese men; some think it unmanly to like sweet things, which are conceived of as being a feminine preserve. But that is no reason for you, as the guest, not to have one if you wish. The dessert, which generally includes a wide variety of fruits in season, is followed by green tea or often coffee as an alternative.

Provided that it is not getting too late for the last train home to the distant suburbs, everyone will probably adjourn to a hostess bar for a final drinking session. Even if you have paid for the dinner, it is better to allow the Japanese to look after this part of the evening for several reasons. Usually you will be taken to one of the bars which make their living from business entertainment and charge astronomical prices. It is also likely to be one of the regular haunts of your Japanese companions, who might be given some consideration for that reason. They will probably have their own bottles of whisky behind the bar and will be well known to the *mama-san*, a lady of a certain age who runs the establishment, often on behalf of a patron, and keeps the hostesses in order. They are there to flatter the men by giggling at their jokes, listening to their problems and stoically putting up with the most appalling behaviour till all hours of the morning. Usually their command of English is limited to a few phrases, so this is not the time for philosophical discussion. But there is a lot of fun to be had in trying to make yourself understood, not least because everyone has had a few drinks. For that reason, nothing of great import is decided at a gathering such as this. Indeed, much of what was said may be hard to remember the following morning.

Home invitations

Even for foreigners who have been residents for some time in Japan, home invitations are rare. This is not because the Japanese are inhospitable, they are. But they remain painfully aware that their homes are tiny by the standards of other countries and that any visitors may feel cramped and uncomfortable. If you are invited, it is all the more important, therefore, to show that you appreciate this honour and ensure that you bring the obligatory gift for the lady of the house. Japanese homes are, in any event, an object lesson in neatness and the use of space; living room space usually doubles as sleeping space in all but the larger urban dwellings. On arrival, you must remove your shoes and don the slippers that you will be given. You will then be seated cross-legged round a low table, with other members of the family, and offered the first of seemingly endless rounds of Japanese tea and satsumas or tangerines. The conversation may be awkward at first, in that it is still a novelty for many Japanese to have foreigners in their home, but this is more because of shyness than anything else.

The seasons of giving

The Japanese are so generous with gifts as to make most other nations appear tight-fisted. It is not all altruism, as a major component of their social behaviour is the giving and receiving of favours. Equally, the exchange of gifts is important for foreigners seeking to build business relationships. Although they are excused the highly ritualized and strict reciprocity of Japanese gift-giving, it is appropriate to mark the successful conclusion of a visit with the exchange of presents. If you are the first to receive one, it will probably be handed over after hours and should not be opened in the presence of others unless you are requested to do so.

When making your trip to Japan it is vital to bring in a supply of high-quality products from your country to give away as presents. If you choose whisky, ensure that it is a top-quality brand – Japanese know and appreciate their whisky. This should be handed over as soon as possible. Thereafter, make presents of your stock of brand-name Western goods – which will no doubt be available in Japan but at much inflated prices – but have them exquisitely wrapped. To the Japanese, the presentation and value of the gift is an indication of the recipient's standing in the eyes of the giver.

The commitment

Assuming that the first visit has gone well, there should be time to consider what sort of commitment you and your company are going to make to the Japanese market. Traditionally, with a few honourable exceptions, British firms decide that it is not worth the effort of a long-term engagement in a far-off market, when there are quick profits to be made in Europe.

There are numerous cases that prove that this is not so, provided that the long-term commitment is there. The classic, oft-quoted example is that of BMW, which set about the Japanese market in determined style with its own marketing and other organizations. So successful has it been, that today the BMW 3 Series is nicknamed the 'Roppongi Corolla', because it is as common a sight in Tokyo's fashionable Roppongi district, a haunt of the young and well-to-do, as the Toyota Corolla is in the rest of the world.

Recently, the British have been making the running, selling to the young and affluent Japanese marrieds and singles who have channelled more of their earnings into leisure spending as the prospect of owning their own homes has receded. Architects, furriers, car designers have all made inroads, but even in selling CDs and structural steel – which, on the face of it seems like coals-to-Newcastle – British firms have recently made spectacular breakthroughs. The American giant EMI is selling CDs as fast as it can import them. Even more striking is the success of Virgin Megastores, which has a joint venture with Marui, the department store chain for the Tokyo area. Virgin looked for a Japanese partner for some time after its success in introducing an airline service on the Tokyo route. Nothing quite gelled for two or three years until the 50:50 deal with Marui was struck. Each side has put in 50 million yen, a relatively modest amount by the standards of Japanese business, and the rest of the money has been put up by local banks. After only three years in business, there are eight Megastores and five smaller ones in the Tokyo area, including the main store in Shinjuku, Tokyo, one in Yokohama and one in Kyoto. There are plans for a further 15 stores over the next five years, including one in Osaka where so far no suitable site has been found.

Michael Inman, who runs the Virgin operation in Japan, says he has found his Japanese contacts open to new ideas, and the market wide open to his products, 50 per cent of which are imported. 'There are very few restrictions, no duties, no copyright problems; we can do anything we want,' said Mr Inman. Virgin goes for the slightly older market, of the 20–35 age group, which is rather more affluent than the student-age customers catered for by Tower Records, its American counterpart in the market. On a turnover of 80 billion yen a year, Virgin's sales in the initial stages were increasing annually at 15 per cent. The returns on sales of domestic records are not quite as exciting because there is still a fixed-price system in Japan. Rapid expansion, with the opening of seven new stores in the year to June 1993, ate into Virgin profits at a time of relatively soft demand in a slow economy. However, the bursting of Japan's 'bubble economy' has meant that rents at a share of turnover are easing from 13–15 per cent to 8–10 per cent while other changes on properties, such as demands for key money and guarantee money, are now less common.

A straight export deal that impressed Nippon Steel, Japan's leading steel-producer, has led to a joint venture with the British supplier Watson Steel Ltd of Bolton, Lancashire. Joe Lock, the managing director, describes his firm as both manufacturer and erector of steel products – in this case the enormously complex steel skeleton for the new Kansai International Airport on an artificial island set in 21 m of water in Osaka Bay. Although the company came with an impressive list of successes including work on Charles de Gaulle Airport outside Paris, and the Sellafield nuclear reprocessing plant, the Japanese were doubtful of the company's ability to perform to the required standards within the time allowed. The Lancashire company's cost advantages over its competitors certainly played a role in securing the contract, but central was the skilful use of computer-aided design which made this complex structure readily understandable to the men on the shop floor who were erecting it. 'That was very attractive to the Japanese,' said Mr Lock. When the £13 million project was completed on time and on budget, the managing director of Nippon Steel flew to Britain, in May 1993, to present the company with a commemorative plaque paying tribute to Watson Steel's achievement and looking forward to the two firms bidding for work on the Hong Kong airport.

Another Japan success story is Oxford Instruments, which has had a presence in the market for almost 25 years but only quite recently set up its own sales organization in Japan. The firm owes its success to long-term commitment and the unspoken pledge that there is no such thing as a finite warranty. Having installed, say, £100 million worth of instrumentation, the company will deal with any problems that may arise at any time free of change. Any foreign company establishing a sales office for its products, says Peter Williams, the chairman and chief executive of Oxford Instruments, must ensure that its activities cover the whole gamut, from distribution to service and after-sales support.

With Britain's reputation for quality products recovering rapidly from a period of decidedly mixed reviews, British firms can now make excellent profits by exploiting niches in the market, whether through straight exporting franchising or a joint venture. Given the size and sophistication of the market, there are good export opportunities that can be ascertained through some fairly straighforward market research. Preliminary inquiries can be made through a number of bodies that are now dedicating significant resources to improving Japan's trade balance through building up imports.

They include MITI (the Ministry of International Trade and Industry) and JETRO (the Japan External Trade Organization). *Sogo shosha*, the big trading houses, such as Mitsubishi and Mitsui who pioneered Japan's foreign trade, may well be willing to help out with consultancy, particularly those firms with a history of handling British products such as Itochu. *Senmon shosha*, or specialized trading firms, deal with particular product lines. All will be willing to help if they see a possibility of doing business. But equally, once an approach is made to an agent, it is they rather than you who will be making the running. With their superior knowledge of the market and language, they will take over all the key decisions regarding dealers, distributors, advertising, pricing, positioning and all the other details that go into the successful placing of a new product. Once in charge, an agent is not likely to listen to much advice from people thousands of miles away.

There are nine huge *sogo shosha* but some 8,000 of the smaller *senmon shosha*. The former concerns tend to deal in large volume and large turnover and may not be interested unless a sizeable potential market can be identified. The latter are prepared to deal in smaller volumes but, of necessity, do not have the reach of their larger brethren. Among them are a number of foreign firms, such as Jardine and Dodwell, who have long experience of successfully placing foreign products in the Japanese market.

It cannot be stressed enough how important it is to choose the right agent or trading company the first time, however long it may take. A wrong decision at the beginning can doom the whole project, so do not rush into it. There is usually no second chance, since switching from one trading company to another would not give you a good name in the market. Usually, the only reason for moving away from your chosen trading firm would be to set up your own dealership network – a very expensive, time-consuming and long-term process that is undertaken only by the biggest foreign players. But if you choose one of these two types of trading comapany, make sure beforehand that you examine its list of product lines, which may be in conflict with your own. It is not unknown for a trader to accept responsibility for handling a competing line just so as to ensure, by taking a passive approach to promotion and sales, that it does not compete with products he is already marketing. The managing director of one trading company handling a range of prestige British cars, for example, refused to be seen driving around in any of them – something that would never have been refused a Japanese manufacturer.

Licensed manufacture or franchising of your product are two alternative approaches which have worked extremely well for some British and American firms, notably Kentucky Fried Chicken and McDonald's hamburgers. Indeed, so successful have McDonald's been, that a young Japanese boy about to visit the United States is supposed to have asked his father, 'Will we be able to get hamburgers there, too?'

This method appears to work well for products that have a particular foreign national flavour about them and have a highly visible image. Therefore, there should be a franchisee who can reproduce precisely the ambience of the product in its home market. The success of this approach can be seen in the marketing of Wedgwood in Japan, which manages to convey just the right touch of cosy English quality in its prestige department store displays. The sort of tightly controlled management of its outlets practised by McDonald's lends itself to this form and is well understood by Japanese managers. Outlets through department stores can be a successful medium, but it is important that clothing and other fashion-sensitive products for sale should be the very latest lines. At least one British venture has failed because it was assumed that Tokyo would be slightly behind London in the adoption of new fashions, a highly dubious and – in that case – commercially fatal decision. For food lines, a food processing firm would make an obvious partner. But if franchised outlets for the sale of fast food are being sought, then perhaps it would be better to approach a firm with ready access to land for sites.

The most serious of commitments to the Japanese market is through a joint venture. This takes a higher level of involvement, which has been likened to marriage. The rough times will have to be weathered but the long-term benefits can very considerable, given the right product and the right partner. Having sold cars into Japan for years without ever achieving its full potential, Jaguar Cars established Jaguar Japan Ltd in 1986 as a joint venture between Jaguar and Seibu, the largest department store in Japan, which already had considerable experience of importing European cars. Jaguar Japan has since built up a distribution and sales-service network tailored to the Japanese market. In 1991 a pre-delivery and inspection centre was added to ensure that imported cars met the high expectations of Japanese buyers. Seibu holds 60 per cent of shares and the top three executives are all Japanese. The firm has been successful in attracting senior mangement from Seibu and the Daiichi–Kangyo Bank, Seibu's main bank.

Now that 100 per cent foreign ownership of Japanese ventures is permitted, it is possible to go it alone. However, given the special nature of the market environment, many feel that the joint venture is the best way forward because it relieves the foreign company of some of the more intractable problems of the market, such as staff recruitment, getting the right premises and managing in a style to which Japanese employees have become accustomed – not to mention finding a productive route through a distribution system that has little to do with logic.

One of the principal problems for foreign firms is getting the right calibre of personnel. Too often, foreign managers have to put up with second-rate staff because many Japanese still believe that it is not socially acceptable to work for a foreign company; or they fear that they will not find the same commitment to their future from foreign companies as they can get from Japanese firms. This has been changing, especially since Japanese firms themselves began to make staff redundant in times of difficulty, but the concern nonetheless remains. A joint venture gets over some of these problems by making them the responsibility of the Japanese partner. But then the need arises for close monitoring of the venture by the foreign partner to ensure that all commitments are being honoured. For their part, the foreign participants in the joint venture must be aware of the long-term view taken by the Japanese and the need to plan their finances accordingly. Most Japanese firms go into new fields not expecting to see any return for five or even 10 years, so there is little point in entering on a joint venture unless you see things the same way.

On not being Japanese

Although it is essential broadly to follow Japanese practices when moving into that market, you should not necessarily abandon all your domestic ways of working. Shelving every facet of your home operations in the hope that you will thereby qualify as a 'Japanese' company is an illusion. Even the longest-resident foreign companies do not come into that category, so it is much better to try to make positive use of the differing approaches that you may have. After all, the Japanese are nothing if not flexible when it comes to business and business opportunities.

11 FOREIGN AFFAIRS
Japan and the wider world

The late Willie Brandt, former Chancellor of West Germany, once said that Japan was a nation without friends. It was a truism of which the country was only too well aware. But since the mid-1970s the Japanese government and corporations have been actively trying to build diplomatic, commercial and cultural bridges to the rest of the world. Many millions of dollars have gone into explaining Japan to the outside world and into government campaigns to make the country seem less threatening to its neighbours and industrial competitors.

Japan's centuries of isolation under military rulers left it more cut off from the rest of the world than the lack of technological and diplomatic connections could possibly suggest. It left the nation with a feeling of 'otherness' that even in the 1990s has not been overcome despite increasing dealings with foreign countries and much greater awareness abroad of the country's products and popular culture. The nation remains torn between the feeling that it is unwanted and ultimately alone in the world – the insecurity of isolation – and the desire to retain its character untainted by foreign influences. This tendency to schizophrenia leaves Japan a prisoner of its history despite the best efforts of its friends in helping it to escape.

Japan's invasion and brutal occupation of countries on the Asian mainland and in South-East Asia during World War II alienated its near neighbours. The effect might have been significantly mitigated had the government and people of Japan sought to apologize wholeheartedly. But as history has unfolded since the war, Japan has not yet fully regained the confidence or trust of its neighbours. Imperial apologies, hampered by the constraints of non-interference in politics, may seem adequate at home but are not always deemed sufficient abroad. So, as has been said before, the country remains in Asia but not of it; when Japanese refer to Asia they refer to a concept and a geographical location that do not necessarily include themselves.

Whereas much of Asia nevertheless looks east to Japan for an economical and social role model, Japan has looked west to the United States and the industrial countries and, until quite recently, sought to emulate them. But these countries are so distant and their cultures are so different from Japan's that it has been difficult to develop close relations, especially as there has been such competition in industry and commerce. The war, however, did produce the 'elder brother' relationship with the United States, whereby a nation much younger in history and culture assumed the role of

Japan's mentor and protector after it had defeated the military government.

With the defeat, the Japanese people took to their occupiers with great enthusiasm, adopting their novel democratic ways with alacrity. The occupation transformed the defeated nation from an aggressor into a peace-loving state. Even though today Japan has the world's third-largest defence budget, the social status of the armed forces has been dramatically downgraded by the events of the war. Japan's first peacekeeping force, which was dispatched to Cambodia under the auspices of the United Nations in 1992, is heavily circumscribed by conditions that preclude it from assuming an aggressive, peace-enforcing role.

The US occupation was intended to shape Japan in the likeness of its mentor: a democracy of unrestrained political activity for all comers matched with a free press and a liberal education system. However, the victory of communism in China and the Korean War worried the Americans that Japan might go the same way. Freedoms began to be circumscribed in order to contain growing communist influence in the trades unions and among the intellectuals. Industry started to benefit from large sums of money spent on the repair and maintenance of the US war machine fighting in Korea. Japan's industrial renaissance was under way, but the country was denied the full-blown benefits of the occupation's idealists while some of its warmongers were rehabilitated in the service of the fight against international communism.

The US–Japanese relationship is considered by the two parties to be the most important bilateral relationship in the world. But economic competition between them has grown to such an extent that the two countries can be likened to two tectonic plates, constantly pressuring each other and occasionally erupting with volcanic force when the tensions become too great. While publicly being content to be number two in this partnership, Japan shows every sign of wanting to become the world's number-one economic power. Can commensurate political power be far behind? Ever since the end of the occupation, Japan has been happy to follow the US political lead, benefiting from the protection of locally based US forces and the US nuclear umbrella. But Americans are uncomfortable with the thought that their erstwhile student may surpass the US economy by the year 2000, while the Japanese are equally uncertain about what life will be like without Uncle Sam's guidance.

The economic equation

Starting with conflict over Japanese exports of textiles to the United States, the recent period has been one of almost ceaseless tension between the two countries over economic questions, which has overshadowed the importance of their security arrangements. Manipulation of the yen–dollar exchange rate from time to time, and negotiations on access for US exports, may have temporarily relieved the pressure but the underlying tension remains. For years, Japan traded with a yen vastly undervalued at 360 to the US dollar, an exchange rate fixed in the early postwar period to define an economic relationship that assumed continued US superiority. Trading under this umbrella, often at much more realistic rates of exchange, Japanese firms, beginning with the electronics sector, built up a strong presence in the US market. First they targeted the market for television sets in the mid-1960s, vigorously undercutting the prices of their American competitors by a sophisticated system of recompensing their dealers for their losses through third-country bank accounts. There followed successful penetration of the computer, photocopier and car industries – Japan became the world's leading car maker in 1981. These successes have given rise to steadily escalating trade imbalances with the United States, which resulted in a Japanese trade surplus of $49 billion in 1992, more than half the global US deficit.

Different US administrations have taken different tacks with Tokyo over what the Americans believe is a disruptive imbalance that ultimately can only lead to a catastrophic breakdown in world trade. As far back as the Nixon administration of 1968–74, the United States sought and obtained assurances that Japan would 'open its markets' to American manufactures, and each time, US officials would be satisfied until the next set of annual trade figures showed that there had been no fundamental change. Successive US governments have failed to formulate a policy towards Japan despite the evidence that, sector by sector, its industries were intent on adversarial trade and world domination. Moreover, no institutional memory has been established that would permit continuity and consistency of policy. Rather, Japanese lobbyists have succeeded in luring successive US trade negotiators into jobs lobbying for Japanese interests.

Trade with Japan has nevertheless been of great benefit to the United States as the high quality of Japanese goods has ensured that American manufacturers have had to follow suit to compete. In the case of the motor industry, however, there is still doubt that the American industry will learn the requisite lessons. Thirty per cent of car sales already go to Japanese firms, and the giant General Motors has been reduced to a market share of 35 per cent and is saddled with multibillion dollar losses. Elsewhere, rapid innovation in Japanese electronics has helped upgrade the quality and accuracy of American weaponry. Indeed, without advanced Japanese microchips many sophisticated US weapons would not be able to function. But it is the lack of two-way trade that has created in the United States an increasingly distrustful attitude towards Japan, which is mirrored by declining respect for all things American on the other side of the Pacific. The seeming impossibility of making any headway with Japan frustrates Americans. The United States runs trade deficits with other nations, but American business is able to sell successfully into those markets and feels it has a fair chance to recoup the balance. With Japan those parameters do not seem to apply.

Until recently, even trade frictions seemed unable to dent the fundamentally sound relationship between the two countries. But the end of the Cold War has helped change all that, and the joke 'The Cold War is over and Japan won' has come to have more than a ring of truth about it. The fact is that, for many Americans, Japan is replacing the former Soviet Union as 'the enemy'. With the threat of nuclear war a thing of the past, the greatest fear for many Americans is the loss of their job to a Japanese competitor after a decade when the American public has watched as prestige buildings and businesses have been taken over by Japanese interests. The British and Dutch, in fact, may own more and invest more in the United States but it is the Japanese acquisitions that make the headlines and cause resentment.

Occasional outbursts of anti-Japanese feeling, such as the public smashing of Japanese stereos or the banning of Japanese cars in company parking lots, are as a crude as they misdirected. With Japan holding some $180 billion of the United States' paper debt by 1992, and the made-in-America Honda among the best-selling cars, the two economies are clearly intertwined. Where there is increasing divergence is on the question of Japan's shouldering of more of the international burdens that fall on nations with such wealth and potential influence. Although Japanese governments have occasionally grown frustrated with playing second political fiddle to the United States, it has, for the most part, suited them to do so. Ever since World War II Japan has escaped paying the real cost of national defence and, until the Gulf War, was able to stand aloof from major international conflicts. Tokyo has gradually assumed much of the cost of the stationing of US forces on its soil, but its initial reluctance to do anything to help keep open the Gulf oil supply routes, which are essential to its own industry, earned widespread criticism. By the time Japan made a sizeable contribution, it was too late to attract much public interest.

The issue of aid to the former Soviet Union has also brought tension between what the rest of the world perceives as Japan's international responsibilities, and its own domestic policy considerations. The bad relations between Japan and the Soviet Union over Moscow's continued refusal to part with the occupied northern islands captured by the Soviet military at the end of the World War II made it politically difficult to grant economic assistance to Moscow. Yet the United States, in particular, believed this an important responsibility of Japan's and it was only Washington's arm-twisting that persuaded the Japanese government to agree with Western plans for assistance to Russia after the breakdown of the Soviet Union. This issue goes to the heart of the US political relationship with Japan. Japanese often feel that, under the old Boston Tea Party rule of thumb 'no taxation without representation', Tokyo is too often pressured by Washington into making commitments it does not agree with. The Allied agreement to take military action against Iraq was a case in point. It is for this reason, if no other, that Japan will increasingly seek to be treated as an equal partner with the United States rather than a mere purveyor of international cheque book diplomacy.

The failure of President Bush, on his visit to Japan in January 1992, to treat his opposite number, Kiichi Miyazawa, as an equal upset his hosts. To make matter worse, the president was accompanied by the leaders of the US motor industry who demanded that Japan buy more of their products even though these were not tailored for the Japanese market. Nevertheless, the Japanese government committed the country's top 23 manufacturing firms to increasing their imports of finished manufactures by $10 billion. None of this was apparent in the Tokyo Declaration that the two leaders endorsed at the end of their meeting. Its main themes were that the two countries had a 'special responsibility' to shape a new era and that the two should build a 'global partnership' for a 'just, peaceful and prosperous world' while strengthening and reinvigorating the GATT (General Agreement on Tariff and Trade) multilateral trading system and the United Nations. The two countries, it said, should open their commercial, financial and investment markets, oppose protectionism and reduce structural impediments to trade while developing new areas of cooperation 'in a manner that provides for an equitable sharing of responsibilities and benefits'. President Bush's being taken ill at a state banquet set the seal on a visit from which neither side could take much comfort. However, Japanese officials knew that, under Republican administrations, the two countries' mutual security policies would always take precedence over trade: when the United States' ultimate interests were at stake, Japan's role as an anti-communist bulwark and crutch for American budget deficits took precedence over pursuing the trade issue to its conclusion. With the advent of the Clinton Democrat administration, that may no longer be so.

The initial meeting between President Clinton and Mr Miyazawa in early 1993 confirmed the new tone when it became clear that the new American leader was going to put trade at the top of his agenda with Japan, with specific proposals about managed trade. The Japanese media saw the tough talking on both sides as evidence that a new, more equal, partnership was now in prospect. 'We've entered an era of fighting with real swords,' said the newspaper *Asahi Shimbun*, alluding to the samurai of old who discarded their wooden swords when martial arts practice became real combat. 'America and Japan', it went on, 'have entered a new relationship with no sugar coating, equal to equal and adult to adult.'

President Clinton's advisers, who are strong in their expertise on China rather than Japan, mapped out a confrontational strategy that would oblige Japan to cut its worldwide trade surplus by 50 per cent over three years. Basing its findings on the fiscal year ended 31 March 1993, it said that Japan had run up a trade surplus with the rest of the world equivalent to more than 3 per cent of its gross national product, or US $126 billion. Washington wants that surplus cut to between 1 and 2 per cent of GNP over three years. The plan calls for the leaders of the two countries to meet twice a year, not only to review progress on the overall surplus but also to examine measurable progress in improving American companies' access to several sectors of the Japanese market. These include computers and supercomputers, purchasing by Japanese government agencies, and cars and car parts. The plan also calls for improved business opportunities for banks, insurance companies and other service industries.

Managed trade is something that Japanese government and industry have dreaded for years, and the Ministry of International Trade and Industry (MITI) was quick to signal that the Clinton plan would be robustly opposed. A Ministry report claimed: 'This report is defending not only Japan. It is to protect the world. We have to say "no" to managed trade.' In view of MITI's having carefully managed Japan's trade for three decades until the 1980s, the report raised eyebrows in many quarters, but Japan's new stance does find favour in other parts of East and South-East Asia and Australia.

The report drew attention to the decline in Japan's global trading surplus in 1990 to US $64 billion and said that the upsurge in the succeeding years was due to temporary factors such as the recession, which depressed imports. But, it went on, no matter how the trade surplus is calculated, in future it will decline for a number of reasons. These include the aging of the Japanese population, on the theory that retired people consume more than they produce and that this will necessarily lead to an increase in imports. It also said that in the years ahead, imports will grow more rapidly than the economy. Whereas in 1985 each increase of 1 per cent in Japan's gross national product produced an increase of 0.5 per cent in imports, now, it said, that figure was rising to about 1.3 per cent. Moreover, the report claimed, Japanese industry was not the formidable power it had once been, and the bursting of the 'bubble economy' was causing many Japanese companies to behave more like their British and American rivals.

At the grass-roots level, given that in the future more and more Westerners are likely to be working for Japanese employers, one way to greater acceptance is to promote more local nationals to senior positions. This is already happening in some companies, but in others local employees feel that they have no real participatory role in the running of the company, with the real decisions being made at the head office back in Japan. Moreover, there is often a wide gap in salary between those sent from Japan and locally-hired employees and no real understanding of the strength of American feeling on such issues as equal-opportunity employment.

Japan and the new Europe

Britain and Japan enjoy a relationship that appears to be developing as a model for the rest of the European Community. One newspaper columnist has described Japan as Britain's 'perfect ally'. Other EC nations do not see it quite like that. Still, there is no mistaking the change of tone in the relationship, dating from the early 1990s, with both sides attempting to put behind them the endless trade disputes and adopt a more positive approach of seeking out the areas in which they can agree. The turning point came, perhaps, with the joint declaration on EC–Japan relations agreed at The Hague on 18 July 1991. This set out the basic values shared by both sides, a list of mutual objectives in the political and economic fields, and an institutional framework for consultation which includes annual meetings between the President of the Commission and the Japanese prime minister. Even the long-running dispute on the import of Japanese cars appears to have been defused by allowing 'transplants' – Japanese cars made in Britain and elsewhere – to be treated as EC products. Although some countries will retain their restrictions on direct Japanese imports, Japan will monitor its own exports to the Community through to the end of 1999.

Despite these agreements, in individual state-to-state relations there remain some tensions. Having enjoyed good relations through industrial and technical ties, and the common experience of defeat in World War II, Japan and Germany have recently entered a period of disagreement. The Germans complain that the Japanese are unwilling to contribute sufficient resources to the rehabilitation of the former Soviet Union, while Japan accuses Germany of failure to take tough enough action against right-wing nationalists and neo-Nazis. In France relations with Tokyo have certainly improved since the time when Edith Cresson was prime minister and made statements about what she saw as the predatory activities of Japanese companies. But that is not saying a great deal, and the French remain fiercely protective of any encroachment on their state car industry.

Britain has for a number of years taken the lion's share of Japanese investment in Europe, but while that stood at US $2.9 billion in 1992, some way down on the $6.8 billion invested in 1990, it is still 40 per cent of the total for the EC, which was $6.6 billion for 1992. But if the economic relationship is reaching a plateau of maturity, then the British government is working hard to thicken the relationship by sending ministers and junior ministers out to build contacts with their Japanese counterparts and get them used to 'thinking Japan'. The culmination of all these efforts will be Japan's establishment of a fund for the promotion of educational and other exchanges between Japan and Europe, much on the same lines as the Abe Fund which promotes closer relations with the United States. It is not likely to be as generously funded because the times and the relationships are different, but it is an indication of the move towards equivalence in the great trans-world triangle of power.

Until the mid-1980s Britain's attitude to Japan had been much like that of the rest of the community: fearful of the threat posed by Japanese management and technology and suspicious of Japan's motives. Both sides quickly recognized the mutual advantage that could be derived from cooperations. Japan could gain access to what increasingly seemed likely to be a fortress Europe, by investing in British-based plant and manufacturing facilities, while Britain would have access to the latest manufacturing management and techniques, permitting the revitalization of much of its industry. A flood of Japanese firms registered their European subsidiaries in London. The larger ones, such as the big trading companies, were already ahead of European thinking. They structured their trading arrangements along the same lines as those in the United States, treating Europe as already a federal reality, with branches in each principal European centre specializing in different elements of their business. The flagship Japanese firms in Britain, led by Nissan, with its Washington, County Durham car-manufacturing plant, have been championed by the British government in their efforts to sell their goods in the European market as British products. Despite the best efforts of the French to frustrate them, by the early 1990s they were well-established in the European market and on the way to making Britain a net exporter of motor vehicles. Sony's plants in Wales achieved the same in the electronics field, and by 1993 Britain was already a net-exporter of television sets. Since then, Japanese–British relations have levelled off, but not solely because the level of investment, at least for the present, appears to have passed its peak. Britain's obvious reluctance to become fully engaged at the centre of European policy-making also makes it less attractive as a partner for Japan.

But if local successes have pleased both the British and Japanese governments and ensured a solid basis for partnership in the future, Japanese attitudes towards the single market were not always so sanguine. With trade relations with the United States, its best market, oscillating between acceptable and bad, Japan has always been aware that the European market was there as a fall-back position. However, at first, the prospect of a full-blown single market showing every sign of being anti-Japanese caused understandable fears in Tokyo. With a 1990 Gross Domestic Product of US $6,000 billion, and the possibility of another $853 billion from 1995 if the countries of the European Free Trade Area join the EC, Europe offers far and away the biggest single market in the world. To have had even limited access to that market might have been difficult for Japanese firms, but in reality none of those fears has been realized because of the widespread prevarication over ratifying the Maastricht treaty. On the other hand, the Japanese government has always backed the notion of closer European cooperation as a means of strengthening the European side of the Japan–EC–US triangle to counterbalance the power of the United States.

The Chinese puzzle

If Japan's relations with the West are at times strained and, for historical and cultural reasons, complicated, they are the very essence of simplicity compared to its relations with China. That Japan regards itself as a 'Western country' and yet is just a few hours' flying time from Beijing, the capital of a country it regards as 'Asian' even though China is its ancient cultural mentor, indicates the complex mentality that is at the heart of Japan's relations with the mainland.

The Tiananmen Square incident of 1989, when a pro-democracy demonstration in Beijing was brutally put down by the army, illustrated the Japanese dilemma. Sharing China's Asian reluctance to condemn and confront and yet being part of the Western camp, with its professed views on human rights and the freedom of the individual, Japan was torn between the two sides to its character. Given the bloody history of Japan's invasion of China during the World War II, Tokyo was in no position to sit in judgement on the old men in the Chinese government and yet, as a member of the developed industrial, democratic club of nations, it could hardly do less.

The initial Japanese government statement spoke only of concern and a hope that the situation would not deteriorate further. The public response, however, was much less equivocal, with broad condemnation of the Chinese government. A second government statement referred to humanitarian concerns but added that there was no intention of interfering in internal Chinese affairs. It was not until 12 days after the bloody crackdown, that Tokyo found a surer footing with the claim that the events were not 'compatible with the basic values of Japan, which is a democratic state'. The freezing of yen loans to China followed, but without fanfare. Japan would impose no further sanctions for fear of isolating China, and the government came under strong pressure from the business community not to jeopardize economic relations. In response, the Ministry of Foreign Affairs warned businessmen not to act like 'thieves at the site of a fire'. Japan was concerned that it would be seen by Western countries as not sharing their values on human rights. However, at the Paris summit of the industrialized countries in July 1989, Japan successfully headed off tighter sanctions on China and began clearing the way for the resumption of contacts. A year later, after the Chinese freed the prominent dissident Fang Lizhi, Japan was permitted to resume loans to China and there was a gradual return to normality. This resulted in the historic first visit by a Japanese emperor to Beijing in 1993.

The Japanese hope that the imperial visit and the apology tendered by his majesty will put an end to the tensions remaining from the war. In the past, Chinese leaders have played on Japanese war guilt whenever they wanted something from Tokyo or were seeking an external focus to distract attention from growing domestic problems. Japanese chemical warfare experiments on humans, the Nanjing massacre and the trauma of children born of Japanese parents and stranded in China are all issues that the Chinese authorities have at different times raised against Japan. Hitherto, it has been well nigh impossible for Japan and China to develop a long-term stable relationship relatively free of the emotional and other complications that arise from the difference between the two countries' political systems.

China is the key to the future security of North-East Asia, and Tokyo is keenly aware that, with the diminishing US military presence, it must maintain a good relationship with China, particularly at a time when Beijing has been building up its military power. Defence contacts were broken off by Japan after the Tiananmen Square incident. Now, there are growing concerns in Tokyo that rapidly rising expenditures on the People's Liberation Army, given a 14.9 per cent increase in spending for fiscal 1993, will change the balance of power in the region. China has also continued to show a willingness to sell sophisticated military technology to some of the world's less-stable regimes and appears to be in a position to exchange nuclear weapons know-how with Iran. Also, Chinese vessels have been involved in a number of incidents with Japanese ships and the scale on which China is building up its navy can only mean that it intends to dominate the northern Pacific Ocean in the future. North Korea remains a wild card for both Beijing and Tokyo, with the former having the edge in influence over the unpredictable communist regime. But whether the Korean peninsula is unified peacefully or through force, it will most likely become an area where the two countries compete for influence. At present, Chinese ties with South Korea are developing fast because there are many areas in which less-advanced Korean technology is more appropriate for Chinese needs than more advanced offerings from Japan.

The importance of the Sino–Japanese relationship seems likely to grow in the future. Japan needs to ensure that China develops its economy successfully and has political stability: it could not withstand the flood of refugees if, for whatever reason, China fell into chaos. It would also be hard for Japan to avoid involvement in any conflict on the mainland. Yet, at the same time, Japan needs to reassure the West that it will not have to face a Sino–Japanese Asian bloc which would pose formidable economic and political challenges to Western countries.

The Russian frontier

For the vast majority of nations in Europe and the Americas, the Cold War is already history. In just a few, short years it has become difficult to recall the mind-set that predominated at the height of the Cold War. Disarmament programmes have seen the destruction of many aircraft and weapons in Europe while the armed forces of the former Soviet Union have pulled back to the home country from their bases in their former eastern European satellites.

Yet at Russia's eastern extremity the picture is markedly different. Japanese territory captured by the Soviets in the closing phase of the World War II – a group of islands including Kunashiri, Shikotan and Habomai – remains under Russian occupation, even after the dissolution of the Soviet Union. Moreover, Japanese sources claim that while Russian ground divisions have been reduced from 43 to 36, and the number of troop from 390,000 to 320,000, more advanced weapons have been introduced, including T80 tanks and SS21 missiles with nuclear capability. Likewise, while the Baltic and Black Sea fleets have seen a dramatic reduction in their capability, there has been no such change in the Pacific fleets, which may have fewer ships than before, but gross tonnage has increased through the deployment of large, new missile-equipped vessels. Numbers of combat aircraft have also been reduced by about 380, but the Russian air forces are now deploying much more capable third- and fourth-generation jets. Thus, Japanese commentators maintain that the face the Russian bear shows to Europe and the United States is benign compared to the face it shows to the

East. Many believe that this reflects Russia's feelings of inferiority to the West, but they recall that, historically, offensives launched against the West have always alternated with those launched against the East.

The opportunistic capture of the northern territories when Japan was on the point of surrender in 1945 was not the only complaint against the Soviet Union. Some 600,000 Japanese war prisoners, including some in senior Tokyo government positions today, were detained there until 1956 and many of them never lived to be repatriated. The attitudes generated by that period still permeate the relationship, a situation which *glasnost* and *perestroika* have done little to change. Indeed, when Japan looks at Russia's rapidly improving relations with the West, it has more reason to be disappointed than in the Soviet era, when expectations were lower.

In a landmark speech in the mid-1980s, the Soviet president Mikhail Gorbachev promised a new era of peace in the Pacific with significant reductions of armaments. However, Japan has seen none of the promised benefits but has reluctantly been pressed by the West into helping the new Russian government of Boris Yeltsin, almost against its better judgement. Applying its two central tenets on foreign aid, Is it going to a stable government and is the home government itself doing everything possible to impove its own situation?, Japan held off for a long time from a full-blooded commitment to assist Mr Yeltsin. This delay was due not only to the generally poor relations between the two countries, but also to Mr Yeltsin's last-minute cancellation of a crucial visit to Japan. Yeltsin also failed to acknowledge earlier Japanese contributions, running into the hundreds of millions of dollars, which were already in train by October of 1992, telling aides that Japan had never given Russia a cent. The initial Japanese package of bilateral aid came to US $2.8 billion. Tokyo added a further $1.82 billion to the international effort to assist Russian reform at a special ministerial meeting held in mid-April 1993.

The Japan–Russia relationship seems unlikely to change much in the medium term even if there is an agreement on the return of the islands. Historically, Russia has for too long been seen as a major threat to Japan and has done nothing recently to change that impression. However, Japan has shown, through its willingness to give state financial assistance to Russia at a time when most of the Japanese private sector is unwilling to invest there, that it is determined that the relationship should not deteriorate further. Japan already has enough to contend with in its uncertain relations with China to contemplate a hostile Russia to the north.

South-East Asia and Australia

Japan's relationship with the countries at the southern end of the Pacific Rim have shown a surprising turn around in the early 1990s. Here, investment and trade are growing faster than with any of Tokyo's other partners. Over the years Singapore, Thailand, Malaysia and Indonesia have all built up sizeable portfolios of Japanese investment which, given their shared anti-communist and pro-Western capitalist ideals, has helped to underpin a natural confluence of interests. But Japan's claim to represent the region at world forums remains ambivalent since the region covers such a wide variety of countries and Japan is planted firmly in the developed nations' camp. However, Japanese influence continues to grow apace with the reduced need for US security guarantees, now that the Cold War is over, and the competitiveness of American companies in the Asian market.

The new growth is partly due to the fact that this is the world's most economically dynamic area and partly because Japan's foreign relations are now more focused on Asia than in previous decades, as trade and investment relations with Europe and the United States have either matured or run into difficulties. The ending of the war in Cambodia and the improving relations with Vietnam have also permitted increased trade with those countries. Vietnam seems likely to grow into a major trading partner with Japan despite the bitter legacy of occupation in World War II.

At the heart of this dynamic new relationship will be the 15-nation Asia Pacific Economic Cooperation group, which was set up at Australia's initiative in 1989. It comprises Australia, New Zealand, Canada, the United States, Japan, South Korea, China, Taiwan and Hong Kong and, in South-East Asia, Thailand, Malaysia, Singapore, Indonesia, the Philippines and Brunei. It is intended as a loose economic federation in the Asia–Pacific region, designed to prevent the creation of trade barriers in the region and deter any that might be established in Europe or elsewhere. Having a better chance of success than other regional blueprints, it includes the United States both to bind that country into Asia and to prevent charges that the group is Japanese-dominated. The shift away from traditional patterns of trade is clear from recent statistics. East Asia takes 60 per cent of Australia's trade while Canberra's manufactured exports to Japan reached US $2.36 billion in 1991, compared to its total exports to the United Kingdom of $1.19 billion.

Australia's central role in the launching of the group is part and parcel of a newly-emerging relationship in which both Australia and Japan are to maintain an open, non-discriminatory global trading system. Australia's significance as a trading partner is an important element in a partnership which is boosted by the fact that Australia is one of the few Western countries to enjoy a trade surplus with Japan – US $2.97 billion for 1992. Australia supplies more than half the raw materials needed for Japan's steel production as well as large amounts of coal and natural gas for its energy needs. Australia has already supported Japan in its disputes over airline services with the United States, and this mutual cooperation seems likely to grow. As one newspaper commentary has observed, they are each other's best friend in a region which is remote from the world's major centres.

The importance of the western Pacific region, and of the potential importance of the new grouping, can be gauged from the fact that the countries of North-East and South-East Asia along with Australia and New Zealand supplied 28.8 per cent of Japan's imports in 1992 and took 31.7 per cent of its exports. Two-way trade between Japan and the western Pacific countries stood at US $181.6 billion, compared to $148.9 billion with the United States.

Although it has so far attracted little attention, there are increasing contacts between the armed forces of the region and those of Japan, despite the sensitivities of history. Japanese naval vessels have paid goodwill visits to the region quite apart from periodic exercises in joint manœuvres with the United States. There are growing ties too between Australian and Japanese defence forces, and while it is far too early to talk of cooperation, Australian planners seem to be heading in that direction.

12 TRAVELLERS' JAPAN
Practical hints

The Japanese often say their country is a paradise for foreigners, and no-where is this more true than in the public and private transport systems, both arguably the best in the world for punctuality, speed and reliability. From the Boeings that whisk the traveller into the country's international airports to the local commuter trains that feed workers daily into the gaping maws of the metropolitan areas, Japanese efficiency and attention to detail allow journey times to be predicted to the minute with a reliability that is legendary.

The country has now lost the most taxing aspects of its mystery as far as foreigners are concerned: travel in and out of Japan and throughout the country is much easier than it used to be. Major airports are now as easy to negotiate as any in the world even for the lone traveller with no previous experience. The nationals of most industrialized nations no longer need visas for short-term visits to Japan, but be prepared for health checks and have details of your available cash and onward travel arrangements ready for officialdom at the airport: Japan is now a favoured destination for many people seeking work and, despite the demands of internationalization, there is increasing interest in keeping this under control.

Getting into Tokyo

One of the first stops for any first-time traveller after crossing the arrivals hall should be the Tourist Information Centre. Here, you will find a good range of free publications in English, such as maps, a list of the more reasonably-priced accommodation for budget travellers, timetables for onward travel, and magazines carrying advertisements for all the latest Japanese electronics products that their manufacturers expect you to fall for. Other ads will show you that they can be bought in Akihabara, Tokyo's 'electronics town', at well below list price.

Announcements and signs in foreign languages are common and there are always staff on hand to guide you through any last-minute snags. At Narita airport, outside Tokyo, a variety of means of transport into the capital is available from a large ticket-sales desk as you come out of the arrivals hall. The fastest, if not the cheapest way, is to take a short bus ride to the Narita airport station for 130 yen from where the Skyliner train will take you into Tokyo's Ueno station. Ueno is one of the city's main rail intersections with the nationwide Japan Rail system and is also integrated into the subway system and the Yamanote Line, which loops right round the capital.

The Skyliner costs 1,240 yen, but if you are less pressed for time the Toei subway line will take you right into the central Ginza district for half that price. Bear in mind that on the subway there is little room for luggage. At 14,000 yen the taxi ride is expensive so, for first-time visitors who do not feel like tackling a main-line railway station, the limousine bus to the Tokyo City Air Terminal (TCAT) for 2,300 yen is probably the best compromise. Alternatively, Japan Rail runs a cheaper service to Tokyo station which also appears to be slightly faster. The coach for the TCAT leaves from a stop almost directly opposite where travellers emerge from the customs hall. From the airport, the coach will take about an hour and 10 minutes along a good, though crowded, expressway. Most of these buses now have telephones that can be used by passengers while the bus is in motion. From the TCAT there is an extremely well-managed taxi service which offers larger cars for those with a lot of luggage for onward travel to anywhere in the city.

Local transport

Taxis. The life of the Tokyo taxi-driver is as hard as in any other capital city, but for the most part the taxi-drivers are helpful. There are designated taxi ranks throughout cities but it is generally easy to hail a cab, except when it is raining, when they become scarce, or when the bars and nightclubs are turning out. Remember to get in through the nearside rear door, which is controlled by the driver, and do not try to alight through the offside door either, as this will worry the driver. Tipping is not expected but not unwelcome. Late at night the drivers want Japanese customers seeking long rides to the suburbs rather than foreigners who will most likely just be going somewhere in the centre of the city, so you have to offer well above the going rate. This is indicated by holding up two or three fingers to indicate whether you are willing to offer twice or three times the standard fare. When in doubt about getting a cab, head for the nearest railway station where there will almost inevitably be a line of them waiting.

Foreign faces can sometimes cause concern about the ability to communicate, so you should be as well equipped as possible to assist the driver in the search for your destination. Unless it is one of the better-known hotels or localities, it is as well to have not only the address written out, preferably by a Japanese friend, but also a small map showing the area immediately around your destination. Japanese cities were not built according to any logical development plan and even the longest resident will not know local areas in detail. After the war, Tokyo just grew, despite being offered the services of some British town planners. As a result, the houses on any street are numbered according to when they were built and only major streets are named. Even Japanese residents need all the help they can get to move around the city. It is, therefore, not unusual to show a taxi-driver a map and visitors should not be embarrassed about it.

The fount of all local knowledge is always the local *koban*, or police box, which will have an officer on duty at all times. He will either know the area you are seeking or will have access to a map showing the location and ownership of all the properties in his area. Frequent stops for consultation or much scratching of the head do not necessarily mean trouble, and if your taxi-driver exhibits signs of frustration it is usually because of the difficulty of tracking down your ultimate destination, but none has ever been known to give up the struggle.

Above all, the Japanese will go to inordinate lengths to direct a helpless-looking foreigner, and it is worth memorizing the simple phrases that you need to ask for directions or to indicate that you need assistance. Your Japanese hosts will often break off what they are doing and go out of their way to help you.

Trains and subways. Many's the time that a foreign businessman has lunged towards the nearest taxi rank in the hope of making up time in a hectic round of appointments, only to spend the next 30 minutes stuck in traffic. It is better to spend five minutes walking to the nearest subway or railway station. These are all easy to use with the aid of your colour-coded map.

The Yamanote Line – colour-coded green – links all of Tokyo's principal rail and subway centres so, at least to begin with, it is a good basis for moving around the city. The city's 11 private railway lines and 10 subways all interconnect with this line at some point. Should you lose your way, the Yamanote Line (or in Osaka, the Kanjo Line, a similar loop line) will always bring you back to your departure point.

Usually, the transfer from one line to another requires the purchase of another ticket. Virtually all lines show maps of their routes above their ticket-dispensing machines and most show the scale of fares for different destinations. That way, the exact fare can be calculated and the ticket obtained from the banks of vending machines that are a feature of every station. The alternative is to buy stored-value cards for a particular line, or a day's go-anywhere ticket for Japan Rail for approximately 700 yen. Another important purchase, before leave for Japan, are the Japan Rail period tickets which can only be bought outside the country. These permit unlimited travel for a period of, for instance 10 days or a month, depending on how much you pay. Their validity starts on the day of their first use and they are relatively cheap compared to regular rail fares.

Arriving at your chosen destination is best assured by first counting the number of stations from your starting point. You can check on your progress by listening for the guard to announce the name of each station as you pull in. Also, look at the station name board. Each one contains not only the name of that particular station in *romaji*, romanized Japanese characters, but also of the preceding station and the next one. Long-term foreign residents sometimes find this constant stream of seemingly obvious information irritating, but for newcomers and sleepy, or even tipsy, commuters it is invaluable. But when setting off on an extended trip, which may take you to distant parts of the capital, be sure to conclude your travels before midnight

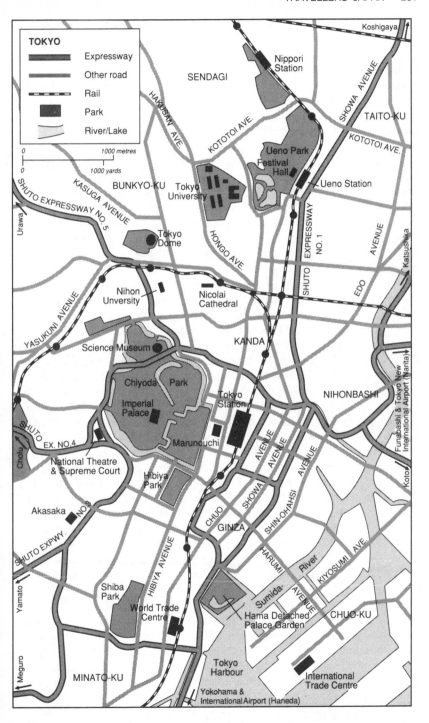

when most train services cease. After that, an expensive taxi ride is your only option.

Long-distance travel

Japan Rail and the numerous private railway lines offer excellent services to all parts of the country, as do Japan Airlines, All Nippon Airways, Japan Air Service and a host of new regional services that have sprung up as the airline business has gradually become liberalized in recent years. For those who are less pressed for time, there are also long-distance bus services, which are a much cheaper alternative. The principal rail services by Japan Rail to the south and west run from Tokyo station. Of these, the Shinkansen, or Bullet Train, is the fastest and most luxurious, with 100 trains a day to Osaka to choose from. This is rail travel *par excellence*, especially if you travel in the Green Car, which is the equivalent of first class. Ordinary express services are much cheaper but do not have the extraordinary speed advantage of the Bullet Train, which can whisk you from Tokyo to Japan's industrial heartland in 3 hours 10 minutes.

Train services across the country are generally organized on three levels: the super express, express and ordinary or stopping train. For example, on the route from Osaka in western Japan to the ancient capital of Kyoto, the private Keihan Line runs a super express service which goes non-stop to Kyoto, the express make a single stop at the midway point, Hirakata, and a stopping train covers the balance of the route by halting at every station along the line. The same applies to commuter lines out of Tokyo. A traveller can save much time by choosing a *kyuko*, or express, which can speed to an outlying suburb to an intermediate point on the way from where a stopping train (*futsu densha*) completes the journey. The express trains usually have red designators or a special livery so they are easily identifiable.

Tickets for all ordinary services can be bought from vending machines at the station of departure. But Shinkansen tickets are usually purchased from a special window at a main line station or from a travel agent. Information on everything you could conceivably need is available from the excellent Tourist Information Centres which are to be found at Tokyo's Narita airport and in all other principal cities. However, they do not do bookings. That is in the capable hands of the Japan Tourist Bureau (JTB), *Nihon Kotsu Kosha*, which often has an office close to a railway station. Their main office is at Nihon Building Annex, 2–7–1 Otemachi, Chiyoda-ku, Tokyo (Tel: 03 / 270–0372).

The myriad private railway systems in Japan are usually geared to servicing a well-travelled commuter line and terminate in a main-line station that often features a department store owned by the same railway company. The two elements of the company's business are thus mutually reinforcing, with the store subsidizing the railway. These private lines often have a higher level of service than that found on the old Japan National Railways. This national rail service has now been privatized, having accumulated

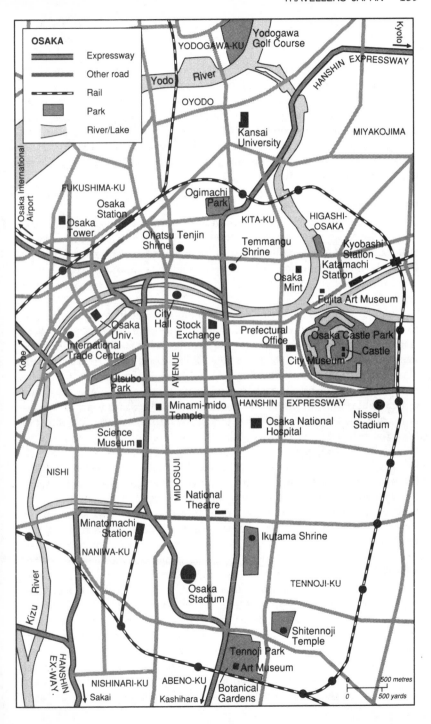

debts that dwarfed the GNP of many nations. Most of the services that have been privatized by region have made profits since the move into the private sector.

Buying tickets to travel on the local private lines is the same procedure at for the main inter-city services. On entering the station, you will see a big, illuminated map of the company's lines with the fares and key intermediate stations marked with large, colour-coded circles. Tickets are available from machines and it is also possible, if you are making a return journey or several journeys on the same route, to buy an electronic stored-value ticket. This is the same size as a telephone card and is inserted in the ticket barrier machine each time you travel.

Face to face

Following a few simple guidelines should make any visit to Japan successful provided that you bear in mind the Japanese concern for good manners and for doing everything by the book. An important factor in the visitor's favour is the Japanese determination that everyone should go away with a good impression of their country, and to ensure this they will go to extraordinary lengths.

A quiet approach, especially when meeting for the first time, will make most Japanese feel more relaxed. Few feel at ease with a boisterous, back-slapping foreigner, at least until they know him or her well. Most will not be very forthcoming about their families, unless they are particularly well-versed in Western ways, and it is best not to probe but to allow your Japanese host to control the exchange of information on such matters. Some Japanese have relationships with foreigners extending over years and never say much about family life, a trait that some find irritating because it can limit the extent to which friendship can develop. But such things may be deemed trivial or irrelevant by a Japanese and are therefore best left alone.

The Japanese expect foreigners to be individualistic and self-reliant, but these are not necessarily characteristics that are widely admired in Japan, particularly by the older generations. Although more and more young Japanese may be adopting this sort of lifestyle, to many of their compatriots they are merely manifesting selfishness and a lack of concern for others. Their detractors see that lifestyle as partly responsible for the problems of drugs, homelessness and poverty that plague many Western societies. Yet while Japanese society does not necessarily offer the same sort of freedoms as the West, it has compensatory attractions in the high levels of personal security and low levels of crime. Above all, remember that the Japanese are ultra-sensitive to Western criticism and that no one is requiring you to live as a Japanese. Here, as in so many other areas, comparisons may be neither relevant nor welcome.

An inquiring mind will help to compensate for what will almost certainly be an imbalance between your knowledge of Japan and your host's knowledge of the West. This is partly because the number of English-language books translated into Japanese is vastly greater than the number of Japanese books that get translated into English. That is a pity. Japanese society may have much to offer the West, particularly in the way that social unity has been preserved.

One to one

For all their world travel and experience, it is common for Japanese to feel uncomfortable in the presence of Westerners. This is not merely because they are unused to speaking English, though that may be problem enough. There also may be the perennial feelings of, at one time, inferiority, at another, superiority, which so often feature in East–West relations. The first requirement is to try to put your Japanese contact at ease by showing a genuine warmth, without being patronizing. Lacking the signs that are present in his normal social relations, a Japanese may feel quite at a loss as to how to manage a relationship with a foreigner.

Throughout your visit, the generosity of your hosts can be almost overwhelming and your efforts to pay for meals or entertainment may well be rebuffed. If so, accept it all with good grace but not before following the general Japanese rule of thumb, which is to offer to do the honours three times. If, on the third time, your offer is again refused then that can be taken as final. The Japanese dislike a public scene or disagreement more than anything; to them, above all, things must go smoothly.

Like many Europeans, the Japanese tend to build their friendships slowly: it may take years before you really get to know each other, so do not expect to be entertained by your host at home. If you are invited into someone's home make sure your socks are presentable: shoes are left at the door. It is not just enthusiam for cleanliness which demands this; shoes can do irreparable harm to expensive tatami mats.

Making yourself understood

Despite the well-rehearsed stories about Japanese being unable to speak foreign languages, most younger people have sufficient command of English to be able to help out a visiting foreigner. English is by far the most common foreign language in Japan and all foreigners are assumed to be able to speak it. In most cities there will be a Japanese with good English within reach, and it is surprising how often they appear when they are most needed. As long as you speak clearly and slowly, you will probably get an answer to your question even if it is only in the form of frantic pointing. Keep questions direct and simple without the complications of negative constructions. For example, if you frame a question thus, 'Can't I get to the station this way?' a Japanese will often answer, in the logic of his own tongue, 'Yes', meaning you cannot.

As with any country, a few words of the language serve to break down barriers even if Japanese are still unaccustomed to hearing foreigners speak their language. If you are prepared to try out your linguistic skills, remember that, however much you may think young Japanese women chattering sound like a clutch of young birds, Japanese is not a sing-song language and has none of the swooping cadences of English. Don't stress syllables and bear in mind that while it is excusable for foreigners to use the language directly, it is more polite, and therefore more common, for Japanese to use circumlocution.

Pronunciation

Japanese vowels are pronounced like those in the Romance languages, with Italian probably the closest. A is long like an 'Ah' of satisfaction, the e is short as in pen, and i is short when it occurs in the middle of a word or long when it occurs at the end. The o is rounded, as in the English exclamation and pronunciation of the names of the Japanese cities Osaka and Nikko, while the u is rounded, as in the Japanese word *deguchi*, meaning exit. Note that vowel length can change the meaning of a word: you plan your route on a *chizu*, or map, but *chiizu* is almost instantly recognizable as the English word cheese. Consonants are always followed by vowels.

Japanese is unrelated to other oriental languages in the immediate neighbourhood. Here are a few basic rules:

1 The word order is subject–verb–object while modifiers go in front of the word modified.

2 There are no plurals. More than one is understood by the context or is spelt with a series of special counting words applicable to specific types of object.

3 Adjectives have tenses and moods.

4 Verbs have only present and past tenses. The future is designated by use of the present tense and an adverb indicating time.

5 *Ka* at the end of a sentence indicates a question.

Verbally the Japanese language uses a system similar to Roman numerals but just to complicate matters there are, in fact, two number systems. One is used with objects and is Chinese in origin while the other stand-alone system is Japanese.

The Japanese system goes thus:

1 *hitotsu*
2 *futatsu*
3 *mitsu*
4 *yotsu*
5 *itsutsu*
6 *muttsu*
7 *nanatsu*
8 *yattsu*
9 *kokonotsu*
10 *to*

The number object system is like this:

1 *ichi*
2 *ni*
3 *san*
4 *shi* or *yon*
5 *go*
6 *roku*
7 *shichi* or *nana*
8 *hachi*
9 *ku*
10 *ju*

The word *shi* for four is often avoided as it sounds identical to the Japanese word for death and is therefore thought likely to bring bad luck. For the same reason *nana* is often preferred for seven. Building up numbers from 10 onwards is relatively simple: 11 is *ju-ichi*, 18 is *ju-hachi* and so on. Thirty is *san-ju* and 100 is *hyaku*.

Useful words and phrases

Yes	*hai*
No	*iie*
No it is not so	*so j'arimasen*
I understand	*wakarimasu*
I don't understand	*wakarimasen*
Do you understand	*wakarimasu-ka?*
Speak slowly please	*yukkuri iite kudasai*
Say it again please	*mo ichido iite kudasai*
Write it please	*kaite kudasai*
How much is it?	*o ikura desu-ka?* (the o at the beginning is more polite)
Just a moment please	*chotto matte kudasai*
Not yet	*mata*
Let's go	*ikimasho*
I like it	*suki desu* (when i and u follow h, k, p, s or t they are voiceless so it sounds more like *ski des*)

Getting to know you

Hello	*haro*
Good morning	*ohayo*
Good day	*konnichi-wa*
Good evening	*konban-wa*
Good night	*oyasuminasai* (when going to bed)
Goodbye	*sayonara* (with a long o sound and two short final *a*s)
Go to it	*ganbatte (kudasai)*
Good health	*o genki de*

See you later	*mata ne*
Take care	*ki o tsukete*

Politeness

Thanks	*domo*
Thank you	*domo arigato*
Thank you very much	*domo arigato gozaimasu* (polite, formal expression)
Excuse me	*shitsurei shimasu* (literally, I am committing a rudeness, for use when squeezing past someone)
Excuse me	*sumimasen* (the standard form)
Excuse me	*gomen-nasai* (when there has been real inconvenience)

Questions

What?	*nan desu-ka?*
Who?	*dare desu-ka?*
Where?	*doko desu-ka?*
Why?	*doshite desu-ka?*
Which?	*dochira desu-ka?*
When?	*itsu desu-ka?*
Whose?	*dare no desu-ka?*

Time

The scheduling of trains and other modes of transport is on the 24-hour clock while for the ordinary person the expression for morning is *gozen* and for the afternoon *gogo*. The hour is expressed by a number with the suffix *ji*, as in *ichi-ji*, one o'clock. Sixteen minutes past four then becomes *yoji ju-roppun*, *pun* or *fun* meaning minute.

Days of the week

Sunday	*Nichi-yobi*
Monday	*Getsu-yobi*
Tuesday	*Kai-yobi*
Wednesday	*Sui-yobi*
Thursday	*Moku-yobi*
Friday	*Kin-yobi*
Saturday	*Do-yobi*

Months

Months are expressed by a counter followed by the word *gatsu*, meaning month, as in *Ichi-gatsu* for January. When standing alone, the word for month is *getsu* and the word for year is *nen*.

Transportation

Station	*eki*
Train	*densha*
Bus stop	*basu noriba* (The word *taminaru* is also used for terminal)
Ferry	*ferri*
Aircraft	*hikooki*
Subway	*chikatetsu*
Ticket	*kippu*
Return	*ofuku*
First	*saisho no*
Last	*saigo no*
Next	*tsugi no*

For the taxi-driver

Straight (on)	*massugu*
Right	*migi*
Left	*hidari*
Up	*ue*
Down	*shita*
That way	*achira*
This way	*kochira*
Here	*koko*
Over there	*asoko*
Place	*basho*
Street	*michi, dori*
Highway	*kokudo*
Is it near (far)?	*chikai (toi) desu-ka?*
Show me on this map, please	*kono chizu de oshiete kudasai*
How long does it take on foot?	*aruite dono gurai kakarimasu-ka?*

Restaurants and food

Breakfast, please	*choshoku kudasai*
Lunch, please	*chuushoku kudasai*
Dinner, please	*yuushoku kudasai*
No thank you	*iie, kekko desu*
Delicious	*oishii*
It looks delicious	*oishii-so*
Bill	*okanjoo*
Restaurant	*resutoran*
Coffee shop	*kissaten*
Snack bar	*sunaku*
How much?	*oikura desu-ka?*
Expensive	*takai desu*
Big	*ookii*
Small	*chisai*

Shopping

Department store	*depato*
Supermarket	*supa maaketo*
Camera shop	*kameraya*
Travel agent	*ryokoo dairiten*

Emergencies

I'm ill	*watashi wa byooki desu*
Get a doctor	*Oisha-san o yonde kudasai*
Get help	*sugu ni tasuke o yonde kudasai*
Quickly	*hayaku*
Help!	*tasukete kudasai*
Hospital	*byooin*
Police	*keisatsu*
Pharmacy	*kusuriya*

Appendix 1 NATIONAL HOLIDAYS

January	1	New Year's Day
January	15	Coming of Age Day
February	11	National Foundation Day
March	20/21	Spring Equinox
April	29	Greenery Day
May	3	Constitution Day
May	5	Children's Day
September	15	Respect for the Aged Day
September	23/24	Autumn Equinox Day
October	10	Physical Education Day
November	3	Culture Day
November	23	Labour Day
December	23	Emperor's Birthday

'Golden week' from April 29 to May 5 is usually taken as a full week's holiday by most businesses.

Appendix 2 THE CONSTITUTION OF JAPAN (Extracts)

We, the Japanese people, acting through our duly elected representatives in the National Diet, determined that we shall secure for ourselves and our posterity the fruits of peaceful cooperation with all nations and the blessings of liberty throughout this land, and resolved that never again shall we be visited with the horrors of war through the action of government, do proclaim that sovereign power resides with the people and do firmly establish this Constitution. Government is a sacred trust of the people, the authority for which is derived from the people, the powers of which are exercized by the representatives of the people, and the benefits of which are enjoyed by the people. This is a universal principle of mankind upon which this Constitution is founded. We reject and revoke all constitutions, laws, ordinances and rescripts in conflict herewith.

We, the Japanese people, desire peace for all time and are deeply conscious of the high ideals controlling human relationships, and we have determined to preserve our security and existence, trusting in the justice and faith of the peace-loving peoples of the world. We desire to occupy an honoured place in an international society striving for the preservation of peace, and the banishment of tyranny and slavery, oppression and intolerance for all time from the earth. We recognize that all peoples of the world have the right to live in peace, free from fear and want.

We believe that no nation is responsible to itself alone, but that laws of political morality are universal; and that obedience to such laws is incumbent upon all nations who would sustain their own sovereignty and justify their sovereign relationship with other nations.

We, the Japanese people, pledge our national honour to accomplish these high ideals and purposes with all our resources.

Chapter I The Emperor

Article 1. The Emperor shall be the symbol of the State and of the unity of the people, deriving his position from the will of the people with whom resides sovereign power.
Article 2. The Imperial Throne shall be dynastic and succeeded to in accordance with the Imperial House Law passed by the Diet.
Article 3. The advice and approval of the cabinet shall be required for all acts of the Emperor in matters of state, and the cabinet shall be responsible therefor.
Article 4. The Emperor shall perform only such acts in matters of state as are provided for in this Constitution and he shall not have powers related to government. The Emperor may delegate the performance of his acts in matters of state as may be provided by law.
Article 5. When, in accordance with the Imperial House Law, a Regency is established, the Regent shall perform his acts in matters of state in the Emperor's name. In this case, paragraph one of the preceding article shall be applicable.
Article 6. The Emperor shall appoint the prime minister as designated by the Diet. The Emperor shall appoint the chief judge of the supreme court as designated by the cabinet.
Article 7. The Emperor, with the advice and approval of the cabinet, shall perform the following acts in matters of state on behalf of the people:

Promulgation of amendments of the constitution, laws, cabinet orders and treaties.
Convocation of the Diet.
Dissolution of the House of Representatives.
Proclamation of general election of members of the Diet.
Attestation of the appointment and dismissal of ministers of state and other officials as provided for by law, and of full powers and credentials of ambassadors and ministers.
Attestation of general and special amnesty, commutation of punishment, reprieve, and restoration of rights.
Awarding of honours.
Attestation of instruments of ratification and other diplomatic documents as provided for by law.
Receiving foreign ambassadors and ministers.
Performance of ceremonial functions.

Article 8. No property can be given to, or received by, the Imperial House, nor can gifts be made therefrom, without the authorization of the Diet.

Chapter II Renunciation of War

Article 9. Aspiring sincerely to an international peace based on justice and order, the Japanese people forever renounce war as a sovereign right of the nation and the threat or use of force as means of settling international disputes.

In order to accomplish the aim of the preceding paragraph, land, sea and air forces, as well as other war potential, will never be maintained. The right of belligerency of the state will not be recognized.

Chapter III Rights and Duties of the People

Article 10. The conditions necessary for being a Japanese national shall be determined by law.

Article 11. The people shall not be prevented from enjoying any of the fundamental human rights. These fundamental human rights guaranteed to the people by this constitution shall be conferred upon the people of this and future generations as eternal and inviolate rights.

Article 12. The freedoms and rights guaranteed to the people by this constitution shall be maintained by the constant endeavour of the people, who shall refrain from any abuse of these freedoms and rights and shall always be responsible for utilizing them for the public welfare.

Article 13. All of the people shall be respected as individuals. Their right to life, liberty and the pursuit of happiness shall, to the extent that it does not interfere with the public welfare, be the supreme consideration in legislation and in other government affairs.

Article 14. All of the people are equal under the law and there shall be no discrimination in political, economic or social relations because of race, creed, sex, social status or family origin. Peers and peerage shall not be recognized. No privilege shall accompany any award of honour, decoration or any distinction, nor shall any such award be valid beyond the lifetime of the individual who now holds or hereafter may receive it.

Article 15. The people have the inalienable right to choose their public officials and to dismiss them. All public officials are servants of the whole community and not any group thereof. Universal adult suffrage is guaranteed with regard to the election of public officials. In all elections, secrecy of the ballot shall not be violated. A voter shall not be answerable, publicly or privately, for the choice he has made.

Article 16. Every person shall have the right of peaceful petition for the redress of damage, for the removal of public officials, for the enactment, repeal or amendment of laws, ordinances or regulations and for other matters; nor shall any person be in any way discriminated against for sponsoring such a petition.

Article 17. Every person may sue for redress as provided by law from the state or a public entity, in case he has suffered damage through illegal act of any public official.

Article 18. No person shall be held in bondage of any kind. Involuntary servitude, except as punishment for crime, is prohibited.

Article 19. Freedom of thought and conscience shall not be violated.

Article 20. Freedom of religion is guaranteed to all. No religious organization shall receive any privileges from the state, nor exercise any political authority. No person shall be compelled to take part in any religious act, celebration, rite or practice. The state and its organs shall refrain from religious education or any other religious activity.

Article 21. Freedom of assembly and association as well as speech, press and all other forms of expression are guaranteed. No censorship shall be maintained, nor shall the secrecy of any means of communication be violated.

Article 22. Every person shall have freedom to choose and change his residence and to choose his occupation to the extent that it does not interfere with the public welfare. Freedom of all persons to move to a foreign country and to divest themselves of their nationality shall be inviolate.

Article 23. Academic freedom is guaranteed.

Article 24. Marriage shall be based only on the mutual consent of both sexes and it shall be maintained through mutual cooperation with the equal rights of husband and wife as a basis. With regard to choice of spouse, property rights, inheritance, choice of domicile, divorce and other matters pertaining to marriage and the family, laws shall be enacted from the standpoint of individual dignity and the essential equality of the sexes.

Article 25. All people shall have the right to maintain the minimum standards of wholesome and cultured living. In all spheres of life, the state shall use its endeavours for the promotion and extension of social welfare and security and of public health.

Article 26. All people shall have the right to receive an equal education correspondent to their ability, as provided by law. All people shall be obligated to have all boys and girls under their protection receive ordinary education as provided for by law. Such compulsory education shall be free.

Article 27. All people shall have the right and the obligation to work. Standards for wages, hours, rest and other working conditions shall be fixed by law. Children shall not be exploited.

Article 28. The right of workers to organize and to bargain and act collectively is guaranteed.

Article 29. The right to own or hold property is inviolable. Property rights shall be defined by law, in conformity with the public welfare. Private property may be taken for public use upon just compensation therefor.

Article 30. The people shall be liable to taxation as provided by law.

Article 31. No person shall be deprived of life or liberty, nor shall any other criminal penalty be imposed, except according to procedure established by law.

Article 32. No person shall be denied the right to access to the courts.

Article 33. No person shall be apprehended except upon warrant issued by a competent judicial officer which specifies the offence with which the person is charged, unless he is apprehended, the offence being committed.

Article 34. No person shall be arrested or detained without being at once informed of the charges against him or without the immediate privilege of counsel; nor shall he be detained without adequate cause; and upon demand of any person such cause must be immediately shown in open court in his presence and the presence of his counsel.

Article 35. The right of all persons to be secure in their homes, papers and effects against entries, searches and seizures shall not be impaired except upon warrant issued for adequate cause and particularly describing the place to be searched and things to be seized, or except as provided by Article 33. Each search or seizure shall be made upon warrant issued by a competent judicial officer.

Article 36. The infliction of torture by any public officer and cruel punishments are absolutely forbidden.

Article 37. In all criminal cases the accused shall enjoy the right to a speedy and public trial by an impartial tribunal. He shall be permitted full opportunity to examine all witnesses, and he shall have the right of compulsory process for obtaining witnesses on his behalf at public expense. At all times the accused shall have the assistance of competent counsel who shall, if the accused is unable to secure the same by his own efforts, be assigned to his use by the state.

Article 38. No person shall be compelled to testify against himself. Confession made under compulsion, torture or threat, or after prolonged arrest or detention shall not be admitted in evidence. No person shall be convicted or punished in cases where the only proof against him is his own confession.

Article 39. No person shall be held criminally liable for an act which was lawful at the time it was committed, or of which he has been acquitted, nor shall he be placed in double jeopardy.

Article 40. Any person, in case he is acquitted after he has been arrested or detained, may sue the state for redress as provided by law.

Appendix 3 USEFUL ADDRESSES FOR BUSINESSMEN

Offices of the Japan External Trade Organization (JETRO)

JETRO London (Japan Trade Centre)
6th Floor, Leconfield House
Curzon Street
London W1Y 7FB
Tel:44 71 493–7226
Fax: 44 71 491–7570

Japan Ship Centre
St Clare House
30–33 Minories
London EC3N 1DD
Tel: 44 71 488–0311
Fax: 44 71 488–1148

Japan Metal Centre
Chancery House
Chancery Lane
London WC2
Tel: 44 71 405–7301
Fax: 44 71 242–0661

JETRO Dublin
BP House
Setanta Place
Dublin 2
Ireland
Tel: 353 1 714003
Fax: 353 1 714302

JETRO Paris
2 Place du Palais Royal
75044 Paris
CEDEX 01
France
Tel: 331 4261–2727
Fax: 331 4261–1946

JETRO Hamburg
Colonnaden 72
2000 Hamburg 36
Germany
Tel: 4940 356–0080
Fax: 4940 346837

JETRO Berlin
Internationales
  Handelazentrum Berlin
12th floor
Friedrichstrasse 95
0–1086 Berlin
Germany

JETRO Dusseldorf
Konigsalle 58
4000 Dusseldorf
Germany
Tel: 49211 136020
Fax: 49211 326411

JETRO Frankfurt
Rossmarkt 17
6 Frankfurt 1
Germany
Tel: 4969 593459, 4969 284221
Fax: 4969 283359

JETRO Munich
Prielmayerstrasse 3/1
8000 Munich 2
Germany
Tel:4989 593459, 4989 594411
Fax: 4989 592014

JETRO Amsterdam
World Trade Centre
Tower C 4th Floor
Strawinskylaan 447 1077 XX
Amsterdam
The Netherlands
Tel: 3120 676–5075
Fax: 3120 664–7597

JETRO Rotterdam
Groothandelegebouw
B3 Weena 695,3013
AM Rotterdam
The Netherlands
Tel: 3110 4113360

JETRO Brussels
Rue D'Arlon 69–71
Bolte 2
B1040 Brussels
Belgium
Tel: 322 230–4858
Fax: 322 230–0703

JETRO Copenhagen
Vesterbrogade 1c
1st Floor 1620
Copenhagen V
Denmark
Tel: 4533 147312
Fax: 4533 110136

JETRO Stockholm
Kungsgatan 48, 4th Floor
11135 Stockholm
Sweden
Tel: 468 118173
Fax: 468 111888

JETRO Oslo
Parkvelen 55
0256 Oslo 2
Norway
Tel: 4722 558611
Fax: 4722 558610

JETRO Zurich
Stampfenbachstrasse 38
8023 Zurich
Switzerland
Tel: 411 362–2323, 411 362–2387
Fax: 411 362–7056

JETRO Geneva
82, rue de Lausanne
1202 Geneva
Switzerland
Tel: 4122 732–1304
Fax: 4122 732–0772

JETRO Vienna
Mariahllferstrasse 41
1060 Vienna
Austria
Tel: 431 587–5628/9
Fax: 431 586–2293

JETRO Milan
INA Building
Via Agnello 6/1
20121 Milano
Italy
Tel: 392 866343, 392 865546, 392 72000037
Fax: 392 72023072

JETRO Rome
Via San Filippo Martire 1/B
00197 Rome
Italy
Tel: 396 808–4752
Fax: 396 807–5230

JETRO Athens
4 Kubari St Kolonaki
Athens
Greece
Tel: 301 363–0820
Fax: 301 362–1231

JETRO Madrid
Plaza de Colon 2
Torres de Colon 1, 7
28046 Madrid
Spain
Tel: 341 319–5584
Fax: 341 310–3659

JETRO Lisbon
Empreendimento Des
   Amoreiras
Av Eng Duarte Pacheco
1000 Lisbon
Portugal
Tel: 3511 659381
Fax: 3511 691818

JETRO Warsaw
c/o IPL Business Centre
Ul. Koszykowa 54
00–675 Warsaw
Poland
Tel: 482 6808 508
Fax: 482 6808 512

JETRO Bucharest
Hotel Bucuresti
Strada Luterana
Compound D
Entrance C2
4th Floor
Apartment 14
Bucharest
Romania
Tel: 4006 148876
Fax: 4003 120432

JETRO Sofia
World Trade Centre
Room 818
36 Dragon Tsankov Boulevard
1057 Sofia
Bulgaria
Tel: 3592 7146
Fax: 3592 705127

JETRO Budapest
1012 Budapest Logodi u
22–24, Budapest
Republic of Hungary
Tel: 361 201–4799
Fax: 361 201–5189

JETRO Moscow
c/o Sotobo Moscow Office
Suite 231
Hotel Mezhdunarodnaja-2
Krasnopresnenskaja Nab 12
123610 Moscow
Russia
Tel: 7095 253–2705
Fax: 7095 253–1562

Appendix 4 BIBLIOGRAPHY

MITI and the Japanese Miracle, Chalmers Johnson (Stanford University Press)
Mirror, Sword and Jewel, Kurt Singer (Kodansha)
Kaisha, the Japanese Corporation, James Abegglen and George Stalk (Tuttle)
The Anatomy of Dependence, Takeo Doi (Kodansha)
Election Campaigning Japanese Style, Gerald Curtis (Kodansha)
Japan Past and Present, Edwin Reischauer (Tuttle)
Inside the Japanese System, Daniel Okimoto and Thomas Rohlen (Stanford University Press)
Bureaucrats and Policy Making, Ed. Ezra N Suleiman (Holmes and Meier)
The Myth of Japanese Uniqueness, Peter Dale (Croom Helm)
The Japan that can say No, Shintaro Ishihara (Simon and Schuster)
A Japanese Mirror, Ian Buruma (Jonathan Cape)
Pink Samurai, Nicholas Bornoff (Grafton Books)
The Enigma of Japanese Power, Karel van Wolferen (Macmillan)
The Bubble Economy, Christopher Wood (Sidgwick and Jackson)
Japan's Commercial Empire, Jon Woronoff (Macmillan)
Doing Business in Japan, Jonathan Rice (BBC Books)
A Modern History of Japan, Richard Storry (Pelican)
Inside Japan, Peter Tasker (Penguin)
The Japanese Conspiracy, Marvin Wolf (Empire Books)

INDEX